LIVING ROOM
DIALOGUES

LIVING ROOM DIALOGUES

Edited By

William B. Greenspun, C.S.P.

*National Director, Apostolate of Good Will,
Confraternity of Christian Doctrine*

and

William A. Norgren

*Executive Director, Department of Faith and
Order of the National Council of
Churches of Christ*

**National Council of the Churches
of Christ in the U.S.A.**

and

**Paulist Press
Glen Rock, New Jersey**

Living Room Dialogues is a joint publishing project of the Division of Christian Unity of the National Council of Churches and the Apostolate of Good Will of the National Confraternity of Christian Doctrine (Roman Catholic educational agency). Both the Division of Christian Unity and the Apostolate of Good Will warmly recommend and encourage its use as a resource book for the conduct of dialogues among Catholic, Orthodox and Protestant laity. Endorsement by the Division of Christian Unity in no way commits the individual member Churches of the National Council or the Council itself to the views expressed in this book. The Apostolate of Good Will speaks for itself and not for the National Confraternity in offering this program. The Catholic writings in this volume appear with proper ecclesiastical permission.

ACKNOWLEDGMENTS

"Nine Steps to Unity" by Robert McAfee Brown and "Ten Commandments for the Ecumenical Age" by John Cogley, from STEPS TO CHRISTIAN UNITY, edited by John A. O'Brien. Copyright © 1964 by John A. O'Brien. Reprinted by permission of Doubleday & Company, Inc.

"Word and Sacrament in Protestant Worship" by Cyril Richardson, reprinted by permission of the publishers from ECUMENICAL DIALOGUE AT HARVARD, edited by Samuel Miller and G. Ernest Wright, Cambridge, Mass.: The Belknap Press of Harvard University Press, copyright, 1964, by the President and Fellows of Harvard.

"Liturgy, Unity and Church" by Michael J. Taylor, S.J., excerpted from LITURGY AND CHRISTIAN UNITY by Romey P. Marshall, O.S.L. and Michael J. Taylor, S.J., © 1965 by Prentice Hall, Inc., Englewood Cliffs, N. J.

"The Liturgy and Orthodoxy" by John Meyendorff is reprinted from THE ORTHODOX CHURCH by John Meyendorff. Copyright © 1962 by Pantheon Books, A Division of Random House, Inc. Reprinted by permission.

"Reform—An Essential Element in the Church" by Julius Cardinal Döpfner from THE QUESTIONING CHURCH. Copyright © 1964 by Burns & Oates Ltd. Reprinted with permission of The Newman Press, Westminster, Md.

"The Way of Renewal" by W. A. Visser 't Hooft from THE RENEWAL OF THE CHURCH by W. A. Visser 't Hooft. Published in the U.S.A., 1957, by The Westminster Press. Used by permission.

"Report of the Section on Witness" from NEW DELHI SPEAKS, reprinted with permission of the publishers, Association Press, New York, N.Y.

"The Nature of Christian Witness" by Philip Berrigan, S.S.J. Reprinted with permission of The Macmillan Company from NO MORE STRANGERS by Philip Berrigan, S.S.J. Copyright © by Philip Berrigan, S.S.J., 1965.

Library of Congress
Catalog Card Number: 65-28465

Printed and Bound in the
United States of America

Contents

INTRODUCTION 7

DIALOGUE NO. 1
CONCERN, PRAYER, LOVE:
FOUNDATION FOR DIALOGUE

CHRISTIAN DIALOGUE 12

DIALOGUE NO. 2
GOOD CONVERSATION IN CHRIST

CHRISTIAN DIALOGUE 24
NINE STEPS TO UNITY 31
    Robert McAfee Brown
TEN COMMANDMENTS FOR THE ECUMENICAL AGE . 43
    John Cogley

DIALOGUE NO. 3
HOW DO WE WORSHIP?

CHRISTIAN DIALOGUE 58
WORD AND SACRAMENT IN PROTESTANT WORSHIP . 66
    Cyril C. Richardson
LITURGY, UNITY, THE CHURCH 82
    Michael J. Taylor, S.J.
THE LITURGY AND ORTHODOXY 96
    John Meyendorff

5

6   **Contents**

DIALOGUE NO. 4
OUR COMMON CHRISTIAN HERITAGE

CHRISTIAN DIALOGUE 102

OUR COMMON CHRISTIAN HERITAGE 110
    Clement Welsh and Wilfred F. Dewan, C.S.P.

DIALOGUE NO. 5
RENEWAL OF GOD'S PEOPLE

CHRISTIAN DIALOGUE 138

REFORM—AN ESSENTIAL ELEMENT IN THE CHURCH 145
    Julius Cardinal Döpfner

THE WAY OF RENEWAL 160
    W. A. Visser 't Hooft

DIALOGUE NO. 6
OUR COMMON CHRISTIAN WITNESS

CHRISTIAN DIALOGUE 176

REPORT OF THE SECTION ON WITNESS 183
    Third Assembly of the W.C., New Delhi, 1961

THE NATURE OF CHRISTIAN WITNESS 200
    Philip Berrigan, S.S.J.

DIALOGUE NO. 7
WHY WE DON'T BREAK BREAD TOGETHER

CHRISTIAN DIALOGUE 212

WHY WE DON'T BREAK BREAD TOGETHER 219
    Wilfred F. Dewan, C.S.P. and Clement Welsh

EVALUATION SHEET 256

Introduction

Americans enjoy friendly conversation. Whatever our faults brooding silence is not one of them. Our land reverberates with voices discussing politics, business, the weather, sports and anything of interest. Thanks to the ecumenical spirit, we now find that religion gets more and more of its share of vocal attention accented not by the polemics of the past but by a new spirit of sincere inquiry.

Living Room Dialogues builds on our natural affinity for friendly discussion and, more importantly, on our accelerating and urgent concern for Christian unity. Already laymen from our various Churches have formed dialogue groups to pray over and study the problems of Christian unity. These groups need literature and resource material to help them develop and grow. *Living Room Dialogues* hopes to meet their needs and to encourage others to embark on an exciting adventure in Christian friendship.

The plan calls for 12 to 15 people—Catholic, Orthodox and Protestant—men and women, married and single, of different races and different age groups, to meet in one another's homes once a month for bible reading, prayer and discussion. The purpose is to help individual laymen and women become personally concerned about Christian unity and to pray for the reunion of all Christians. In addition, this book aims to remove confusion and misunderstanding among the laity of different Christian traditions and to nourish understanding and appreciation for the faith and worship of each other's Church.

The seven dialogues which follow were designed primarily for experimentation by pilot groups. For this reason a variety of materials will be found in the chapters. Some of the resource readings were written especially for these dialogues. Others were selected from a wide range of existing publications.

Each dialogue begins with prayer and bible readings. This is followed by a section entitled *Christian Dialogue* which provides discussion material for the meeting. The discussion leader or leaders should study this section carefully before the dialogue and decide how best to use this material for a successful discussion. Groups will naturally vary in their backgrounds and interests. Each group should, therefore, select and adapt the discussion outlines and questions according to the intellectual and theological background of its members and the pace of its discussion. Some will want to delve more deeply into a topic and perhaps spend two sessions on it; others will find a single discussion sufficient.

Each dialogue, except the first one, contains resource readings that should be read by each member before coming to the meeting. You will also find a selected bibliography for each dialogue. Experimental dialogue groups have discovered that if members come to the meetings with insights from extra reading, their discussion is more lively and fruitful. In order to allow the opportunity for some additional reading your group should plan to meet only once a month. Normally, it is expected that no priest or minister will be present at these sessions but that they will be consulted by the discussion leaders after each dialogue to clear up difficulties and answer questions which were raised during the meeting.

The following guidelines are offered for the benefit of discussion leaders:

Guidelines for Discussion

1. You will want to choose a moderator or discussion
   leader, or you may rotate this responsibility each

time. You may want co-leaders, a Roman Catholic and a Protestant, a man and a woman.

2. How about an observer, a different one each time, not to take part in the discussion, but to observe the process and to give positive suggestions for improving it next time?

3. In the first session, take time for each person to identify himself or herself—who each is—something of his interests and concerns—his church, etc.

4. Help to set the stage for learning, growing, sharing, caring, by listening to what is really being said, by accepting each person's contribution and by not judging them. Be open to all ideas and suggestions whether you agree with them or not. By your own attitude of willingness to learn and change, you will encourage others to do the same.

5. Take responsibility for helping with the discussion, not having to talk all the time, not having to be right or to prove a point. Help to keep some from monopolizing by encouraging each person to participate. If this is difficult, you might take turns at first to give everyone a chance to participate.

6. Help to distinguish facts from opinion, but encourage both.

7. If the group seems to wander, help to recall them to the subject under discussion. Don't try to cover more than one subject in an evening.

8. Set a firm closing hour and stick to it. Better to go home eager for more than exhausted! Two hours should be the maximum time.

9. By your own prayer and worship life, help the members of the group to center their interaction, their questioning and seeking in shared and varying kinds of prayer within the group.

10. Become better acquainted yourself with the wealth of resources of the Churches involved, and of the Christian Faith, and share these with others.

11. Ask God the Holy Spirit to lead and to change the

members of the group, so that individually and corporately they may find new ways of behaving as Christians, in the Church and in the world. Ideas will change but so will lives.

If you find this experience as rewarding as early experimental groups have, you may want to continue beyond the seven sessions suggested here. For those who do, we plan another series to follow this one and we want your help in preparing it. For this reason, an evaluation sheet will be found in the back of the book. Please use this form to evaluate your dialogues and to make suggestions for future dialogues. Please tell us, in particular, of any successful innovations in your meetings. Send your reports to:

Living Room Dialogues
c/o The Paulist Press
304 West 58th St.
New York, N.Y. 10019
          or
Living Room Dialogues
Room 804
475 Riverside Drive,
New York, N.Y. 10027

May God bless us all as we seek to do his will.

DIALOGUE NO. 1
Concern, Prayer, Love:
Foundation for Dialogue

CHRISTIAN DIALOGUE
Concern, Prayer, Love

OPENING PRAYER (ALL)

Let us pray. O Lord Jesus Christ, who on the eve of your Passion prayed that all your disciples might be one, as you are in the Father, and the Father in you, grant that we may suffer keenly on account of disunion.

Grant us the loyalty to recognize and the courage to reject our hidden indifference, mistrust and our mutual hostility.

Grant that we may find each other in you, so that from our hearts and from our lips may ceaselessly arise your prayer for the unity of Christians, such as you will and by the means that you will.

Grant that in you, who are perfect charity, we may find the way that leads to unity, in obedience to your love and to your truth. Amen.

BIBLE READING *(Each member of the group in turn reads a bible passage and leads the response.)*

Truly, I say to you, whoever says to this mountain, "Be taken up and cast into the sea," and does not doubt in his heart, but believes that what he says will come to pass, it will be done for him. Therefore I tell you, whatever you ask in prayer, believe that you receive it, and you will (Mark 11, 23-24).*

And I tell you, Ask, and it will be given you; seek, and you will find; knock, and it will be opened to you. For every one who asks receives and he who seeks finds, and to him who knocks it will be opened (Luke 11, 9-10).

* Scriptural quotations in every Christian Dialogue are taken, for the most part, from the *Revised Standard Version* of the Bible.

RESPONSES

Leader: Lord, by your words and deeds you taught us the need for faith in the power of prayer.

All: Help us to deepen our beliefs in the power of prayer. Impress upon us that to find ourselves once again united in you, we must continue to seek and to ask together.

BIBLE READING

Again I say to you, if two of you agree on earth about anything they ask, it will be done for them by my Father in heaven. For where two or three are gathered in my name, there am I in the midst of them (Matthew 18, 19-20).

RESPONSES

Leader: Lord, we are gathered together for your sake.

All: You are here in the midst of us.

Leader: We agree on the need for our unity; with you we ask for it in prayer.

All: According to your word, we hope it shall be done for us by your Father in heaven.

BIBLE READING

Holy Father, keep them in thy name, which thou hast given me, that they may be one, even as we are one (John 17, 11).

I do not pray for these only but also for those who believe in me through their word, that they may all be one: even as thou, Father, art in me, and I in thee; that they also may be in us, so that the world may believe that thou hast sent me (John 17, 20-21).

RESPONSES

Leader: Lord, on the night before your passion you prayed for unity.

All: Unite us so the world may believe that you have sent us.

BIBLE READING

And in the morning, a great while before day, he rose and went out to a lonely place, and there he prayed (Mark 1, 35).

But so much the more the report went abroad concerning him; and great multitudes gathered to hear and to be healed of their infirmities. But he withdrew to the wilderness and prayed (Luke 5, 15-16).

In these days he went out into the hills to pray; and all night he continued in prayer to God (Luke 6, 12).

RESPONSES

Leader: Lord, your Gospel tells us of your constant prayer during your ministry.

All: Teach us to put prayer at the heart of our Christian witness and mission.

BIBLE READING

And he told them a parable, urging them always to pray and not lose heart. He said, "In a certain city there was a judge who neither feared God nor regarded man; and there was a widow in that city who kept coming to him and saying, 'Vindicate me against my adversary.' For a while he refused; but afterward he said to himself, 'Though I neither fear God nor regard man, yet because this widow bothers me, I will vindicate her, or she will wear me out by her continual coming.'" And the Lord said, "Hear what the unrighteous judge says. And will not God vindicate his elect, who cry to him day and night? Will he delay long over them? I tell you, he will vindicate them speedily" (Luke 18, 1-8).

RESPONSES

Leader: Lord, help us to persevere in our prayer for Christian unity.

All: Do not let us lose heart when the novelty of praying with one another wears off.

BIBLE READING

Then Jesus went with them to a place called Gethsemane, and he said to his disciples, "Sit here, while I go yonder and pray." And taking with him Peter and the two sons of Zebedee, he began to be sorrowful and troubled. Then he said to them, "My soul is very sorrowful, even to death; remain here, and watch with me." And going a little farther he fell on his face and prayed, "My Father, if it be possible, let this cup pass from me; nevertheless, not as I will, but as thou wilt." And he came to the disciples and found them sleeping; and he said to Peter, "So, could you not watch with me one hour? Watch and pray that you may not enter into temptation; the spirit indeed is willing, but the flesh is weak" (Matthew 26, 36-41).

RESPONSES

Leader: Lord, we are sorrowful and troubled over the scandal of our divisions.

All: There is agony within your body, the Church.

Leader: If it be possible, let these divisions pass from us.

All: Not as we will, but as you will.

Leader: We have been sleeping in the face of our divisions; help us to watch and pray.

All: Our spirit is willing but our flesh is weak.

Christian Dialogue

Introduction

As we begin our *Living Room Dialogues* tonight, we should share a strong desire that it grow and deepen into a fruitful instrument for God to use in bringing about the unity of all Christians. In our succeeding meetings we will be involved primarily in discussion based upon study and reading done beforehand. Tonight, in our first meeting, we seek motivation and insights through meditation on Holy Scripture and our conversation.

It is important that we enter into our dialogue with correct motives and attitudes. We must have a clear idea of why we have come together, what we hope to accomplish and how we will benefit as individuals. Unless our goals are clear at the outset, our chances of persevering in the dialogue will be slim.

We must be aware that we enter into the *Living Room Dialogues* as pioneers, one of many groups formed throughout the country to conduct a pilot program. The content of this book is given to us to test, criticize and revise.

Through our dialogues we aim to create a ground swell of prayer and concern for Christian unity in America and to give depth to the movement. For now we are experiencing the honeymoon stage of ecumenism in this country. Good feelings and friendly gestures must mature into a solid ecumenical outlook. Unless such concern and prayer for Christian unity develops in local Christian communities the present hope for the reconciliation among Christians will fade.

What Does Concern Have To Do With Christian Unity?

Hopefully, something will happen to each one of us in the course of our *Living Room Dialogues*. We will become Christians sincerely concerned over the scandal of a divided Christendom.

To feel personal anguish over Christian disunity a Christian needs a universal outlook and sensitivity. He becomes aware that Christianity is not being extended throughout the world; it is dwindling. He sees the Christian community exerting less and less influence on exploding non-Christian populations and new emerging nations.

Divided Christianity presents the greatest single obstacle to the spread of Christ's Gospel in the world today. Since the world can find peace in the nuclear age only through Christ, the urgency of a common witness for Christ becomes more acute each day.

Christians also realize the diminishing influence of Christianity in their own culture. Many religious writers refer to our own society as de-christianized. Yet our divisions impede and sometimes paralyze effective witness. Pressing social problems cry out for a united Christian voice and action in every neighborhood of our land.

DISCUSSION QUESTIONS

Do you feel it is more important for Christians to be concerned about Christian unity today than it was 100 years ago? Why? From your own experience and observations can you give examples which would point to a lessening of Christian influence in your neighborhood or community?

What are the pressing social problems in America that cry out for united Christian action?

Can you honestly say that in the past you have been personally distressed because the Christians in your neighborhood were not united in Christ? Have you personally regretted the scandal this disunity gives for Christ in your community? Or must you as a Christian admit that Christian unity has not been a major concern in your life?

What Does Prayer Have To Do with Christian Unity?

We begin our dialogue with certain assumptions. We have to agree that the greatest force for the uniting of all Christians is prayer, for without prayer our initial interest in Christian unity will consume itself in shallow enthusiasm. Humanly speaking the goal of Christian unity faces insurmountable odds. Our own concern and work for Christian unity will quickly dissolve in frustration and discouragement unless they are based on three things:

1. Prayer and trust in the power of God
2. Deep personal commitment to *the unity that Christ wills.*
3. Patience and resignation to the coming of unity *in Christ's own time.*

A member of an ecumenical study group made this statement at a planning meeting, "Taking part in common prayer for Christian unity has given me a new insight into my own personal prayer life. I realized that most of my private prayer had been negative and selfish. I prayed to Christ only when I had a personal need. I turned to him only in times of my own personal tragedies and crises. For the first time I am praying for something Christ desires and prayed for, 'That all may be one in him.' For the first time I see the social implications of private prayer. I have begun to pray for the sufferings of my fellowman. My prayer now embraces world peace, the poverty stricken of Asia and social justice for the American Negro."

DISCUSSION QUESTIONS

Do you feel that private prayer is just an individual thing (between Christ and you) or do you believe it also has a social side?

If an atheist who was a community leader asked you what you asked for when you prayed to your Christ, would your answer edify him? Or would you have to admit your own private prayer to Christ was too selfish and too much centered on your own needs and fears? Could you tell him you have been praying daily for Christian unity because Christ desires it?

Suppose the members of this group decided that each time they walked or drove past any Christian Church they would say quietly to themselves, "O Lord, that they all may be one." Do you think this would help to make the members of the group personally concerned about Christian unity? Would you be willing to say this prayer each time you pass a Christian Church?

Do you think that meetings such as these could help to spread concern and prayer for Christian Unity? How?

What Does Love Have To Do with Christian Unity?

Now we consider another important goal for our *Living Room Dialogues:* understanding rooted in love. Tonight we strive to create a new atmosphere of Christian love and understanding among ourselves. We will build this new friendship in Christ by praying and listening to

God's Word in Holy Scripture together, by studying and talking together.

By these actions we will penetrate more deeply the things that already unite us in Christ; we will grow in our understanding of each other's faith and we will acquire more balanced insights into our differences.

Once we as a group discover new depths of love and friendship, then we can eliminate the hard core of prejudice and apathy within us. Finding out why we are brothers in Christ, we will discover why we are *separated* brothers. We must avoid, however, the temptation to dwell only on areas of agreement and gloss over our differences. An unsentimental facing of the issues that divide us is necessary if the dialogue is to be fruitful. We may discover that some of the differences are not as great as they seemed at first. Others, of course, may prove to be more serious than we had suspected. But it is necessary to face them honestly if they are to be dealt with in a constructive way.

DISCUSSION QUESTIONS: *(Each member of the group should comment briefly on the following questions.)*

Before we can build a friendship on the Christian elements we hold in common we have to know what these elements are. Let us go around the room and see how many we can name. What are the things we already share in Christ?

In future meetings we will examine some of the things that divide us. What are the chief areas of misunderstanding among Christians? What subjects do we feel we will have to face honestly to deepen our understanding of one another?

SUMMATION OF THE DISCUSSION *(Given by the discussion leader.) Also at this time all the necessary arrangements should be worked out for the next Living Room Dialogue.*

CHORAL PRAYER
Leader: Where charity and love are, there is God.

All: The love of Christ has gathered us together.
Leader: Let us rejoice in him and be glad.
All: Let us fear and love the living God.
Leader: And let us love one another with a sincere heart.
All: Where charity and love are, there is God.
Leader: When, therefore, we are assembled together, let us take heed, that we be not divided in mind.
All: Let there be an end to bitterness and quarrels, an end to strife.
Leader: And let Christ, our God, dwell in our midst.
All: Where charity and love are, there is God.
Leader: Let us also with the blessed see
All: Your face in glory, O Christ our God,
Leader: There to possess pure and unbounded joy
All: For infinite ages and ages. Amen.

BIBLE READING: *(Each member of the group in turn reads a bible passage and leads the response.)*

If I speak in the tongues of men and of angels, but have not love, I am a noisy gong or a clanging cymbal . . . and if I have all faith, so as to remove mountains, but do not have love, I am nothing (1 Cor. 13, 1-2).

RESPONSES

Leader: Lord, this is our first meeting to come to know and love each other as Christian neighbors.
All: Inflame us with your charity. Do not allow us to become noisy gongs or clanging cymbals.

BIBLE READING

If anyone says, "I love God," and hates his brother, he is a liar; for he who does not love his brother whom he has seen, cannot love God whom he has not seen. And this commandment we have from him, that he who loves God should love his brother also (1 John 4, 20-21).

Put on then, as God's chosen ones, holy and beloved, compassion, kindness, lowliness, meekness, and patience, forebearing one another and, if one has a complaint against another, forgiving each other . . . And above all these put on love, which binds everything together in perfect harmony. And let the peace of Christ rule in your hearts, to which indeed you were called in the one body (Colossians 3, 12-15).

RESPONSES

Leader: Lord, we desire to unite in a bond of Christian friendship.
All: Help us to put on a heart of mercy, kindness, humility, meekness and patience.
Leader: Lord, we desire to remove all mistrust of one another.
All: Teach us to bear with one another and forgive one another.

BIBLE READING

Now the company of those who believed were of one heart and soul, and no one said that any of the things which he possessed was his own, but they had everything in common. And with great power the apostles gave their testimony to the resurrection of the Lord Jesus, and great grace was upon them all (Acts 4, 32-33).

And they devoted themselves to the apostles' teaching and fellowship, to the taking of bread and the prayers (Acts 2, 42).

RESPONSES

Leader: Lord, we stand before you as separated brothers.
All: Help us to become believers of one heart and one soul.
Leader: We do not have all things in common.
All: Hasten the day we will share the breaking of bread in Holy Communion.

CLOSING PRAYER

Leader: O Lord, you have loved the Church and given yourself for it;
All: Sanctify and cleanse it by your Word.
Leader: Remove all needless divisions,
All: Take away the spirit of rivalry and jealousy.

Leader: Rebuke all our uncharitable judgments of one another,

All: Unite us all in your holy work.

Leader: Bless all who love the Lord Jesus Christ,

All: By whatever name they are called.

Leader: Guide them into closer fellowship with you.

All: Preserve your Church in unity and peace.

Leader: Give her increasing trust in the power of prayer and holiness,

All: In the unfailing guidance of your Spirit.

All: O God, Father of our Lord Jesus Christ, our only Savior, the Prince of Peace, grant us the grace to take to heart the scandal of our divisions. Deliver us from all hatred and prejudice, and from all that hinders our unity, in order that, as there is but one body and one spirit, one hope in our calling, one Lord, one faith, one baptism, one God and Father of all, so we may also be of one heart and one soul, united by the bonds of grace and truth, of faith and of love, in Jesus Christ our Lord. Amen.

DIALOGUE NO. 2
Good Conversation in Christ

Resource Readings

Nine Steps to Unity (pp. 31–42)
Robert McAfee Brown
Ten Commandments for the Ecumenical Age (pp. 43–56)
John Cogley

Suggested Readings

Brown, Robert McAfee and Weigel, Gustave (editors). *An American Dialogue.* Garden City, N.Y.: Doubleday, 1960.
O'Brien, John A. *Steps to Christian Unity.* Garden City, N.Y.: Doubleday, 1964.

CHRISTIAN DIALOGUE
Good Conversation in Christ

OPENING PRAYER

Leader: In spite of our ignorance of one another, of our prejudices and our dislikes,
All: Jesus, make us one.
Leader: In spite of all spiritual and intellectual barriers,
All: Jesus, make us one.
Leader: O God, for your own great glory,
All: Gather together all separated Christians.
Leader: O God, for the triumph of goodness and truth,
All: Gather together all separated Christians.
Leader: O God, that there may be one sheepfold for the one Shepherd,
All: Gather together all separated Christians.
Leader: O God, that peace may reign in the world,
All: Gather together all separated Christians.
Leader: O God, to fill the heart of your Son with joy,
All: Gather together all separated Christians. Amen.

BIBLE READING

Let love be genuine; hate what is evil, hold fast to what is good; love one another with brotherly affection; outdo one another in showing honor . . . Repay no one evil for evil, but take thought for what is noble in the sight of all. If possible, so far as it depends upon you, live peaceably with all . . . Do not be overcome by evil, but overcome evil with good (Rom. 12, 9-10, 17-18, 21).

MEDITATION

Lord, in this meeting we want to build Christian attitudes and guidelines for Christian dialogue . . . We want to heed St. Paul and love one another with fraternal charity, anticipating one another with honor . . . We do not want to be overcome by evil but overcome evil with good . . . Lord, help us.

BIBLE READING

Now the company of those who believed were of one heart and soul, and no one said that any of the things which he possessed was his own, but they had everything in common. And with great power the apostles gave their testimony to the resurrection of the Lord Jesus, and great grace was upon them all (Acts 4, 32-33).

And they devoted themselves to the apostles' teaching and fellowship, to the breaking of bread and the prayers (Acts 2, 42).

Meditation

Lord, we enter into dialogue to hasten the day when we can become believers of one heart and one soul. . . . We want to have all things in common. . . . We pray that through listening to your Word together we will one day unite in the communion of the breaking of the bread and in the prayers. . . . Lord, help us.

Christian Dialogue

Introduction

In this outline we offer guidelines to help you to dialogue about dialogue. Each group will have its own characteristics. Each will want to proceed according to ground rules with which it feels comfortable. Our purpose is to help you work out such a framework for your future meetings. Your resource reading presented a number of principles for dialogue. These plus your discussion on the following points should be the raw material for your own set of guidelines.

What Is Dialogue?

"A dialogue is not a speech in which one person talks and the other listens, or in which one participant has certain advantages which are denied the other. A dialogue implies that two people, or two groups, are both speaking and listening (though not, one hopes, simultaneously), each saying what he has to say, and each listening to what the other has to say."*

Dialogue is an encounter between Christians. It aims to create a true Christian friendship among them *through coming to know each other as Christians*—what they believe, what they aspire to, what they hope for the Church, what their commitment to the Lord actually is.

DISCUSSION QUESTIONS

At this point each member of the group should recall his own personal experiences in discussions about religion —at school—in the service—at work—with relatives, etc. How many of them could be called dialogue in the true sense of the word? Did any of them end up in arguments? Why do we hear about so many discussions on religion ending up in arguments? What factors turn a dialogue into an argument? How can our group guard against these factors?

The Spirit of Dialogue

Participants must trust one another to be speaking the truth as each one sees it, in good faith and without any secret motives. All must assume a common devotion to truth and above all to Jesus Christ who said, "I am the truth . . ."

According to Robert McAfee Brown and John Cogley, what other attitudes and virtues must one bring to dialogue?

What other attitudes and virtues do you feel are important for Christian dialogue?

*Brown and Weigle, *An American Dialogue* (New York: Doubleday, 1960), page 25.

How Will Dialogue Affect Knowledge of Your Own Church?

Each Living Room Dialogue will center around some point of Christian life and belief. A participant will need, therefore, a basic understanding of his own Church's position, a willingness to state it and to have it questioned and criticized. For some of us this may require some homework—reading or asking a pastor for clarification or information. At the outset it is important that the members of the group admit to one another that they are not professional theologians—that they do not know all the answers about their own beliefs—that they will not be embarrassed to say, "I don't know but I will try to find out." One of the benefits of dialogue is that the members experience a renewed interest and deepening of their own commitments. The challenge of discussion becomes a new motivation for reading and learning.

In what areas do you feel you need more knowledge about your own Church?

How will dialogue help you to acquire this?

What Will Dialogue Teach You About Other Churches?

Each member of the group must really work to understand the position of the others. Much of this understanding will develop in the course of the dialogues but again some serious homework should be undertaken. At least a minimum of honest reading and study will save the group from time-wasting which could result from total ignorance of the others' positions or beliefs. A limited bibliography will be found at the conclusion of each chapter. Each member should try to do a little outside reading during the year. Some groups make room at some point in their dialogue for members to share insights from their outside reading.

In the process of dialogue, when a new or strange point of view is expressed, it is often advisable for someone to restate it as he heard it, "Do you mean. . . . ?" Then listen to see if the original speaker agrees with the restatement. Needless to say, such understanding requires an eagerness to see the beliefs of others in their best light, not their worst, and a willingness to revive previous ideas about another's position—to give up caricatures which may have long been cherished.

DISCUSSION QUESTIONS

What are some of the things you admire in the tradition of others in the group and would like to know more about?

What things puzzle you in the tradition of others?

Honesty and Humility in Dialogue

All participants must be willing to be humble and penitent about the things which their own groups are doing or have done which cause or perpetuate divisions. No true dialogue can take place if some are intent on proving all fault lies on one side. We need to recognize that we are all sinners and that we have contributed to the disunity of the Church and to say together, "Forgive us our trespasses . . ."

DISCUSSION QUESTIONS

What do Robert McAfee Brown and John Cogley have to say on this point?

Do you feel that Dr. Brown and Mr. Cogley were accurate when they commented on the faults of Protestants and Catholics? Do you recognize any of these faults in yourself?

What does John Cogley mean when he says, "Do not attempt to achieve charity at the expense of truth?"

It has been said that in our culture there is a strong universal emotional need to be liked and accepted. This has led to the fear that laymen in dialogue would be too willing to compromise what they believe about Christ in order to "get along better". Do you feel this fear is justified? How can a set of guidelines guard against a spirit of misguided compromise?

The Results of Dialogue

Dialogue aims to make better Christians of each one of us by deepening our own religious knowledge and commitment and by increasing our love and understanding of our Christian neighbors and friends of other traditions. Its participants aim at doing what God wills for the Church. They realize that these encounters are simple first steps in this process of renewing their own lives and the life of the Church. No one comes away from dialogue unchanged. In this spirit their dialogue must be offered to God for him to use as he sees fit.

What led you to become a member of a *Living Room Dialogue?*

What personal benefits do you expect to get out of dialogue?

Dialogue and Prayer

Prayer and the bible should be prominent in the activity of any dialogue group. When prayer and Holy Scripture surround dialogue, the dialogue itself becomes prayer. Once dialogue becomes prayer it is guided and enriched by the action of the Holy Spirit.

DISCUSSION QUESTIONS

Why is reading from the bible a key to creating the right spiritual climate for dialogue?

How much time should a dialogue group give to scriptural reading?

Formulating Rules of Dialogue

Now as you close your dialogue on dialogue it would be worthwhile to draw quickly a brief set of ground rules by which you plan to conduct your future meetings. They will not, of course, be hard and fast rules but a set of norms outlining the spirit in which you hope to reach out to one another in a truly Christian way. They will spell out your expectations about the nature of your dialogues, what you hope to achieve, how you wish to conduct them.

Future chapters in the book will aid you in dialoguing on specific doctrinal questions and Christian practices. But this discussion is important because it outlines the spirit and purpose of these encounters, the spirit of Jesus Christ and the hope of doing his will.

This discussion should begin with the observer giving his summation of the foregone discussion in which he points out the guidelines that have been already suggested by the members of the group.

CLOSING PRAYER

Leader: Let us pray, that we may be delivered from all in us that hinders the coming of unity;

All: From selfish unwillingness to leave old ways;

Leader: From a sectarian spirit;

All: From pride masking prejudices as principles;

Leader: From willingness to sacrifice conviction to expediency;

All: From pessimism and defeatism, impatience and sloth;

Leader: From setting either the hopes or fears of men before the will of God;

All: That we may serve the cause of unity according to the gifts that are in us;

Leader: That we may not set back the good cause by lack of charity;

All: That honoring the convictions of others we may seek the truth in love.

All: O God, Father of our Lord Jesus Christ, our only Savior, the Prince of Peace, grant us the grace to take to heart the scandal of our divisions. Deliver us from all hatred and prejudice, and from all that hinders our unity, in order that, as there is but one body and one spirit, one hope in our calling, one Lord, one faith, one baptism, one God and Father of all, so we may also be of but one heart and one soul, united by the bonds of grace and truth, of faith and of love, in Jesus Christ our Lord. Amen.

Nine Steps to Unity

Robert McAfee Brown

1. Our concerns about Christian unity must be steeped in the life of prayer, which is always the "next step" toward greater unity. This almost sounds platitudinous, but I stress it because I am discovering that prayer *for* one another can gradually, by the power of the Holy Spirit, be transformed into prayer *with* one another. Twice a week all fall during Vatican II the Protestant observers met in a Methodist Church near St. Peter's to pray *for* the Council. Every morning, however, we were also present at Mass in St. Peter's, and we found ourselves more and more engaged in praying *with* the Council.

There were many portions of the Mass in which we felt we could participate without doing violence to our own faith or appearing to trivialize the faith of our Catholic brethren, portions that have been part of our own Protestant liturgical heritage as well—the *Kyrie*, the *Gloria*, the *Credo*, the *Sanctus*, the *Pater Noster*, the *Agnus Dei*. I think that I have been brought closer to an understanding of the real meaning of Roman Catholic faith by attending Mass five times a week for ten weeks and praying with the Council fathers, than by all the many books of Catholic theology it has been my responsibility to read in the past five years.

During the discussion of the schema on ecumenism, a number of bishops quite independently of one another called attention to the difficulty we experience in sharing common worship. As a result, bishops from missionary areas, bishops from Eastern rite Churches, and bishops from Europe, asked for relaxations in the regulations forbidding Catholics to participate in common worship with non-Catholics. This is particularly vexing on family occasions such as baptisms, weddings, and funerals, but it is also vexing when it obstructs our learning how to join together in the simplest acts of common prayer.

Some of these barriers are in process of being overcome during that period each January when Catholics are celebrating the Christian Unity Octave, and Protestants are celebrating the Week of Prayer for Christian Unity. And I am persuaded, not only for theological reasons but out of my experience last fall in Rome as well, that we must proceed to more, rather than less, common worship together, actively sharing in those prayers and responses that are part of our common heritage as Christians, and at least observing in respectful silence those portions of the worship of one another that we cannot, as yet, share.

On the night of President Kennedy's death I was at the Canadian Theological College in Rome—the lone American and the lone Protestant in the building. But as we all said together the *Pater Noster,* upon learning of the President's assassination, I knew that I was in the midst of fellow Christians, with whom it was possible to join in a common act of prayer to a common Father, and in my time of personal bereavement I was sustained by that fact.

2. A second "step to Christian unity" is a common acknowledgment of our guilt for the events that separated us in the past. It has often been difficult for Catholics to feel that they should acknowledge responsibility for the rifts that now divide Christendom. Since the Second Vatican Council, however, it should no longer be difficult for the Pope himself to set forth mutual confession and mutual pardon as the conditions of ecumenical advance. Speaking of the separation of Christians one from the

other, Pope Paul said in his opening allocution on September 29, "If we are in any way to blame for that separation, we humbly beg God's forgiveness and ask pardon too of our brethren who feel themselves to have been injured by us. For our part, we willingly forgive the injuries which the Catholic Church has suffered, and forget the grief endured during the long series of dissensions and separations."

Again and again during the Council sessions this statement was quoted, as bishop after bishop reiterated the conviction that only as sin is acknowledged can forgiveness be granted. When both sides engage in mutual confession, both sides can engage in mutual pardon, and when such an attitude is present there are literally no limits that can be built around what the Holy Spirit can do with such a basis for genuine reconciliation.

3.   Another step toward unity, and one that is perhaps even harder than to acknowledge one's fault, is the attempt to engage in inner renewal. Protestantism's best gift to the ecumenical future will be a purged and purified Protestantism. Catholicism's best gift will be a purged and purified Catholicism. Our task is not to point out the faults so obviously and glaringly present in the other's life, but rather to work to remove the faults so insidiously present in our own life.

This need for inner renewal was vividly illustrated by the speeches made in the Council. South American bishops inveighed against the Church's identification with the rich and its lack of concern for the poor. A German cardinal insisted that the Church purge itself of every trace of anti-Semitism. A Mexican bishop urged a more charitable attitude toward the sect groups. A French bishop wanted more concern for those in need, whether Catholic, Protestant, Jewish, or non-believer. An American bishop reminded the fathers that they must give the layman more to do than "obey, pray and pay". Over and over again the theme was: the Church as it now is, is a far cry from the Church as it ought to be. Many of the fathers put the ecumenical overtones of this point as follows: The Church cannot simply "wait" for people to return to it; the Church must engage in the inner renewal which removes the legitimate reasons people have had for being unwilling to relate themselves to it.

4.   Before we can take active steps toward unity, we must be clear about the nature of the unity we do and do not share. The phrase so commonly used nowadays is a good symbol of what our true situation is. That phrase is the phrase "separated brethren". The basic word, of course, is the noun. We are brethren. Why are we brethren? Not simply because we share a common humanity, but because we share a common baptism. As Catholic ecumenical thinkers have been pointing out with increasing vigor, this fact of our common baptism underlies the whole ecumenical venture. By virtue of baptism, we are all, in some sense, united with Christ; we are all, in some sense, within the Church. The Catholic may feel that the Protestant shares this membership within the Church very imperfectly, but baptism is nevertheless the basis of a real and indelible bond between us, on which we can build.

We are not only brethren; we are also separated brethren. No satisfaction at our underlying brotherhood can be allowed to make us complacent about the fact of our separation; but no despair over our separation can be allowed to make us forgetful of the fact that we are brothers. Here, then, is both the glory and the agony of our situation. We can never act as though the other did not exist, and we can never accept our separation from the other as a satisfactory situation. We are already bound to one another in deeper ways than we usually acknowledge, and only as we see one another in these terms—as brothers, albeit as separated brothers—can we get to the heart of our problem. Any "steps to Christian unity" that do not proceed from this fundamental assurance are likely to be steps in the wrong direction.

5. Since we are brothers, albeit separated brothers, who must enter into union with one another, one of our basic tasks is to become better acquainted. This means exploration, at all levels, both of those things we share and of those things that divide us. Theologians must engage in this enterprise in theological discussion groups. Catholic seminarians must pursue deeper acquaintance with Protestant seminarians, and vice versa. And laymen in local parishes must seek ways to reach out and come to know their counterparts in neighboring parishes. The Vatican Council itself furnishes a good basis for beginning such attempts at acquaintance on the latter level. Any Catholic parish that invites neighboring Protestants to an evening of discussion about the Vatican Council can be assured of a good response, and one hopes that the reverse would be true also. Catholics willing to discuss a book like Hans Küng's *The Council, Reform and Reunion* will find Protestants amazed, delighted, and rejoicing in what they find therein. Such local study groups, beginning with a discussion of the Council, could then move into other areas: the place of Scripture, the message of the prophets, the significance of baptism, and out of such exchange not only become acquainted with one another's convictions, but also become acquainted with one another as persons.

As such acquaintance deepens it is more and more possible to discuss differences as well as similarities, and to do so without self-consciousness or rancor. I discovered during the second session of the Vatican Council that the longer I was there, the more free and unstrained were the conversations I could have with Roman Catholics at the coffee bar. Catholics did not just want to hear polite praise from me; they wanted to know what I "really thought", and before long an atmosphere of enough trust and confidence had been established so that I could tell them what I "really thought"—that I really thought the liturgy schema was a stunner, and that I really thought the communications schema was a disaster. Both things.

Not just the first, and not just the second. For if carping criticism is no help neither is routine praise.

I also discovered, by virtue of the privilege of being in attendance at all the Council sessions, that some things that bother Protestants very much about the Catholic-Protestant situation bother Catholics equally. For years, Protestants have chafed over the rules and regulations surrounding "mixed marriages", and have felt that these make genuine ecumenical encounter on the local level next to impossible. But I discovered at the Council that this matter bothers many of the bishops as well.

Since there was no mention of this problem in any of the *schemata* under discussion, it was all the more impressive to discover how many bishops from different parts of the world raised the matter of mixed marriage regulations as one of the thorniest of the problems with which *they* had to cope, and recommended changes in Catholic legislation on the matter. I had previously thought that most Catholics lived in bland indifference to the fact that there was a "problem" here. Perhaps now that we both acknowledge that there is a problem, we can begin to talk together about ways of coping with the problem— ways that will not compromise the convictions of either side, but can help to make religion a creative rather than a destructive factor in a mixed marriage, once the latter has taken place.

It is one of the signs of maturity to be able both to give and to receive criticism in a spirit of charity. If the criticism is surrounded by bonds of mutual concern and love, it need not be destructive but can actually be creative. When we have reached this point in our relationship with one another we have taken a gigantic "step to Christian unity".

6.   Sometimes it is this awareness of the issues that divide us at present that can force us to a reassessment of the past. Both Protestants and Catholics need to re-study their own past history. The conventional Catholic

polemic against the Reformers is beginning to change. I heard one bishop on the Council floor say that Catholics must recognize that the Reformers' *intention* was a recovery of the Gospel and not a disruption of the Church. And the conventional Protestant polemic against Catholic liturgy ("magic . . .") is beginning to be replaced by a more responsible attempt to understand why the Mass is so central to Catholic faith—and somehow the charge of "magic" just doesn't fill the bill any more, if it ever did.

A look at the past—an attempt to understand where we *are* by examining where we *came from*—may be one of the most important things we can do together. And to the degree that we can do this without emotional polemics, we may both be able to grow in the process, and to grow toward one another.

A good example of this "step to Christian unity" is the treatment accorded the Mariological material at the Vatican Council. By a narrow margin, but nevertheless by a sufficient margin, the Council fathers voted not to have a separate *schema* on Mary, but to incorporate material on Mary into the *schema* on the Church. Part of the reason for this decision was their feeling that separate treatment of Mary tends to encourage Mariological devotion in isolation from the rest of Catholic faith. Another part of the reason was their recognition that ecumenical relations would be helped rather than hindered by the relocation, particularly if the material were recast in predominantly biblical terms.

Such an action has all sorts of creative ecumenical possibilities. If the new material on Mary, to be presented at the next session of the Council, does have a predominantly biblical orientation, then this fact will place a real obligation on the shoulders of Protestants. It will force us to re-examine in a new way the biblical materials about Mary. Protestants have not really done this before, due to emotional biases engendered by a feeling that Mariology has gotten out of hand by straying so far from the biblical materials. But the Council's recent action creates at least the possibility that an issue which has been ecumenically divisive in the past could become ecumenically creative.

Our examination of our differences, then, must include a willingness to re-examine past reasons for those differences, in the hope that we can gradually overcome at least some of them.

7. This suggests another "step to Christian unity" that can be taken promptly. One of the French Protestant observers at the Council told me that there are over two hundred joint Protestant-Catholic bible study groups in France today. In America we have scarcely begun to explore the beneficial possibilities of such an endeavor. Catholics and Protestants have the good fortune to share substantially the same Scripture. (The Catholic canon is a little longer than the Protestant, but with sixty-six books still shared in common we have enough to keep us busy for the foreseeable future.) We agree, furthermore, that in a unique way God has spoken to men through the Scriptures. We agree that the Scriptures are the fountainhead of our faith and that within them we find the Bread of Life. If we want to know about the heritage we share, as brethren in Jesus Christ, it is to the Scriptures that we must go.

What could be more obvious, therefore, than that we should go to them together? It is a commonplace that Catholic and Protestant biblical scholars have shared one another's research and findings for close to three decades now, and there are resources of biblical interpretation that both Catholics and Protestants can use together. If two neighboring parishes, one Catholic and one Protestant, want to come together to renew their understanding of the Christian faith, there could be no better place to embark upon this quest than through common bible study. With a priest and a minister available as resource people, such groups can genuinely ask themselves, "What is this book trying to say to us today in the midst of our divisions, and in the midst of our solidarity despite our divisions?"

Every morning at the Council, before the work of the day began, there was the ceremony of The Enthronement of the Gospel. An early illuminated manuscript was brought forward and placed on the altar for the duration of the session, as a reminder to the fathers that their proper work was the elucidation of that Gospel, and the presence of the book upon the altar served as a useful reminder of that proper work, whenever anyone began to stray away from the content or the spirit of the Gospel.

The bible is the basic resource of the faith we share. Consequently, as we share our study of the bible, we will share yet more of the faith we share.

8. In the midst of the above activities, and in the midst of cultivating the above attitudes, there is another thing we can do specifically and tangibly. We can join forces in the sharing of our common civic responsibilities. We do not need to agree about the Dogma of the Assumption, to agree that all men are of equal worth to God and that the color of one's skin is an irrelevance to God and to those who call themselves God's children. Even while we explore our doctrinal divisions, we can experience our civic unity. No true Catholic and no true Protestant can accept the notion that restrictive housing covenants are right, or that a member of a minority group should be denied the privilege of eating in a restaurant.

Where civic injustice exists, in other words, Catholics and Protestants can already make common cause. Not only that, they *must* make common cause. It is a cheap evasion to say that we cannot share civic responsibility together at the city planner's table because we cannot yet share bread and wine together at the Lord's Table. If we cannot demonstrate our solidarity in Christ by our united action against racial and economic injustice, we have little cause to believe that the world will take much notice of what we say or do elsewhere.

As was suggested earlier, it is often the case that as

we work together on "getting out the vote", or mobilizing opinion for a bill in the state legislature, we really come to know one another for the first time. If Catholics and Protestants are discussing a fair housing bill together, they will finally find themselves discussing the doctrine of man together—which is what a fair housing bill is all about in the first place.

The solidarity that is gained by these common forays into the body politic is a most sustaining experience. Anyone who participated in the March on Washington will understand this feeling. There were many Protestant and Catholic clergymen present on that occasion. Since most of them, whether Protestant or Catholic, wore clerical collars that day, it was hard to tell one from the other. And the important thing is that *on that day it didn't particularly matter*. What mattered was that the Church of Jesus Christ was finally beginning to involve itself in the racial struggle, and at that point of involvement in the racial struggle there was neither Jew nor Greek, bond nor free, black nor white, Catholic nor Protestant. On that day, making even that minimum social protest, Catholics and Protestants were brought close to one another. If it is true that "the world is too strong for a divided Church", it is also true that a divided world needs a strong Church. The whole cause of Christ is strengthened at those points where, without compromising our own basic conviction, we can still work together.

9. The final "step to Christian unity" must be put as a caution and a warning, as well as the sounding of a hope. Many people thrust themselves into "Catholic-Protestant relations" with fervent zeal and enthusiasm, discovering that all sorts of barriers due to misunderstanding can be demolished. But when they get to the hardcore differences that still remain, despite all the goodwill, and when they discover that unity is not just around the corner, they lose hope. If they are Protestants they mutter about Catholic intransigence *("Why* must they stick

to their belief in the infallibility of the Pope?"). If they are Catholics they mutter about Protestant stubbornness ("Why can't they see that Christ intended to found one Church, and that the Church he founded is the Roman Catholic Church?"). Some Protestants go as far as to decide that Catholic ecumenism is only a "trick"—a kind of soft-sell to make it easier for non-Catholics to submit to Rome.

There are indeed awesome barriers that stand in the way of full unity, and it is paradoxically a "step to Christian unity" to recognize the apparently discouraging fact of those barriers. Nothing but disillusionment will come of a naïve hope that unity can be achieved by just a little more talking. The differences that will remain when all the talking has been done are still monumental differences. It is admittedly hard to see what ultimate good can come of all the talk, and even of all the action, if the end product is still Catholic insistence that the Catholic Church is the only true Church, coupled with Protestant insistence that reunion can come only as Catholicism renounces its claim to be the only true Church.

This sounds like an ultimate impasse if there ever was one. It would be an ultimate impasse were it not for the Holy Spirit. And the only condition under which Protestants and Catholics can take genuine "steps to Christian unity" is at some kind of real risk. The risk is that what will emerge at the end of the road will not simply be the Catholic Church as it now is, with all Protestants absorbed into it, nor will it be the Protestant Church as it now is, with all Catholics absorbed into it. What will emerge is something we do not yet really see. Unity will not come if either group simply waits for the other to move toward it. Unity will come only as both groups move out *toward* one another, recognizing that after their confrontation with one another, neither will be quite the same as it was before the encounter took place.

This means, as the first chapter of Vatican II's proposed *schema* on the Church insists, that we have to do, at the heart of our faith, with a mystery. We cannot totally and definitely outline or blueprint the structure of the Church. Its boundaries are known only to God, and cannot be exhaustively stated in any formulae, however inspired. This means that both Catholics and Protestants must be open to insights about the nature of the Church that may thus far have been denied to both of them, and it also means that neither group can be content to be quite as static as it has been in the past.

If such talk sounds strange to Catholic ears, I can only insist that both Pope Paul, in his talk to the Protestant observers, and Cardinal Léger, in a speech to the Council fathers, inveighed against what they called "theological immobilism", the notion that God's truth has been captured in some kind of final form by man's doctrinal statements. We must always believe that the Spirit can lead us to a *new* grasp of "the faith once delivered to the saints".

We can believe, for example, that it is the will of Christ "that all may be one", without being absolutely sure how that oneness is to be achieved. But if we do believe that Christ wills his children to be one, we must do all within our power to destroy whatever barriers we can that are still keeping his children divided. This will not destroy all the barriers, but it will destroy some of them, and will thereby create a new situation. And that, indeed, is the main "step to Christian unity" that must be taken in our day—the creation of a new situation. We do not know what will emerge out of the new situation. But God does. And that is sufficient.

Ten Commandments
for the Ecumenical Age

John Cogley

1. *Remember that saints and sinners are to be found
in all branches of Christianity.*

In the pre-ecumenical period, what might be called
the Age of Polemics, it was customary to check with
the saints of one's own tradition and the sinners of other
traditions. The villainy of some historic figures was exaggerated and the simon-pure sanctity of others traced
uncritically, depending on which side they were found.
For example, many Catholics, anxious to belittle Martin
Luther, dismissed him simply as a monk who broke his
vows in order to marry an ex-nun. The tremendous spirituality of Luther, his anguish of soul, vibrant faith, and
awesome love of God were blithely ignored. All that
remained of him when these Catholic apologists finished
their work was a strong-willed, stubborn, egocentric, sensu-
ous, disobedient cleric who betrayed his priestly vocation
and led millions into willful heresy. Protestant simplifiers,
on the other hand, portrayed a Brother Martin who was
almost a single light shining in the total darkness of
monastic corruption and superstition of his time. Neither
did justice to the complex man Luther actually was, nor
to the tangle of issues that resulted in the Reformation.

The modern layman of whatever faith who wishes to
participate in the ecumenical movement has to rid his
mind of such stereotypes. The Protestant, for instance,

would do well not to be caught exaggerating the number
of "bad Popes" and the enormity of their crimes. The
Catholic would do well not to be caught denying that
any such Popes ever existed or claiming that clerical corruption played only a minor part in creating the scandal
of Christian disunity.

The people of one tradition should be better acquainted with the works of charity and prayer carried on
by others. Protestant speakers might be asked to address
Catholic groups and Catholic speakers to address Protestant groups. They could describe, for example, the work
carried on at the Protestant parish in Harlem, the Mary-
knoll clinics in Korea, the string of colleges established by
American Presbyterians in the Middle East or the missions
of the Medical Missionary Sisters of Philadelphia, who
look after sick and pregnant women in Pakistan.

Protestant libraries might emphasize from time to time
the biographies of saintly Catholic heroes and Catholic
libraries might do the same for Protestant heroes. Schools,
colleges, and the organizations of one faith might honor
outstanding work done by persons of the other faith.
There is no reason why all Catholic medals, awards, and
honorary degrees should always go to Catholics or to
persons whose religious affiliation is vague (which in the
past often seemed to count as a higher recommendation
than forthright Protestantism). Nor is there any reason
why Protestant honors should not be given to Catholics
whose accomplishment, even judged by Protestant standards, deserves recognition.

There are many ways in which we can show that
we both take seriously what St. Paul said about the primacy of charity. Unhappily, we are still in disagreement
about certain articles of faith and indeed about the nature of faith; we may actually have serious differences
about what is to be hoped for, in the life to come; but
the greatest of these, charity, can be a point of agreement
here and now. There are many different ways of showing
that it is. For no Christian community underestimates love

of God and of neighbor, and none has a monopoly on it. If that were not true, the ecumenical movement would be doomed from the start.

2. *Do not look to conversion as the proper result of ecumenism.*

The ecumenist who tries to exploit the desire for Christian unity to make converts to his own faith is doomed to failure, on both counts. For he is not forthright about either of his two purposes. The convert-maker has one end in view, the winning of hearts and minds to his idea of what is true—a perfectly laudable, apostolic motive. The ecumenist has another aim: the creation of bonds of charity between different Christian communities and the healing of Christian schism in accordance with the will of God. Any "fifth-column" proselytizing activity on the part of the ecumenist, Catholic or Protestant, will quickly undo what he set out to accomplish. His proper role in relation to other Christian communities engaged in the common pursuit of unity is then not so much to preach the Gospel as to live it.

Of course it is always possible that as a result of ecumenical activity some conversions may follow, from Protestantism to Catholicism or from Catholicism to Protestantism. This is one of the risks involved in the movement. But such an effect is accidental and unsought, so to speak, and based on a purely personal decision, which must be respected. It can never be counted on.

Convert-making involves a persuader and the one persuaded in a teacher-student relationship. Ecumenicity, on the other hand, involves a confrontation of persons who regard each other as equals. Neither sets out to "work on" the other. The purpose of ecumenism is not to persuade but to understand a position other than one's own, to build bridges across chasms of historic hostility, and to seek out what is held in common rather than to sharpen differences.

From the beginning the ecumenical movement has

been inextricably tied in with the idea of dialogue. Dialogue should not be confused with debate or argument or dialectic. As Martin Buber, the great Jewish thinker, explained it, it does not involve the conflict of ideas so much as the confrontation of persons, each taking the other as he is. No one comes out of a dialogue a winner or a loser but simply as a fuller person enriched with a deeper understanding of how another person thinks, why he thinks as he does, and what at the innermost core of his being are his convictions.

Charity is built on such knowledge. And it is the belief of ecumenists, whatever their faith, that if, in the providence of God, the unity of truth is one day to be realized among Christians, it must first be preceded by the unity of charity. Achieving that unity—the oneness of love—is the special task of our generation. It is sought in the belief that if it is found the rest will one day be added unto us, in a manner and according to means which God has not yet revealed.

3. *Do not attempt to achieve charity at the expense of truth.*

During all the years since the Reformation, especially since the Council of Trent, the Catholic Church has laid down very strict rules regarding the participation of Catholics in non-Catholic worship, the acceptance of non-Catholic sacraments, etc. In some places at certain times, these regulations may have been too rigidly enforced, as they still seem to be in a few dioceses where Catholics are forbidden to pray together with their Protestant brethren, sing mutually accepted hymns together, or listen to a reading from the Scriptures. Since the Ecumenical Council began, though, there is a general loosening up and the joint prayer meeting or Bible service is fairly commonplace.

Still, the Catholic Church has not completely backed away from its former position, nor is it likely to. The reason is that the Church does not believe that charity can be bought at the expense of truth, for God is the Author of both. Catholics are forbidden, by their active participation in Protestant services, to seem to be endorsing Protestant theological teachings and the principles of the Reformation. In accordance with the same reasoning, Protestants by and large would not think of participating in the Mass to the extent of receiving Holy Communion, presenting themselves for Confirmation to a Catholic bishop, or telling their sins in a confessional in order to receive a priest's absolution.

No intelligent Catholic would expect them do so. Nor would any Catholic with a brain cell working expect his Protestant neighbors, in the interests of ecumenism, to abstain from meat on Friday, attend Mass on the Holy Days of Obligation, or submit themselves to the Catholic Canon Law regarding marriage. Ecumenicity makes no such foolish demands.

Most people become Catholics or Protestants because they were born into one or the other faith; they had no choice in the matter. Hence conversion is always a possibility. But the mature Christian stays with his faith because he is convinced that it provides the means of salvation in accordance with the will of the Lord. Because Martin Luther no longer believed that of the Catholic Church he was born into, he bolted it. His famous "Hereon I stand . . ." is a magnificent statement of the claim that truth and personal conscience should have on the Christian. In its way, it is the basis of all Protestant thought, as the ancient Catholic proposition *extra ecclesiam nulla salus*—understood as meaning that Christ and his Church are one—is the basis of the Catholic claim.

There is no reason, then, why either Protestant or Catholic should feel that the ecumenical spirit requires them to slight particular doctrines, state other than true beliefs, act as if one belongs to a community of prayer based on theological positions one does not truly accept, or settle for a vague indifferentism which holds it really doesn't matter what one believes as long as one's inten-

tions are good. That attitude used to be described by con-
servative Catholic theologians as a "false irenicism". Many
of them feared that the laity, being unschooled in theology,
would quickly fall into it if they were encouraged to
participate in the ecumenical movement.

I believe that these theologians underestimated the intelligence of the laity and the layman's grasp of the
theological essentials. But, in recognition of the danger so
assiduously pointed out by them, and so as not to raise
any false hopes among a certain kind of Protestant who
sometimes seemed to feel that Catholic "exclusiveness"
was based more on fear of exposure to Protestant worship than on devotion to Catholic truth, it is included in
this list of "commandments".

4. *Do not attempt to serve truth at the expense of
charity.*

If the foregoing "commandment" is one likely to be
broken by Protestants, the fourth is particularly directed
to Catholics.

Not long ago, a reader asked Monsignor Conway, who
conducts a question-and-answer column in a number of
diocesan papers, whether a Catholic who is innocently
served meat on Friday by a non-Catholic hostess must
turn it down. The good monsignor said that he saw no
reason why the guest should not eat the meat without
comment, in order to avoid embarrassing the hostess.
After all, the law of charity comes before even ecclesiastical laws, as our Lord himself indicated when he had no
hesitations about performing cures on the Jewish Sabbath.
It was not, Monsignor Conway pointed out, a matter of
choosing between the service of God and the service of
man, for charity toward one's fellows is a kind of service
to God.

The primary emphasis of ecumenism is on charity.
This means that, while one never denies his faith or says
it is other than it is, one does not at the same time delib-
erately wave red flags which might needlessly arouse the

anger and annoyance of others or bring the personal encounter to a bad end. For instance, the Catholic does not flaunt his belief in the prerogatives of the Blessed Virgin Mary before he has established his belief in the uniqueness of Jesus Christ who alone gained eternal salvation for mankind. An ecumenical-minded Anglican does not immediately proclaim his disbelief in the authority of the Pope before he establishes his belief in the authority of the apostles. Catholics do not launch into a discussion of the miracles of Lourdes or Fatima, to get an ecumenical discussion off the ground, any more than Presbyterians demand to know immediately why Catholics put so little stress on the Bible in their worship.

In time, even issues as touchy as these can be discussed, and should be. But in ecumenism as in everything else, a sense of timing is all-important. There is a time to speak and a time to remain silent. Not every misunderstanding has to be corrected immediately nor does every thoughtless or tactless statement have to be challenged on the spot. This requires, of course, a certain comprehension of another's feelings and at least some understanding of another's mind-set—and such insight does not come easily to some people. Perhaps the best thing for them to do then is to avoid ecumenical conversations and let others carry that ball, while they confine themselves to the sidelines.

5. *Do not question another's sincerity or lightly impute superstition, ignorance, or fear in order to explain why they believe as they do.*

I have known Protestants who felt that the Catholic Church was little more than a cultural relic, a vast sociopolitical phenomenon that had almost lost touch with the life of faith. Its customs, traditions, liturgy, and the mental processes of its members seemed so alien to them that they found difficulty in even connecting Catholicism with Christianity. I have likewise known Catholics who felt the same way about Protestantism. They felt that the average Protestant's attitude toward doctrine was so cavalier as to cut the Churches of the Reform from the living Christian tradition.

Though Protestants, by and large, find satisfactory Biblical justification for their position on such matters as birth control and divorce, these Catholics took it that only capitulation to the world or compromise with basic Christian teaching could explain it.

There are Protestants who regard the Mass, the central act of Catholic worship, as a meaningless mumbojumbo of superstition, and Catholics who look on the Protestant emphasis on private interpretation of the Scriptures as a kind of moral and theological anarchy. Of course, each is judging the other by different standards from those arising out of the total thought-system of the two traditions. Each, consequently, is unjust to the other, as a deeper understanding of the unknown system would reveal. The Catholic, for example, may look amiss at the Protestant's neglect of the Mother of Christ, asking how one can honor the Son by giving so little attention to the Mother; but the Protestant in turn may be equally put off by the Marian emphasis he finds in the Catholic life, asking if the Son has not been deprived of his due rights by the glorification of the Mother. Each as a result may be tempted to make cruel and uncalled-for charges against the other. But to do so, each has to speak out of an ignorance of the other's total theological orientation.

To avoid misunderstandings of this kind, then, one should be very, very slow indeed to make charges. Protestants, for instance, might do well to realize that Catholics in obeying their Popes, bishops, and even parish priests, do so because they believe that Jesus Christ established a hierarchical Church and that in obeying the men set over them, they are obeying the Lord himself. It is not because they fear men but because they love God that they obey. Catholics, for their part, might do well to understand that in rejecting any final ecclesiastical authority and relying on the Scriptures alone, the Protestant is also obeying the Lord, according to his best lights.

Imputation of unworthy motives can be death to the ecumenical spirit. Charges, made out of ignorance of a tradition other than one's own, can not only be unjust but cut off any possibility of future understanding.

6. *Respect what others deem holy.*

A Protestant who believes the doctrine of the Real Presence is a total misunderstanding of the Lord's Last Supper cannot reasonably be expected to genuflect before the altar in a Catholic church. He can, however, be expected, and properly so, to behave decorously and with a reverential attitude in the place his Catholic brother holds sacred. A Catholic who finds himself in a bare Protestant church where the center is the pulpit rather than the altar may find the setting strange. But he would be a boor to show that he looks upon it as nothing more than an auditorium. It is a dedicated place of prayer and he should acknowledge that fact by his deportment. Such behavior can be taken for granted in a civilized society. It is only in most unusual cases that this "commandment" is broken.

But ecumenism would seem to require that the attitude of reverence be carried further. For instance, one would hope that the new spirit would mean the end of the tasteless "theological" joke. An after-dinner story involving the confessional, for instance, may seem perfectly harmless to one who does not believe in the sacredness of the confessional, but it can wound and embarrass those who do. A raucous rendition of a Gospel hymn may be a source of delight to those who are not used to such music in their worship, but it may easily shock the sensibilities of those who are. Funny stories involving the flippant use of the name of Mary, like some I have heard, can be a source of great annoyance to Catholics. Tasteless stories involving priests, ministers, nuns, and other consecrated persons certainly don't promote better feelings between religious groups. If through the ecumenical spirit they disappear completely, the benefits to religious brotherhood will only be exceeded by the contribution made to lessening of the total amount of boorishness in the world.

Religious communities don't think of their tradition in abstract, conceptual terms. The tradition, rather, is incarnated in certain rites, ceremonies, customs, music, buildings, monuments, shrines, and even persons. The ecumenical spirit requires that all these be treated as holy because they are invested with a symbolic as well as a real meaning by those who identify with what they stand for.

7.   *Don't defend the indefensible.*

Religious history, involving as it does sinful man, has many dark chapters. Intolerance, persecution, ignorance and social reaction have all played a part. Protestants have persecuted Catholics, and Catholics have persecuted Protestants. Both groups have in their collective past examples of cruelty and barbarism, carried out in the name of religion, which are a shame to Christianity. Both can claim martyrs who bore witness to one or the other faith with great courage and integrity. In the Age of Polemics, out of a mistaken sense of loyalty, it was commonplace to hear even gentle, saintly religious folk justifying and explaining away the most monstrous deeds committed by their spiritual ancestors and finding excuses for the most outrageous intolerance.

But perhaps, in this regard, the contemporary is even more important than the historic. Intolerance, persecution, and ignorance have not disappeared from the world. When they appear, victimizing either Catholics or Protestants, it would be reassuring to see members of one group come to the defense of the persecuted in the other. For example, American Catholics stanchly and unmistakably using their influence to protest against unfair, intolerant treatment of Protestants in certain European and Latin

American countries would point up the fact that there are Catholics who are genuinely interested in religious liberty. A more vigorous defense of persecuted Catholics in Communist countries on the part of Protestants would certainly promote interfaith amity.

A mistaken, sectarian sense of loyalty on either side which feels it necessary to defend the indefensible can be most harmful to the ecumenical spirit. In the first place, it gives the impression that the intolerant, the dishonest, the cruel, or the double-dealing, when all is said and done, are really representative of the faith. Secondly, it gives the impression that loyalty to the group outweighs loyalty to the standards verbally upheld by the group. Thirdly, it gives the impression that Catholics feel that any Catholic is better than any Protestant, or that Protestants feel that any Protestant is better than any Catholic, and hence more worthy of defense and support. A man who gets that impression really has no reason to look forward to Christian unity, since he comes away with the idea that what is being offered is a kind of second-class citizenship.

8. *Work together for the common good, as citizens equal before the law.*

One of the better developments of modern times, without which ecumenism might have been totally out of the question, is the constitutional establishment of religious liberty, or the civic equality of all persons whatever their faith. This means that Protestants and Catholics (Jews and unbelievers as well) share a common obligation to promote the public welfare. It also means that cooperation between members of different faiths is a necessity as well as an opportunity.

It is foreign to the ecumenical spirit for such work to be conducted in the spirit of warfare as between competing religious blocs or pressure groups. Any suggestion that Catholics are ganging up on their Protestant fellow citizens to get more than their share, for example, can hurt the ecumenical movement. Likewise, any hint that religious prejudice is keeping one or the other group from getting a full share is harmful. Preferential treatment of whatever kind—and the "preferred" can change from place to place—is sure to be resented.

In this area of life, the political order, arise many touchy issues that can be the source of tensions between different religious bodies. In the first place, depending on the interests involved, the groups see things differently. Currently in the United States, the school question is a prime example. Deeply held doctrines have also led to controversies—over birth control, for example, or divorce laws, Prohibition, or gambling. All the goodwill in the world, plus great measures of patience, intelligence, and political prudence, are necessary to resolve such issues. Ecumenism provides no magical formula by which they can be resolved.

But the ecumenical spirit does add a new ingredient. The ecumenical spirit means that one side will go to great pains to understand the position of the other; that both sides are as interested in protecting the rights and needs of the other as of their own; that neither side is imperialistic in its demands or dedicated to translating its particular beliefs into the law that is binding on all. Such issues are too complex, manifold, and far-reaching to be discussed fully here. It is enough to say that the ecumenical spirit can be an important contribution to their ultimate solution.

It is important to note, too, that Protestant-Catholic collaboration in the civic area is not all controversy-laden. There are goals for our society—peace, civil rights, public education, and abolition of poverty come to mind—which members of both groups share. Here the possibilities for united Christian action are unlimited, especially as between laymen and indeed entire parishes. We shall be sure that the ecumenical spirit has taken hold when it becomes commonplace for the members of Blessed Sacrament parish and the congregation of the Elm Street Methodist Church to hold meetings with a view to, say, desegregating the north end of town, providing employment for the drop-out teenagers in town, or improving the standards of science teaching at the local high school. "By their fruits you shall know them." By the work they accomplish together, Protestants and Catholics may yet come to recognize each other as true Christians.

9. *Pray together.*

Here of course there are certain limitations. Until the great day when full unity has come, Protestants and Catholics cannot share the Sacrament of Unity. But there are many opportunities for joint public prayer—common public displays of faith, the celebration of feasts held in common—and reading the Scriptures together.

There are also opportunities galore, so far generally unused, for study clubs to bring together Christians of both faiths to investigate the conditions of our society, judge what is needed to Christianize it, and make plans to act as a "leaven in the loaf". There is no special reason why the two laities should confine their joint activities to insipid church bazaars or cake sales.

The important thing is that there be more contact *as Christians,* more public acknowledgment that both groups worship the same Lord, acknowledge the same Scriptures, and yearn for ultimate unity. This yearning cannot be left forever an abstract commitment but must be expressed visibly, humbly, and penitentially. Only then will it become meaningful to the millions whose imaginations have not yet been aroused by the ecumenical movement and who take the present scandalous division of Christendom as inescapable.

10. *Leave theology to the theologians.*

At one level of the ecumenical encounter the laity will, by and large, be out of place, because they do not have the knowledge or training for it. This, of course, is the meeting of theologians who are dedicated to straightening out the doctrinal issues that must be settled before unity can, at the official level, move forward. This is an important aspect of the movement but, to my mind, far from the most important. Because it is so specialized and has involved such articulate, thoughtful people, I believe its importance has been exaggerated. What the parish minister and the local priest do and the attitudes prevailing among their parisioners strike me as much more significant in the long run.

Nevertheless, the theological dialogue is essential—and it can only be carried out by theologians ready for it. An untrained layman sounding forth on issues he really knows little about is an absurd figure. The theological dialogue requires subtlety of thought, the study of history, a grasp of two theological traditions, and a sharp awareness of where doors may be opening or of where lines must be drawn. Even a thorough knowledge of the catechism or a teaching certificate from the Sunday school association is not enough to meet the challenge.

There may be a few laymen better equipped than most clerics to meet it. It is only realistic, however, to accept the notion that most laymen are not ready for it, nor can they be expected to be. The layman, unprepared for it, might do more harm than good by trying to engage in theological dialogue. He may well mislead the other participants, closing doors that should be left open and drawing lines that should be left undrawn.

DIALOGUE NO. 3
How Do We Worship?

Resource Readings

Word and Sacrament in Protestant Worship (pp. 66–81)
Cyril C. Richardson
Liturgy, Unity and Church (pp. 82–95)
Michael J. Taylor, S.J.
The Liturgy and Orthodoxy (pp. 96–99)
John Meyendorff

Suggested Readings

Dalmais, I. H. *Introduction to the Liturgy.* Baltimore, Md.: Helicon, 1961.
Davis, Charles. *Liturgy and Doctrine.* New York: Sheed and Ward, 1962.
Edwall, Pehr, Hayman, Eric and Maxwell, William D. *Ways of Worship.* New York: Harper and Row, 1951.
Schmemann, Alexander. *Sacraments and Orthodoxy.* New York: Herder and Herder, 1965.
Sloyan, Gerard. *Worship in a New Key.* New York: Herder and Herder, 1965.
The Constitution on the Sacred Liturgy. Commentary by Gerard Sloyan. New York: Paulist Press, 1964.
Thompson, Bard. *Liturgies of the Western Church.* Cleveland, Ohio: World Pub. Co., Meridian Books, 1961.

CHRISTIAN DIALOGUE
How Do We Worship?

OPENING PRAYER

Leader: Remember, O Lord, all your children who carry the sign of Christ upon their foreheads.

All: Lord, have mercy on us.

Leader: Draw them, who were purchased by your blood, closer to you in the union of love.

All: Lord, have mercy on us.

Leader: Remove from their hearts all stubbornness and pride and whatever impedes respect and love for fellow Christians everywhere.

All: Lord, have mercy on us.

Leader: Make your Church, O Lord, to shine more gloriously before men through that unity which is your gift alone.

All: Lord, have mercy on us.

Leader: Hasten the day, O Lord, when your scattered children will be drawn together in that unity for which you did pray.

All: Lord, have mercy on us.

All: Glory be to the Father, and to the Son and to the Holy Spirit. As it was in the beginning, is now and ever shall be, world without end. Amen.

BIBLE READING

Praise the Lord, all nations!
  Extol him, all peoples! (Psalm 117, 1)
Make a joyful noise to God, all the earth;
  sing the glory of his name; give to him glorious praise!
Say to God, "How terrible are thy deeds!

So great is thy power that thy enemies cringe before thee.
All the earth worships thee;
  they sing praises to thee, sing praises to thy name."
                                    (Psalm 66, 1-4)

Praise the Lord!
Sing to the Lord a new song,
  his praise in the assembly of the faithful!
Let Israel be glad in his Maker,
  let the sons of Zion rejoice in their King!
Let them praise his name with dancing,
  making melody to him with timbrel and lyre!
For the Lord takes pleasure in his people;
  he adorns the humble with victory.
Let the faithful exult in glory;
  let them sing for joy on their couches.
Let the high praises of God be in their throats . . .
                                    (Psalm 149, 1-6)

MEDITATION

Lord, this evening we want to tell each other how we give praise and glory to you in our churches. . . . We begin by meditating upon the Psalms of praise from Holy Scripture. . . . Even though we stand before you divided in your new covenant we can offer praise to you together through the prayers of Israel which we cherish in common. . . . We are your people, Lord. . . . We know you love us. . . . Adorn us once again with your unity. . . . We long to face the world united and proclaim "Praise the Lord, all nations! Extol him, all peoples!"

BIBLE READING

And all who believed were together and had all things in common; and they sold their possessions and goods and distributed them to all, as any had need. And day by day, attending the temple together and breaking bread in their homes, they partook of food with glad and generous hearts, praising God and having favor with all the people. And the Lord added to their number day by day those who were being saved (Acts 2, 44-47).

Meditation

Lord, we do not continue daily with one accord in your temple. . . . We are in separate temples, ignorant of each other's worship. . . . Tonight we want to begin to remove this ignorance. . . . We offer our mutual learning to you. . . . Use it as a means to gather us into your temple where we can praise God. . . . Be in favor with all the people. . . . Add to our company those who are to be saved.

Christian Dialogue

Introduction

In this discussion we hope to learn about each other's worship. We see each other going to church on Sunday morning and although we may understand in a general way what goes on during our service, we do not know what happens to each of us. How are our hearts changed? How do we listen and speak to God in worship? What does it mean to us?

Tonight we want to speak humbly and frankly to each other out of our own experience as worshippers. The most important resource we will draw on is the understanding we have of our own worship and the Christian faith which it expresses and nourishes.

Before beginning, one important note: we will not discuss in detail the doctrinal differences concerning the Eucharist tonight. A later dialogue will treat this question fully.

You and Your Worship

Everyone in the group goes to church. Presumably you do this for the purpose of worshipping, not out of any less worthy motive. But our worship can become routine. We want to tell each other what our worship means and thus discover or rediscover the value of our life of worship.

DISCUSSION QUESTIONS

Let each member of the group tell briefly how he worships in church on Sunday. What is the main part of your worship? How do you listen and speak to God in your worship?

What does your worship do for you? Which parts of the service mean the most to you? Why? How does your worship give praise and thanks to God? What is the role of Jesus Christ in your worship? Do you have the eucharist or Lord's Supper in your service? What briefly is its meaning?

Why Worship in a Group?

Today both Catholic and Protestant scholars stress the corporate aspects of Christian worship. They emphasize how God calls us together to worship him through his Son, Jesus Christ. Yet Christians in their worship often forget the essential notion that worship is communal. Recapturing the authentic Christian idea of the Church as a worshipping community characterizes the renewal of public worship in all the Churches.

DISCUSSION QUESTIONS

Why is the worship of the Christian community better than the worship of an individual? Where in the Bible does God indicate that he wants his people to come together and worship him?

St. Paul's teaching about Jesus provides the doctrinal basis for our corporate worship. What is this doctrine? Can you explain it?

Drawing on your experience in civic, business and family life, what is the value of bringing people together for important celebrations? Most Christian Churches celebrate the Lord's Supper regularly or at least occasionally. How does the "sacred meal" give greater depth and meaning to corporate worship?

Focusing on Jesus

The center of Christian worship is, or should be,

Jesus. By his suffering, death and resurrection, Jesus redeemed us. His merciful word strengthens, consoles and heals us when we gather together to worship him. Yet some Christians are tempted to focus on other concerns in their worship.

DISCUSSION QUESTIONS

How is your worship centered on Jesus? How does it fail in this respect? Are there any peripheral things in your worship which deflect your worship from the Lord?

When you pray in Church, do you find that your own personal or family needs come before giving praise and thanks to God for what he has done for you in Jesus Christ? How can we get the right balance and emphasis in our worship?

The Bible and Worship

The bible contains the history of our salvation, the story of the great deeds by which God saved us. When Christians gather to worship, they listen to the account of these events proclaimed once again to them. Hearing these holy words they are renewed in faith and their spirits are healed and strengthened. But Christian Churches use the bible in different ways in their services. For some it is the main element in worship; for others it relates closely to the eucharist in worship.

DISCUSSION QUESTIONS

Why are the bible and the liturgy or worship so closely related? How did the people of Israel use the word of God in their temple worship? Can you give some examples in the New Testament where worship involved using the sacred books? Describe how reading the bible in your family or alone helps you to worship better on Sunday.

After hearing God's Word proclaimed on Sunday, how do you respond in your worship? If your worship has a eucharistic liturgy, how does the liturgy of the Word (the bible readings) relate to the liturgy of the eucharist (the

Lord's Supper)? How is the sermon related to the bible readings? Why is this description of the sermon appropriate—"to break the bread of the Word"?

Worship and Renewal

The next dialogue will discuss in detail the close relationship between the renewal of the Church and the ecumenical movement. Tonight we wish to explore briefly, however, the way in which renewal has affected your worship or ways in which it might affect you. All Christians must honestly face the hard fact that worship has little place in the life of many nominal Christians of all denominations. And for many faithful church-goers it has too little meaning. Renewal of the liturgy seeks to make Christian worship more meaningful to modern man and to bring him closer to the love and mercy of God.

DISCUSSION QUESTIONS

How has the liturgy of your Church been renewed or changed during your lifetime? Has this helped you to worship God better? What other changes do you feel should be made?

Why do so many Christians stay away from church except for the great religious events of their lives? How can the true meaning of worship be conveyed to these people? What do they find wrong with Christian worship? Is it too drab and self-satisfied? Is it too remote and archaic? Has it lost its sense of Christian mystery? Is it based on sound Christian doctrine? Is it too formalistic and automatic? Is it out of touch with the needs and aspirations of modern man? How can these faults, if they exist, be rectified?

Worship and Witness

Christians have grown recently in their awareness of the relationship between worshipping and witnessing to Jesus in their everyday lives. Christianity cannot be confined to one hour Sunday morning. The great social and moral problems of the world cry out for Christian solutions. And

Christians should receive the power and the motivation to witness to Christ from the pulpit and the altar.

DISCUSSION QUESTIONS

How does your worship affect your everyday life? Does it make you more conscious of your responsibility for Christian witness in the community?

What is the leading social problem of your local community? How does your worship give you a Christian orientation to help solve this problem?

Do you do anything in your Church services to make worshippers more aware of their responsibility to witness to Jesus? What more could be done along these lines?

Worship and Young People

All Churches work diligently to initiate their young people into the Christian life. A major part of this training comes through worship. From sermons, hymns, bible readings, reception of the sacraments, our young people learn about Christ and mature as Christians.

DISCUSSION QUESTIONS

Do you have special services in your Church for children or are families encouraged to worship together? Which do you think is better?

What special effort has your church made to reach the young? Has it been successful? Do you think experiments such as bringing in instrumental groups, folk singers and modern dancers are a good idea? Why?

What do your children say around the house about their church worship? How important is the example of parents? How can young people be guided to Christian maturity in their formative years so they will fulfill their responsibilities to worship God as adults?

Signs and Symbols in Worship

The Church in its worship recalls biblical events which are signs of God's intervention in human history. Hence Christian liturgies in one way or another use symbols and signs to bring God's people into touch with the saving events of the past, to show the transcendent power of God here and now and to point us to that day when Jesus will come in glory.

DISCUSSION QUESTIONS

How does reading the bible in Christian worship render present the saving events of the past? Is the history the bible records the same as other kinds of history?

Although their interpretations vary, all Churches believe in baptism and the eucharist. What does the water of baptism symbolize? What do the bread and wine of the eucharist symbolize? What are some other signs and symbols that are used in your worship?

Christians also perform many gestures and actions in their worship which have a symbolic meaning. For instance, why do you think standing symbolized the resurrection of Jesus for early Christians? What is the significance of singing together in Church? What does the response "amen" by a congregation really signify? What does our offering of money symbolize? How can we guard against letting our sacramental acts and gestures become perfunctory and meaningless?

CLOSING PRAYER

O God of peace, who through your Son, Jesus Christ, did set forth one faith for the salvation of mankind, send your grace and heavenly blessing upon all Christian people who are striving to draw closer to you and to each other, in the unity of the Spirit and the bond of peace. Give us boldness to seek only your glory and the advancement of your kingdom. Unite us all in you as you, O Father, with your Son and the Holy Spirit, are one God, world without end. Amen.

Word and Sacrament in Protestant Worship

Cyril C. Richardson

Owing to the wide diversity of Protestantism it is not possible to give as clear and comprehensive a survey of its worship as is possible in the case of Roman Catholicism. While the Latin rite is, of course, not the only one in Roman Catholicism and there are a number of Uniat rites in different languages, nonetheless, there is a basic uniformity which characterizes the vast majority of Roman Catholic liturgical observances. With the Churches of the Reformation it is different. Yet there are fundamental leading themes characteristic of all Protestant services and these we shall survey. We must, however, always bear in mind that the wide range of Protestant services is such that different emphases have tended to characterize the various denominations, and throughout Protestant history there has been no fundamental pattern universally observed.

Before treating the basic concerns of Protestant worship, it is well for us to bear in mind the large dependence of Reformation liturgy upon the forms of worship in the later Middle Ages. Originally Protestant services were revisions of the Roman Mass and of the medieval vernacular service of Prone, which was inserted in the Mass before or after the sermon. Furthermore, a type of devotional piety centered in subjective meditations characterized the Lay Folk's Mass Books which were widely used in the Late Middle Ages. Not a little of the Protestant attitude toward the Holy Communion ultimately derives from these layman's handbooks.

It is thus important to note that in the realm of worship the Reformation represented a continuity with the medieval past as well as a revolution. In the general structure of the service, in the quality of devotion, in the emphasis on the passion of Christ in the celebration of the Lord's Supper, and finally in the continuing idea that the congregation should basically remain passive, there is a clear connection with the Mass of the later Middle Ages. On the other hand, the Reformation stands as a revolution in introducing a fundamental emphasis upon the Word of God, upon the need for corporate worship and for greater intelligibility as well as simplicity. It is noteworthy that many of the features in the schema of the present Vatican Council have a direct parallel in the concerns of the Reformers. In consequence it is likely that the Catholic services will become more like Protestant ones just as, under the impetus of the current liturgical revival, Protestant services are recovering something of their Catholic past and becoming more like Roman ones. This presages well for an eventual unity of the spirit among Christians in so far as they appreciate the many diverse facets of worship and grow closer together in their common concern for the life in Christ.

Basic Concerns of Protestant Worship

Let us now look at some of the basic concerns which have dominated Protestant worship throughout its history. While these concerns have been given varying emphases among the differing denominations, nonetheless they may be said to be characteristics in general of Protestant liturgy.

The first one is this: That the *Word* may prevail. By the Word of God the Reformers meant first and foremost God's disclosure of himself in Jesus Christ. This revelation of God in his freedom is given in the words of

Scripture as well as in the sacramental acts of the Church. Fundamentally, however, it means the declaration of God's forgiveness and the condescension of the divine love in our redemption. It was this aspect particularly which Luther stressed in his liturgies where the warmth of piety centering in the grateful recognition of the divine love is dominant. For Calvin, on the other hand, the Word means primarily the declaration of the *gloria Dei*. This is, of course, not without the note of the divine love, but it gives peculiar prominence to God's transcendence. There is a word of Calvin that very well expresses the whole character of his services: "We are born first of all for God and not for ourselves."

Because the Word is something that is spoken directly to man's understanding in God's self-disclosure, the importance of the sermon and the reading of the Scripture in the vernacular are primary concerns of the Reformers. Luther, for instance, in his *Formula Missae* writes: "But the important thing is this, that everything be done so that the Word prevails and does not become a clamor or a whine and rattled off mechanically as it has been heretofore." Or again, "Where God's word is not preached, it is better that one neither sing nor read or even come together." Hence, it has been characteristic of Lutheran worship that even at sacramental services a sermon is regarded as essential. Unless man is given the opportunity of hearing the Word of God and of intelligently grasping the character of the divine revelation, worship descends to superstition. Calvin equally is concerned with this importance of the presentation of God's revelation by sermon and Scripture. He writes in the *Institutes,* "The principal object of the sacrament, therefore, is not to present us the body of Christ simply . . . we never rightly and advantageously feed on Christ except as crucified and when we have a lively apprehension of the efficacy of his death." It is this "lively apprehension" that is the fundamental point of worship. Sacramental forms can so easily fall into superstition, the intoning of prayers in a foreign tongue can become so unintelligible, that the full significance of participating in the disclosure of the divine glory and love in Jesus Christ becomes obscured.

It is for this reason that the reading of Scripture itself becomes sacramental. In the place of the snippets from the Epistles and Gospels, which the English reformers used to refer to as "pisteling and gospeling", the Reformation stressed the need for much longer passages of Scripture and full and adequate expositions of them in the sermon. The sermon characteristically took on the quality of instruction, and indeed the use of the scholar's gown became indicative of the relation of the minister to the congregation. In some ways the educational and instructional character of worship was overemphasized and its more prophetic meaning along with its more mystical elements tended to be obscured. However, the large emphasis given to Scripture and its exposition was basically an attempt to speak directly to the worshiper about the divine condescension in Jesus Christ.

As a result of the emphasis upon the Word, there was a consequent decline of sacramental worship. While all the Reformers except Zwingli wished that the celebration of the Lord's Supper should be the normal form of Sunday worship, nonetheless the tendency for there to be only a preaching service quickly asserted itself. There were many reasons for this. There were, on the one hand, political reasons, as in Geneva, where the town councils refused Calvin's insistence upon weekly celebrations of the Lord's Supper, because they feared riots and the opposition of the people who might imagine the Roman Mass was being restored. Another reason had to do with the infrequency of communicating in the later Middle Ages. The rule which had been laid down by the Fourth Lateran Council of communicating once a year at Easter was widely followed and attendance at Mass was generally not for the purpose of receiving the elements. Conse-

quently, when the Reformers stressed the corporate character of worship and insisted that the Lord's Supper
should only be celebrated when all communicated, celebrations became infrequent, since the people were disin-
clined to break their medieval habit. The service of the
sacrament could not be celebrated with no one or
only a handful to participate. Thus, the Protestant service
really became a *missa sicca,* in which the service of the
Word, derived from the Synagogue, stood alone without
reaching its consummation in the sacrament.

Yet a deeper reason for the decline of the sacrament
must be observed in the theological understanding of the
Lord's Supper which dominated the thinking of the Reformers. They tended to view the Holy Communion as a
reduplication of the Word. Thus, if the Word had already
been preached and the Scripture read and expounded,
what was done in the Lord's Supper was merely a repetition of the same thing. It expressed in more tangible
and visible form what had already been accomplished in
words. We shall revert again to this point, but it is perhaps the deepest reason why the celebration of the Holy
Communion became monthly or quarterly as a consequence of the Reformation.

The second fundamental concern of Protestant worship
was that superstition should be made impossible. There
should be no "hocus-pocus", which actual phrase is a corruption of the Latin words of consecration "hoc est
corpus meum". The white walls and the streaming day-
light from the large windows of New England churches are
symbolic of this desire to have everything clear and in
the open without any possibility of reverting to magical
tendencies. A number of features of Protestant worship
directly come from this concern. Intelligibility was stressed
above the sense of mystery. Everything was to be done
aloud and spoken in the vernacular, so that there could
be no misunderstanding. The feeling which had developed
from the fourth century that the consecration prayer

should be said in a subdued voice because of the character of the liturgical mystery, was something quite alien to the Reformation spirit. Then, again, simplicity was a dominant concern. Cranmer's objections to what he calls "dumb ceremonies" indicate a typical spirit of the Reformer. Elaborate worship was now superseded by the most simple forms which were regarded as having less danger in them and as being more directly intelligible to the congregation. Finally, the sense of corporate worship was emphasized over against priestcraft. In the revisions of the Roman Mass which the Reformers undertook, a number of the ancient prayers in which the priest addressed God in the first person singular were converted into the first person plural, in order to indicate that the minister is the leader of the congregation rather than one who mediates between the congregation and God. Furthermore, the emphasis upon Psalm singing in the simple Genevan tunes gave point to this feeling for corporate worship, just as the requirement that the Lord's Supper should only be celebrated when the people were willing to communicate, equally emphasized the communal character of worship. All these concerns were directed against any identification of the religious symbol with the reality to which it points. Superstition, which did to some measure characterize the late Middle Ages, was to be offset by a type of worship in which the congregation could participate with understanding and without the dangers of magic. This, of course, posed very serious problems for Protestant worship, in that there was always a tendency for the symbols to be divorced from the realities to which they pointed, and the rational forms to be so emphasized that the sense of mystery in worship was overcome.

A third dominant concern of Protestant worship was that the free spirit of God should be given opportunity. This was particularly developed in the left-wing Reformation among Independents, Congregationalists, and Baptists. Here the emphasis fell first upon extemporaneous prayer.

The immediate, direct experience of conversation with God was to supersede written and traditional forms of prayer. Even the Lord's Prayer was regarded as inadequate for public worship because it could be rattled off mechanically and did not have that immediate and spontaneous freshness which the more left-wing reformers felt to be the note of true worship. John Cotton, for instance, in 1642 could write: "Nor will it stand well with the holy gesture of prayer, which is to lift up our eyes to heaven, if we cast our eyes down upon a book." This is a typical Puritan attitude to the Anglican *Book of Common Prayer*. Barrow could ask, "May such old, written, rotten stuff be called prayer? May reading be said to be praying?" Or, again, John Owen could write: "All liturgies are false worship (and not the English only), used to defeat Christ's promises of gifts and God's Spirit." There was a consequent opposition to written sermons as well as written prayers. Worship was to be conducted in such a way that one would be open to the immediate and direct influence of God's Spirit and not bound by traditional forms.

This implied giving emphasis to intimacy in worship. In the small congregation of devoted believers, fellowship with God was looked upon from the point of view of a direct and immediate relation in which the worshiper gave personal utterance to that which the Spirit of God evoked in his heart. Not only the minister but the layman prayed aloud, prophesied, and exhorted. Certain of the extreme forms of such worship in speaking with tongues, religious dancing, and so forth, were developed in the more radical of these groups.

Finally, it must be observed that a certain tension between form and freedom has been characteristic of Protestant worship precisely because of this desire to stress the free Spirit of God. Only in the Anglican communion has there been an attempt to enforce uniformity. In general, classical Protestantism has tried to relate form to freedom by providing model services and model prayers, but allowing the minister a good deal of latitude in their use and composition. Calvin himself was not averse to a set form of worship. He even urged its usefulness, contending that it was "to help the unskillfulness and simplicity of some . . . that the consent of the churches with one another may appear . . . that the capricious giddiness and levity of such as effect innovations may be prevented". Yet the forms he provided for Geneva were models rather than forms which had to be followed in detail by the minister. His attitude, as that of Luther, was the same which had characterized the ancient church. Hippolytus had provided his liturgy in the *Apostolic Tradition* as a guide to Zephyrinus, the Bishop of Rome, whom Hippolytus as a learned scholar seems to have felt was in need of some guidance. In the general Protestant scene today some measure of form and freedom is to be observed in practically all denominations, and indeed the 11 o'clock Sunday service is rather similar in the large Protestant bodies.

The final basic concern of Protestant worship has been the revival of the liturgy of the ancient Church. It was the desire of the Reformers to recover the way of worship in the New Testament and the early period. This was the Reformation counterpart of the Renaissance concern to return to the sources. The motto was *ad fontes*. Hence Calvin could subtitle one of his liturgies, "Selon la Coustume de l'Eglise ancienne". It is for this reason that the Reformers felt that Word and sacrament belonged together; and indeed Calvin himself regarded their separation as "a vicious custom", and annual communion as a veritable "invention of the devil". We have already indicated some reasons why the sacrament tended to decline in importance, but it must be stated that the early Reformers, while they did not have the scholarly resources we have today for understanding New Testament and early Church worship, nonetheless were vitally concerned that there should be a return to the original forms of worship in the Christian Church.

The modes of worship that characterize the Protestant denominations today are beginning to betray an increasing uniformity. There is a general Sunday morning service in the Presbyterian, Methodist, Lutheran, and Congregationalist traditions which, while there are differences in detail, nonetheless has assumed a basic pattern. It opens with a choral procession and with a sentence from Scripture, which is followed by a confession of sins and absolution. Then there is a responsive reading from the Psalter followed by hymnody or a chant. After this there comes the morning lesson and then the pastoral prayer, which may be a single long prayer or divided into shorter collects. The service tends to reach its climax in the sermon, which is followed or preceded by an anthem, the collection of alms, and a hymn. The service concludes with a benediction and a recessional.

This structure in essence is, of course, the first part of the Mass. There have been many changes but the main outline of intercessory prayer, psalmody, and sermon goes back to the Synagogue service that the early Christians inherited from Judaism.

While a good deal of variety is introduced into the service of the Word, in the celebration of the Lord's Supper the specific forms of the different denominations tend to be more closely observed. These differ in the various churches, but there are now emerging "ecumenical" liturgies that attempt to recover a good deal of the Catholic past while still preserving fundamental Protestant points of view. Perhaps the most notable of the ecumenical liturgies has been the Anglican, for Cranmer attempted to weave together many diverse sources in his book. In the Holy Communion the basic structure and a good deal of the material comes directly from the Sarum Use, but this has been modified both by Protestant concerns and also by materials derived from Lutheran and other liturgies. In the middle of the nineteenth century in this country the Mercersburg liturgies appeared. They were a notable contribution since the leaders of that movement of the

Reformed Church in America, namely Nevin and Schaff, had a concern for recovering the Catholic heritage. One might also note the liturgy of the United Church of Canada: the uniting Methodists, Presbyterians, and Congregationalists made use of their diverse liturgical heritages, weaving them together in a common service. The more recent revision of Lutheran liturgies both in Sweden and the United States has recovered the traditional pattern of the consecration prayer in the place of the *verba* of the typical Lutheran liturgy. In the Congregational Church in this country the *Book of Worship for Free Churches* indicates the extent to which the liturgical revival has affected that communion. A similar revision of the *Westminster Directory* is now being undertaken and will doubtless issue in an equal concern for recovering the Catholic elements of the past. Perhaps the most notable ecumenical liturgy of the modern day is that of the Church of South India, which has united Catholic and Protestant elements with rare skill and success. Equally interesting though less influential is the Taizé liturgy of the French Reformed community, which is dedicated to Church unity and of which Roger Schutz is the distinguished leader.

The characteristics of these ecumenical liturgies are—first, the attempt to recover traditional structures; secondly, the preference for biblical language in the central prayers where there have been the keenest theological divisions; and, finally, the introduction of responses that heighten the congregation's participation in public prayer. The responses inserted in the consecration prayer of the Church of South India are particularly significant in this connection.

There are a number of other factors that make for ecumenical liturgy among Protestants. One of these is hymnody. Increasingly Protestant churches sing hymns from every period of the Church's development, and indeed one might say that in the realm of hymnody there is the most notable ecumenical spirit. Again, the recovery of the Church year among Protestant groups who formally disavowed it has been important. Nowadays not only Easter and Christmas, but Epiphany, Lent, Advent, and a number of holy days such as All Saints are observed. Then, too, the introduction of silence into worship has been a sign of learning from other denominations. This has not grown extensively, but the impact of Quakerism on Protestant worship is not to be underestimated. Finally, the architecture of churches in which there has appeared the "divided chancel" with the altar in the center and the pulpit at the side, has indicated a desire among Protestants to return to a type of architecture which did not give undue prominence to the pulpit and which followed the norm developed in the early basilica and the Gothic church. In all these ways there has been a movement toward a recovery of the Catholic heritage without compromising the basic concerns of the Reformation.

On the question of the sacrifice in the Lord's Supper, the Protestant position gave the emphasis to three things. In the first place (as is made clear in a recent book by Aulén) the once-for-all-ness of the Cross is given the great stress. In no way can the Lord's Supper repeat it, nor can the action of the Supper participate in the Cross as if the latter were a transcendent and timeless reality. Rather is the emphasis placed upon the uniqueness and the *Einmaligkeit* of the Passion. Thus, the Catholic doctrine in connection with the sacrifice of the Mass is excluded. In its place the Protestant liturgy expresses the themes of the sacrifice of ourselves, our souls and bodies, and also the sacrifice of praise and thanksgiving. Many texts from the early Church which deal with the latter type of sacrifice are quoted; and insofar as the early Fathers attacked the literal sacrifices of pagan and Jewish religion, there is a close connection between the Protestant mind and that of the early Church. However, it must be observed that the full implications of the early doctrine were not grasped by the Reformers.

From these basic ways of looking at the Lord's Supper a fundamental antithesis between the Protestant and the Catholic viewpoint arose. There was a contrast for one thing between table and altar. For the Protestant the table of the Lord's Supper was the table around which the faithful gathered to receive that which God promised, but in no way to participate in an actual sacrifice. Then again there was a contrast of prophet and priest. Protestants stressed the prophetic element of the Word, whereby the declaration of God's forgivenesses was made, over against the action of the priest in converting the substance of the bread into that of the Body of Christ. Finally, we may observe the contrast between the surplice and gown, on the one hand, which were the vestments of Protestants, and the chasuble and alb on the other, which were the traditional eucharistic vestments. The surplice was a medieval development for the choir offices. The gown was either the scholar's gown as Luther had used it to preach in, or else the gown of the upper bourgeoisie which Zwingli had adopted in the Zurich services and which was similarly taken over in Geneva. These vestments symbolized the service of the Word as a choir office, or the educational significance of the exposition of Scripture. The chasuble and alb, on the other hand, while they had their origins in the normal wear of the upper classes in the later Roman Empire, had taken on a sacrificial significance. This occurred in the ninth century when a Judaizing movement overtook the Church in the early Middle Ages. When dress had sufficiently changed for the alb and chasuble to seem somewhat esoteric, they were given the meanings attaching to the priestly vestments in Leviticus. In consequence they came to signalize the garb of the sacrificing priest.

New Emphases to Overcome the Antitheses

It is clear from what we have already said that the basic antitheses of the sixteenth century are still with us.

Reconciliation between Catholic and Protestant positions appears impossible if we continue to think along the lines which led to the sixteenth-century separation. It presages well, however, for some possible ecumenical theology, which will gather together both Catholic and Protestant insights, that the stark divisions of the Reformation are coming to be viewed rather as overemphases on both sides than as truly expressive of the meaning of the Lord's Supper and other sacramental forms. It is patent, for instance, that the concepts of table and altar cannot be separated. If, on the one hand, the significance of the Lord's Supper leads to the Communion as the corporate act of the fellowship of Christ, then, on the other hand, sacrificial ideas cannot be excluded from the Lord's Supper. It is a sacramental act whose significance lies in its relation to the total sacrifice of Christ, and in consequence the altar is not a concept which can be excluded as if it were irreconcilable with the idea of table. In actual fact, table and altar in their Hebrew as well as in their Greek equivalents are words which interchange. An altar is a place on which an offering is made, and this very place is itself a table, for every offering culminates in a communal feast. Similarly the contrast between prophet and priest cannot be held to be one of mutual exclusion. The Word is not something which cancels the priestly act of the sacrament, but rather Word and sacrament belong together in a mutual fulfillment.

Perhaps the most fundamental point at which to begin some reconsideration by means of which these antitheses can be overcome is the notion of worship itself. We are all familiar with the commonplace that worship in its linguistic origin is connected with the word "worth", and worship gives expression to that which man prizes most highly. This, however, while it may be satisfactory for a theology based on the idea of value (as Ritschlianism, for instance), is not fully satisfactory. The underlying notion in worship is that of *being,* the word "worth" itself coming from the

Anglo-Saxon *weorthan,* which means "to be". Worship is the act in which man recovers his being in relation to God. He overcomes the split between himself and his ultimate ground. All worship, therefore, must be looked upon not merely as the expression of what man values, but rather as the means by which man discovers the true meaning of his existence and realizes the basic nature and the destiny for which God intended him. In this light, we have a much larger concept in terms of which we can look at different aspects of the act of worship.

A second helpful approach is that of realizing that the concept of sacrifice cannot be limited to that of death. In this regard all Western theology, whether it is Roman Catholic or Protestant, has tended to lay undue weight on the notion of sacrifice in connection with the passion of Christ. Sacrifice actually is a much broader term. It means to "make holy"—*sacer* and *facere.* The process of making holy or recovering one's "wholeness" in relation to God involves much more than the concept of death. At least four fundamental notions are implied, and all of these should find expression both in the actual liturgy as well as in the understanding of the Lord's Supper. These four moments of the sacrificial act are offering, dying, rising, and finally participating in the eschatological banquet. The significance of the Lord's Supper is that it presents the total sacrifice of Christ in such a way that the believer can participate in it and reenact it in his own being. There is first offering, that is to say, the abandonment of the self to God. There is then dying, the actual experience whereby the ego-centered nature is crucified. But that leads to resurrection. We rise with Christ, and this finds its fulfillment in the communal banquet that gives expression to the End. This banquet is both a present realization of the heavenly sphere and also an anticipation of the final fulfillment. Here both future eschatology and realized eschatology are united. In this larger concept, then, of sacrifice we see worship as the total act in which there is presented the whole work of Christ in such a way that we are able to live through it ourselves and participate in that which he has accomplished in terms of human nature. This further leads us to a consideration of the way in which the sacrificial action of the service so presents Christ that his perpetual relation to the Father is made manifest and made accessible. It is necessary at this point to go beyond the idea of the once-for-allness of the Cross, to appreciate its significance as the historic expression of the eternal reality of the Divine Nature. It is because the Divine Nature is love that the sacrifice of Christ is an eternal act and is thus able to be made present in worship here and now.

A third important consideration in our rethinking of sacramental forms is the notion of participation. In the act of worship we "re-call", "re-present" that which has already been done but whose significance lies beyond the historical moment in which it was done. There is an actualization of Christ in and among us, and not merely a remembering of what was done in the first century A.D. Here it is important that due weight be given both to the objective and subjective aspects of sacramental worship. It lacks reality if the subjective experience of faith is played down. But it lacks power if there is an insufficient appreciation of the way in which the act of Christ is objectively present. The outward forms are not merely reminders of something that was once done, but are themselves the vehicles through which the external significance of what was done is made available. Hence there may be a way of speaking about the sacrifice of the Mass in such a manner that elements of superstition can be eradicated, and all talk about repeating the cross (which certainly is not genuine Catholic talk) can be avoided.

The mystery theology of Odo Casel is perhaps of some help in this connection. It may indeed be said that he derived his material too much from Hellenistic religions and not sufficiently from the biblical notion of *anamnesis*.

It would perhaps be better to take such a celebration as that of the Passover fully to bring out the significance of biblical "remembering." In the biblical notion, the community is able to relive the events of the past and make them genuinely their own, because of the corporate personality of the group. The Jew in celebrating the Passover does not think of the crossing of the Red Sea as something which happened to people long ago. Rather is he bidden to think of *himself* as one who was rescued from Egypt, because he is a participator in the heritage of the people of Israel. In the same way, the Church understands that the crucifixion occurred not only in the first century but occurs in some sense in connection with us here and now. We are the inheritors of a tradition. We are the heirs of the early disciples. And thus in the act of worship there is made present, in a way in which we can grasp it and be grasped by it, the eternal significance of what was once done in Palestine. These events are present events as well as past events, and the whole significance of the act of worship is to make present the past in such a way that we are able to relive it in ourselves and thus recover our true being and destiny. It is along lines such as these that perhaps we shall be able to overcome the false antitheses that were posed in the sixteenth century, and achieve some vital reconciliation between Catholic and Protestant understandings.

Liturgy, Unity, the Church

Michael J. Taylor, S.J.

Liturgy, unity, the Church—to the Catholic these realities are inextricably bound up in the saving mystery of
Christ. Christ has formed us from the many into the oneness of his Church. He had consecrated us a priestly
people whose worship renders full praise to the Father as
it unites us ever more deeply with him and with our
brothers in the sanctifying oneness of his Body.

In our view there can be no doubt (allowing for the
limitations of a Church built on men) what Christ wants
his Church to be. His Incarnation brought us redemption
and gave us a capacity for the perfect worship of the
Father. It gave us a way to God; it offered us a share in
the very truth and life of God himself. And with all the
energies of his Incarnate life, Christ brought into being
a Church whose acts of worship could render perfect
praise to the Father; he set up a kingdom of grace where
men could share in the way, the truth, and the life of
God. This is the divine *koinonia,* as much of it as this
earth will see until the *parousia.*

As prophetic preparation for the Christian Church, the
Father had earlier formed the children of Abraham into
a sacred people, a nation of priests, a worshiping community. In the desert under Moses' leadership, bound
by covenant and law, he fashioned them into a religious
assembly whose life of faith and ritual offered God a true

and pleasing liturgy. Separate from other men, their worship, though only a prophetic shadow of the greater substance to come, was created pure in God's sight, a sign for all the nations to see and emulate.

And Christ, in fulfilling and perfecting the Father's covenant with Israel, did not change the nature of the chosen race as a worshiping, priestly people. He fashioned the believing remnant into a "new Israel", a visible kingdom of priests who would worship the Father in spirit and truth because they actually lived within the perfect priest, worshiper, and temple—Christ. God no longer signed his "chosen people" by circumcision, but sealed them in that sign of victory over death and glory in resurrection which is the miracle of baptism. Their unity was no longer a matter of theocratic loyalties; it was a solidarity worked by the indwelling Spirit of Christ who formed all believers into a universal priesthood. Today the Church is even more God's nation of priests, his worshiping assembly.

The word *assembly* is about as close as we can come in English to the meaning of the biblical word which we translate as *church*. The Church of Jesus, then, is his assembly, a gathering of believers who discover in him a new, special relationship to the Father and to one another. It is a living union, as branches are joined to vine, as members of a body are one with their head. It is a personal union, as a bride is one with her groom in the unifying love-covenant of marriage. It is the union of temple stones whose aggregate rests upon the rock of Christ forming the perfect temple for the worship of the Father.

And the Christian enters this assembly as the ark of salvation, where, cleansed of his sins, he is able to worship God in full truth, to know and love him through grace. That grace brings newness of life, a new life in Christ. Man, since his first taste of divine indwelling, had always sought to live in God, but in his journey toward that life had completely lost his way. By himself he never found God. In fact, he had made himself an enemy through sin; by infidelity he brought on himself estrangement, exile and death. Clothed in sin and guilt he was incapable of happiness, unable to be what he knew he should be. He lived alone and with little hope.

But Jesus gave the answer to man's incapacity, confused searching, and guilt. In spite of our sins he became one of us, and as the Word made Flesh he undertook the human journey toward God himself so that sinful, misdirected man could follow him and be unburdened of sin and death and find a way to God. The pilgrim Christ became one of us and in his victory over sin and death gave us the means of forgiveness, the ability to know God and experience the highest form of unity, unity in the life of God himself. Our pilgrim Christ still lives, still forgives and directs us along the path to God and life; he lives and acts in his Church. And if men would seek salvation, they must enter into the Mystical Christ; they must love God in and with and through the Church, for the Church is Christ; it is his people, his royal priesthood, his consecrated nation.

Sacraments and the Mystery of Christ

Destined for membership in this priestly fellowship where he enters into the life and victory of Christ, the Christian is inserted into his Lord through the liturgy of baptism. It is the rite of initiation, the liturgy of birth. This liturgy prepares for what we believe is the more perfect liturgy of the Mass, which edifies and nourishes the worshiping fellowship, increasing life in its members and creating an ever deeper solidarity between them and Christ. Baptism is a liturgy once-for-all. The eucharist is the ongoing liturgy in which the Church regularly declares and realizes itself more fully in salvation and oneness. The eucharist, or the Mass, is the Church's ritual worship of God. All other rites and sacraments are related and subordinate to it. Here the Catholic believes that he does what Christ commanded him to do "until he comes" (1 Cor. 11, 26). Through the Mass the mystery of Christ is unfolded in Word and Sacrament; the saving acts of our Lord are celebrated and made present. In the Mass the faithful share in the reconciliation and the new life which God in the Flesh has purchased for us; the bonds of oneness with Christ and his Church are renewed and sealed.

Theoretically a Catholic could remove himself from parochial responsibilities and live a life detached from social action and missionary commitment and still be a minimal Christian. But if he refused to worship in the Church, to assist at Mass, in effect he would deny his faith. This is so because Catholics are primarily worshipers; they are secondarily missionaries. This is not to imply that a man could celebrate the Mass without some effect on his daily life, or that he could separate the liturgy completely from the effort to bring Christ to others through love and service. No one can pray the Mass properly without bringing to it and taking away a sense of commitment to love and serve the brothers. But there are many ways to love and serve. There is no substitute for the gathered assembly of Christ and its act of worship.

And a Christian does not gain admittance to this assembly of Christ because he is talented, moral, or intelligent. Jesus' parables make this clear. Wheat and weeds grow together in his kingdom, good fish swim with bad, sheep are herded with goats; cleansing judgment comes only when the earthly kingdom moves into the eternal. One is named a brother in Christ and a Catholic, as St. Ignatius of Antioch wrote centuries ago,[1] because he worships with the brothers in a eucharist at which the apostle-bishop preaches the Word of God and confects the Holy Sacrament. One is named a Catholic because he is a vital part of a eucharistic, priestly, worshiping assembly.

To worship, the community needs an appointed apostle (because our worship is hierarchic); we need an offering (because our worship is priestly); we need the Word of

---

[1] *Letter to the Smyrnaeans*, VI, 8 (P.G. 5714) (New York: Fathers of the Church, Inc., 1947), p. 121.

God (because our worship is dialogue). This is basic. For our community worship act we need Word and Bread and apostle-bishop. All of these are essentially ordered to the common worship in which we go to the Father through Christ, in whom we meet the Father in the Spirit. All are Christ's saving instruments; they exist for him, they communicate his life. None of these elements is independent of him or the brothers; all interdepend, all are essentially related.[2]

Word

First in worship there is the sacred Word of God. Given high respect during the liturgical assembly in homage to the unique character of its message, the bible brings us the living voice of God who comes to teach and inspire. In the divine Word we meet the Lord; his Spirit provokes our hearts to an ever more perfect response of commitment and faith. In Scripture we enter into a divine dialogue which creates within us a union of mind and will in preparation for a union still more profound.

Bread

Our union with Christ is established by faith in his Word; it is also made effectual by contact with his redemptive acts. And so, after the saving activity of the Word is recalled and commented on at Mass, the eucharist takes place. It is well known that the Catholic accepts the eucharist as the sacramental presence of the real and total Christ; he looks upon the sacred bread as the mystery which renders present the supreme act of sacrifice so that we, the lately come members of his body, might identify ourselves with that saving act and participate in it as the unifying, sacramental food of our souls. To deny the eucharist as sacrament and sacrifice for the Catholic is to destroy its reality and chief purpose; the eucharist for him is the sacrament of Christ's sacrifice.

[2] This concept is well developed by Robert W. Hovda in his chapter "What is the Church?" *Sunday Morning Crisis* (Baltimore: Helicon Press, Inc., 1963).

Our Lord left his saving actions to us in the forms of fundamental human actions. These had a solidity of form that enabled them to bear the weight of greater supernatural realities that he would put into them. Thus he made the common act of cleansing into the sacrament of baptism. And in the eucharist he chose bread and wine or the meal as the basic sign which was to support the supernatural realities. The eucharist renews the Last Supper; it is undoubtedly a meal. The early Church celebrated the eucharist as a sacred meal. Today, allowing for embellishments, the observant eye can see that the basic structure of the Mass is still that of a meal.

The eucharistic meal connotes feeding, and it does nourish our souls. But there is more. For Catholics it is a family meal, expressing and strengthening their family life within Christ. The Israelites looked upon the sacred meal as a sign of union with God and with each other, an enjoyment of divine favors, and a pledge of future glory and messianic fulfillment. As a continuation of meal rites inherited from the Old Testament, the new Christian meal becomes the symbol of the family blessings of salvation, but much more. The Christian considers his meal the fulfillment of these figure meals; a perfection and enrichment almost beyond belief.

Christ gave us the eucharist during the week of the Pasch; in fact, he gave it to us as our Christian Pasch. And this was at the Last Supper, the most important meal in the New Testament. Like all major religious meals, there were two important actions that took place during the supper. At the start of the meal the head of the family took, blessed, and broke bread which he shared with all at table; in this way everyone present was drawn into active celebration of the feast. At the end of the meal the head of the table gave the principal festal blessing. This blessing was a thanksgiving, a eucharist, which recalled the mighty deeds which God had done for his people. On the solemn occasion of the Pasch the meal would be accompanied with a cup of blessing; after a

prayer, the celebrant passed the cup to all present in order
that they could echo their thanks to God for his blessings.
We believe that Christ in this context of family thanksgiving, in a spirit of obedience and adoration, at the breaking
of the bread told the apostles that it was his body and at
the blessing of the cup told them that the wine was his
blood sealing the new covenant. And he invited them to
share in it—a participation not only in the religious event
of God-with-us, but a participation in the life of the God-
Man himself; a symbol of oneness—but more, a cause of
oneness with Christ.

And yet there is more. The Lord's Supper celebrated
the death of Christ. His approaching death overshadowed
the occasion. The bread became his body as *offered;* the
wine, his blood as *shed*. In giving the apostles his body
and blood as food and drink Christ gave them himself
also as a redeeming victim. He expressed his offering of
sacrifice in a symbolic way. He thus made his meaningful meal more significant still; he made it the meal of
his sacrifice. The eucharist, the liturgy of the body and
the blood, the Catholic believes, is the sacred meal which
makes present sacramentally the sacrifice of Christ and
feeds us on the unitive, grace-filled life of the victim of that
sacrifice. And if we ask why Christ gave us his sacrifice
in meal form, we would understand that it is because he
wants us to join ourselves to it and make it our sacrifice,
our worship as well. The sacrifice which is peculiarly his
worship to the Father he has given to his worshiping
Church. And in the Mass it is as head of the Mystical
Body that Christ continues his priestly liturgy. The sacrificial meal from that moment until the end of time is the
offering of the whole Christ, head and members—in essence we believe a perfect liturgy.

Apostle-Bishop

Our community is priestly; our worship goes to the
Father through Christ, the perfect priest. Fulfilling all the

prophetic figures of sacrifice, Christ accomplished his redemptive mission by the priestly offering of himself on
the cross. Now, as head of the Mystical Body, he lives in
the Church. It is his prolongation, extension in time, his
priestly body, his sacerdotal community. But in Christ's
present worship of the Father, our bishop-priest or his
delegate stands in a unique relation to Christ as offerer. If
we are a priestly people, we might wonder why we single out one person to be our representative at worship.
Christ's priestly life flows through the souls of all members of his body, but the priesthood is not shared in
the same way by all Christians. This is because the
Church is hierarchical (Paul tells us that not all are
apostles, not all inspired spokesmen and teachers: 1 Cor.
12, 12ff.). There are two ways in which the priesthood
of Christ can be shared: by baptism and by holy orders.
If we distinguish two aspects of the Church, the twofold
sharing of the priesthood will be easier to understand.
First, the Church has official representatives of Christ. This
is the hierarchy, Christ's ministerial members who are
empowered and commissioned by him to make available
the visible means of grace, either by the authoritative
preaching of God's Word or by the administration of his
sacraments; in short, this hierarchic priesthood visibly
and authoritatively represents the invisible Christ until his
Second Coming. Second, there is communion with Christ.
This is the Church which lives within the priestly Christ.
It is the worshiping community that he builds by grace,
whose objective is to live with Christ in a union of love
and prayer. The first aspect is the ministerial, hierarchical
priesthood given by holy orders. The second aspect is the
universal priesthood which makes us able to unite ourselves with Christ's sacrifice and receive the many graces
that flow from it: it is bestowed at baptism. Nor is the
latter priesthood a mere passive receptivity; it means
that we actively and willingly enter into the mystery of
Christ and make it our own.

Thus the Mass manifests the Church as a priestly fellowship united in Christ, praising the Father in the oneness of the Spirit and in this worship act we partake of the unifying and sanctifying life of Christ himself. In the eucharist and the Word we have the nourishment of brotherhood, the common meal and the common Word, ancient signs of brotherly communication and community, now made supernatural by Christ to convey his supernatural life to us. In the apostle-bishop we have the hierarchical minister and preacher who speaks Christ's saving words and confers his sacramental mysteries.

The Church in its life, unity, and worship proclaims to the world that Christ is making good his promise to make men one as he and the Father are one. And the world at long last is slowly moving toward an analogous unity. It is beginning to sense the folly of political, social, and economic *apartheid*. Men fight for brotherhood; they rebel against imperialism and class division; they demand civil rights for all men—it would seem to give expression to an inner conviction they feel that men were not meant to be antagonists but to act in unity under God. These latter-day struggles seem the product of a subtle influence emanating from this community formed in oneness by Christ.

The Church in its unity inspires the world toward oneness and the world in turn looks to the Church to present to man a unity yet stronger, yet more vital. The Church would direct the world in its striving toward the Word, the bread, and the apostle-bishop.

The Catholic Church believes that Christianity must have these for fullness, for oneness—her liturgy and unity without them would be gestures only and without substance. All are related to one another and were created to capacitate the priestly community to give full worship and praise to God. With these instruments, especially in the worship act of Christians, Jesus unites and renews his community, his people, his holy Church, and brings them to God.

Worship in Fellowship

A Catholic looking in on Protestant worship[3] discovers there real fellowship and community. The Protestant congregation is one where the members usually know each other; the minister and the congregation are generally on speaking terms. There is a feeling of brotherhood in a common action of praise and thanksgiving, a sense of mutual discipleship in the witness of Christ. The elements that assist this community spirit are many. Obviously the use of the vernacular is responsible for intelligent participation. Protestants worship in their own language and so are able to understand and follow the service with ease. And the readings, prayers, hymns, and responses, usually cast in a good literary vernacular, are spoken, read, and sung in a reverent and prayerful way. The Catholic, in fact, is impressed at the "art" that Protestants show in the matter of saying their prayers reverently (the Catholic has a tendency to recite his prayers too fast and by rote).

Granting that there were periods in the evolution of Protestant worship that understressed it, Protestants have emphasized strongly the priesthood of all believers and have insisted that participation, involvement by all the members of the community, is an essential mark of worship. The family nature of the Christian flock is given expression when the "we" of the service is spoken by all the faithful.

The Catholic at Mass on the other hand can be overly concerned with himself, his worship obligations, his personal advancement in the Christ-life. The "super" reverence that has surrounded the Mass, the church building, the tabernacle, although it is extremely productive of the essential note of "Christ present" sometimes creates an exclusivist attitude of being "alone before Christ" and not of being "together with the brethren in Christ" (the

[3] The author in his criticism draws not only from Mr. Marshall's enlightening presentation, but also from his own personal observations of Protestant worship over a ten-year period.

aspect that should characterize Mystical Body worship).
Some feel that acknowledging the presence of their fellow
Christians is something of a distraction, almost to be dis-
couraged. It would seem that a blend of reverence and
open community could well be more in evidence at
Catholic Mass. If we believe strongly that we are a community (and we must), then there should be more external, friendly acknowledgment of this belief. Obviously
the reforms of the Second Vatican Council allowing an
increase in community action will help to create an atmosphere of open fellowship at Mass.

If the Catholic can volunteer any criticism here, it
would be more in the nature of degree than of kind. He
is greatly impressed when he finds community among
Protestants. He is only disturbed when he discovers that
the community, though real, is not as theologically
grounded as he feels it should be. The worship is indeed
communal, but the faith of the community is sometimes
highly personalized and fragmented. The Catholic sees
the Church not as an aggregate of private believers but as
a community of common believers who witness in mutual
faith the full Christian mystery. Community worship to be
truly *ecumenical,* he feels, must well from a *united* community of faith.

Also, the Catholic is uneasy when he discovers a sense
of *ad libitum* in the matter of worship attendance. It is
true that Protestants want to worship only with a "willing
community"; this is good. But again the Catholic thinks
that the Church as a whole must be projected and viewed
always as a worshiping assembly; it may be other things
but it is essentially this. Therefore we must stress the
obligations that our Baptism imposes on all of us to live
our priestly consecration by joining our brothers in the
Lord for the saving praise of the Father.

High Respect for the Word

The Catholic is deeply moved by the importance Protestants give to the proclamation of the Word. They obvi-

ously look upon the Book as God's greatest gift to the Church; if another precious gift, the eucharist, seems to be understressed in worship, at least our liturgies coincide in their mutual reverence for Scripture. Protestants and Catholics join each other in believing that the Word becomes active in worship; the bible is no longer simply an apologetical source book, a recorded chronicle of static events in salvation history. When the minister preaches Scripture, it becomes a "living Word". "For the word of God is living and efficient and keener than any two-edged sword . . . extending even to the division of soul and spirit . . . a discerner of the thoughts and intentions of the heart" (Heb. 4, 12). "Is not my word like fire, says the Lord, like a hammer shattering rocks?" (Jer. 23, 29) The Gospel catches us up in that perfect dialogue between God and his people which was established by Christ in whom we know, hear, and speak to the Father. In the Word, Jesus as man speaks for us to the Father; as the Word of God he is the epitome of the Father's will for us. The preached Word lives; it is addressed to us and demands our response here and now. As Jesus asks his disciples: "Who do men say that I am?" the Gospel moves us to answer with Peter: "You are the Christ, the son of the living God!" The whole Gospel account of Christ: his miracles, his commandment sermons, his didactic discourses and parables, the creation of his sacramental gifts —challenge our response, and so often that response has been formed for us in the inspired words of Scripture itself: the Our Father, the Psalms, the Canticles, the many "faith responses" of Christ's first followers: "I do believe, help my unbelief"—"You alone have the words of eternal life"—"Truly this was the son of God"—"My Lord and my God!" Protestants by centering their liturgy in the saving Word are drawn toward Christ as Lord and Savior and are able to make worship a living response of faith.

Lack of the Peripheral

Another commendable aspect of Protestant worship

(and a great help to ecumenism) is its lack of the peripheral. Centered around Christ as Lord and Savior the service proceeds along simple, uncluttered lines. It is directed to the Father, but all proceeds clearly through Christ, our one only mediator. Catholics have much to learn here. Their rite, though intrinsically Christo-centric, has become overloaded, as we have seen. In its elaborateness, the simple structure of the liturgy as saving Word and unifying, sanctifying sacrament has not always been clearly defined. The Second Vatican Council has called for a restoration of simplicity and clarity in this regard and recent enactments have gone a long way toward a clearer definition of the rite.

Protestant liturgies in their Christo-centric direction need no improvement. Still the Catholic feels that Protestant worship could more strongly project a spirit of the *presence* of Christ. Our Lord's incarnational extension in time through his mystical indwelling in Christians (though taught) is not always sensed. As we will see, Christ's sacramental oneness with us is not fully appreciated by Protestants. One would like to see the indwelling of Christ stressed more, an indwelling that is especially manifest at worship when the community formed in him carries out its highest act.

Sacramental Renewal

Perhaps the most ecumenically hopeful aspect the Catholic sees in Protestant worship is the restoration in some churches of Holy Communion as an integral part of the service. Protestants find that our biblical renewal has brought us much closer to them; in like manner Catholics view the Protestant sacramental renewal as a great source of ecumenical hope.

Protestants in "rediscovering" the eucharist are not innovating or imitating, but returning to what the great reformers insisted was an essential part of worship; worship that contained a balanced use of Word and Sacrament had the most meaning for Calvin, Luther, and the Wesleys.

The eucharist is our bread and meal of unity, the sacred grains of wheat which form us into the one bread of Christ, the sign to ourselves and the world that we are one in Christ. "For we being many are one bread, one body, all that partake of the one bread" (1 Cor. 10, 17). If we are to live and act as one, then Christ must solidify and protect that unity in grace.

The Liturgy and Orthodoxy

John Meyendorff

The Christian liturgy has been given various forms and these in turn have gone through various transformations in the course of history, in both East and West, in response to new conditions and in accordance with the peculiar genius of different peoples. The Church of Constantinople, for example, did not have any liturgical tradition of its own prior to the fourth century, but it gradually created a new rite which was greatly influenced by Antioch. This new Byzantine rite already possessed all the essential features which it now has by the ninth century, at the time when it was carried to the far corners of the Byzantine world and became *the* liturgy of numerous peoples. It is celebrated today in many different languages and is regarded as a powerful bond uniting divers nationalities who feel that it is an expression of their one Orthodox faith. The custom of translating it into a language understood by the people has helped to root the liturgy in the minds of the faithful, who look upon their participation in the common prayer of the Church as an important sign of belonging to the Body of Christ. This is not a question of mere ritualism, but an appreciation of the corporate significance of the Gospel message combined with the realization that the new life in Christ is indeed manifested by and communicated in the sacramental nature of Christian worship. This is why the Orthodox layman pays particular attention to the form and manner in which the liturgy is celebrated. He never regards it, as does his brother in the West who is accustomed to a liturgy celebrated in a language which he does not understand, as an act involving only the priest, but feels responsible himself for all that is done in the house of God. This awareness as to what is taking place, it can readily be appreciated, makes it difficult to carry out reforms, whether good or bad in nature. Actual schisms have resulted from attempts to change the liturgy in minor respects. This close control which the Church exercises over its own liturgy causes it to view as suspect rites with which it has not been closely in touch since the Middle Ages, especially Western variations—wrongly so, however. It is also true that this genuinely living liturgy, which is firmly rooted in the language of each country and has often been instrumental in forming that language itself, can often serve to keep the faith alive. Under the Turkish and Mongol yokes the Christians of the East were strengthened in their faith by the celebration of the liturgy, and so it is in Russia today, where the liturgy remains the only means at the disposal of the Church for communicating to the faithful the truths of religion in the midst of a Marxist state. The revival of Christianity in Russia shows once more that the school of the liturgy can be a very potent influence.

It is not possible here to linger over the details of the Byzantine liturgy. Various liturgical cycles, daily, weekly, annual, and paschal, correspond in large part to similar cycles in other traditional liturgies, but in contrast to the rather austere Latin liturgy these cycles are much richer and much more elaborate. The Psalter and other excerpts from the bible which form the basis for the daily office (vespers, compline, nocturn or midnight prayer, matins, prime, terce, sext, none) are supplemented by a great many different kinds of hymns which vary according to the season or feast day.

The custom of celebrating the eucharistic liturgy on a daily basis was of relatively late origin, both in the East and the West. However, it has never become widespread in the East, hence the Orthodox Church is not familiar with any obligation for priests to celebrate daily—the liturgy is not regarded as their private affair but as an act involving the whole Church—and the liturgy has retained some of its meaning as a "common work", a solemnity involving the whole community which normally takes place only on Sundays and feast days. But while Orthodoxy does not attach any particular importance to the frequency with which Mass is celebrated, it has inherited from Byzantium a spirituality strongly oriented toward the sacramental life. Both as a memorial and as an anticipation of the world to come, the eucharist is the place where the Church identifies itself with the Kingdom of God. This is the essential meaning of the celebration held on "the eighth day" of the week, the Lord's Day.

The Byzantine rite has preserved a number of the countless variations which once characterized the liturgy of the ancient Church: for example, it has two eucharistic liturgies which are used on different occasions, that of St. John Chrysostom and that of St. Basil. A third type of liturgy, celebrated at Jerusalem and occasionally elsewhere, is traditionally attributed to St. James, the brother of the Lord. During Lent it is customary not to celebrate the liturgy except on Saturdays and Sundays, in accordance with the canons of ancient councils; the fast is intended to impress on Christians the meaning of the fallen state in which they now are until the Parousia, despite the assurance of salvation which is even now within their grasp. Lent is therefore a period of expectation interrupted only by the dominical liturgies and terminating in the triumphal paschal liturgy, the anticipation of the Second Coming of Christ. On certain days during Lent, however, it is customary to celebrate a form of vespers when communion is distributed which has been reserved from the preceding Sunday. This is called the Liturgy of the Presanctified, a form of service traditionally ascribed to St. Gregory the Great, the pope of Rome.

Like all traditional eucharistic prayers the Byzantine

canon has the form of a solemn thanksgiving which the bishop or priest offers to God the Father. Because the Church is the Body of Christ, the Son of God, it is privileged to address itself directly to the Father in commemorating the redemptive work of the Son and in invoking the descent of the Holy Spirit "on us and on these gifts here present" (Liturgy of St. John Chrysostom) so that they may be changed into the Body and Blood of the Lord. This trinitarian character of the canon, which reaches its culminating point in the solemn invocation of the Spirit (Epiclesis), is regarded as essential by the Orthodox Church, and the lack of this feature in the present Roman Mass since the early Middle Ages is held to be a grave defect. It is the Spirit, actually, who reveals the grace of redemption in the Church after the ascension of Christ: "When the truth-giving Spirit, who proceeds from the Father, has come to befriend you, he whom I will send to you from the Father's side, he will bear witness of what I was" (John 15, 26).

Orthodox teaching always has emphasized the reality of the sacramental change (*metabole*) in the eucharist by which the bread and wine are transformed into the body and blood of Christ. However, neither the liturgy nor the Fathers nor any authentic Orthodox text prior to the sixteenth century uses the term "transubstantiation" (Greek *metousiosis*) to describe this mystery. This term is employed in later Orthodox confessions of faith intended to define the teaching of the Church with respect to Protestant opinions on this matter, but there is always the reservation that the term is only one of several that could be employed and does not imply that the Church intends to adopt the Aristotelian philosophical theory of form and matter.

DIALOGUE NO. 4
Our Common Christian Heritage

Resource Readings

Our Common Christian Heritage (pp. 110–136)
Clement Welsh
Wilfred F. Dewan, C.S.P.

Suggested Readings

Bea, Augustine. *The Unity of Christians*. New York: Herder and Herder, 1963.

Baum, Gregory. *The Catholic Quest for Christian Unity*. New York: Paulist Press, 1965.

Dillenberger, John and Welch, Claude. *Protestant Christianity*. New York: Scribner, 1958.

Horton, Walter Marshall. *Christian Theology*. New York: Harper, 1958.

Neill, Stephen. *Christian Faith Today*. Harmondsworth, Middlesex, Eng.: Penguin Books, 1955.

Tavard, George. *Two Centuries of Ecumenism*. Chicago: Fides, 1960.

CHRISTIAN DIALOGUE
Our Common Christian Heritage

OPENING PRAYER

Leader: Let us give thanks to God for making us one with himself and with one another by the sacrifice of Christ upon the cross.

All: We thank you, O Lord.

Leader: For all your gifts to us in spite of our divisions, and for teaching us to share them with one another in the ecumenical movement.

All: We thank you, O Lord.

Leader: For bringing us together to listen and meditate upon your words of Holy Scripture.

All: We thank you, O Lord.

Leader: For your risen life which you imparted to all of us at baptism.

All: We thank you, O Lord.

All: Heavenly Father, we thank you that you have given us your Son as our Savior and our brother. We praise you that we do not have to trust in ourselves but may come before you in his name. Set his work and his sacrifice anew before our eyes. May we recognize again from what depths he has rescued us. May new thankfulness and love grow in us through his gifts which we still share in common. Grant that the peace which made one body of Jew and Gentile may be made visible in us to the honor of your great name. Amen.

BIBLE READING

Blessed be the God and Father of our Lord Jesus

Christ, who has blessed us in Christ with every spiritual blessing in the heavenly places, even as he chose us in him before the foundation of the world, that we should be holy and blameless before him. He destined us in love to be his sons through Jesus Christ, according to the purpose of his will, to the praise of his glorious grace which he freely bestowed on us in the Beloved (Ephesians 1, 3-6).

And he came and preached peace to you who were far off and peace to those who were near; for through him we both have access in one Spirit to the Father. So then you are no longer strangers and sojourners, but you are fellow citizens with the saints and members of the household of God, built upon the foundation of the apostles and prophets, Christ Jesus himself being the cornerstone, in whom the whole structure is joined together and grows into a holy temple in the Lord; in whom you also are built into it for a dwelling place of God in the Spirit (Ephesians 2, 17-22).

If God is for us, who is against us? He who did not spare his own Son but gave him up for us all, will he not also give us all things with him? (Romans 8, 31-32)

Who shall separate us from the love of Christ. . . . For I am sure that neither death, nor life, nor angels, nor principalities, nor things present, nor things to come . . . will be able to separate us from the love of God in Christ Jesus our Lord (Romans 8, 35-39).

Meditation

Lord, tonight we meet to discuss the Christian elements we share in common. . . . The greatest gift we share and the source of all the others is you, our Lord and Savior. . . . Through you we all have access in one Spirit to the Father. . . . Help us to keep you as the chief cornerstone of our *Living Room Dialogues*. . . . We know you will not fail to grant us the joy of once again sharing all things with you. . . . Begin tonight by impressing upon us that nothing, even our divisions and differences, can separate us from the love of God which is in you.

BIBLE READING

For by one Spirit we were all baptized into one body —Jews or Greeks, slaves or free—and all were made to drink of one Spirit (1 Cor. 12, 13).

Now you are the body of Christ and individually members of it (1 Cor. 12, 27).

I therefore, a prisoner of the Lord, beg you to lead a life worthy of the calling to which you have been called, with all lowliness and meekness, with patience, forbearing one another in love, eager to maintain the unity of the Spirit in the bond of peace. There is one body and one Spirit, just as you were called to the one hope that belongs to your call, one Lord, one faith, one baptism, one God and Father of us all, who is above all and through all and in all (Eph. 4, 1-6).

And I am sure that he who began a good work in you will bring it to completion at the day of Jesus Christ. . . . And it is my prayer that your love may abound more and more, with knowledge and all discernment, so that you may approve what is excellent, and may be pure and blameless for the day of Christ, filled with the fruits of righteousness which come through Jesus Christ, to the glory and praise of God (Phil. 1, 6-11).

So, if there is any encouragement in Christ, any incentive of love, any participation in the Spirit, any affection and sympathy, complete my joy by being of the same mind, having the same love, being in full accord and of one mind (Phil. 2, 1-2).

Meditation

Lord, though the things that divide us are serious and important, the things that continue to unite us are greater. . . . Our bond of union is our baptism in you, making us members of your body. . . . We have one Lord, one baptism, one God and Father of all but we are not completely one in faith. . . . Help us, Lord, to strengthen our love for one another so we can more and more abound in knowledge and discernment. . . . That we may approve the better things . . . That we may think and believe alike with one soul and one mind.

Christian Dialogue

Introduction

Tonight we hope to establish some of the common ground on which all Christians stand. As we talk about these beliefs, we pray the conviction will grow that we are truly brothers in Christ. Our divided histories have made us aware of what separates us. The ecumenical movement thankfully opens our eyes to what binds us together.

Such a discussion will not, of course, remove the differences and disagreements. These will remain and appear in some cases even greater than we thought. But so will the areas of agreement enlarge as we understand our true positions and it is these that the Holy Spirit will use as he guides Christians toward unity.

DISCUSSION QUESTIONS

The resource reading stated that all Christians find their common root not only in a common idea of God but in a more specific point of unity: in Jesus Christ. And that what we believe about Christ himself is what must be set down as the first essential point of agreement among us.

To begin the discussion each member of the group should reflect upon his own relationship with Christ. All the members of the dialogue should give a brief account of how they came to know Christ. Who first introduced them to Christ? What means did their Churches employ to deepen their knowledge and commitment to Christ? Which of the means used do they feel were the most effective?

The following questions should form the basis for further discussion concerning Christ as the center of the common heritage of Christians.

List ways in which Jesus plays a role in your life today: your prayer, your family and social life, your work.

What are the basic things concerning Christ on which Christians agree?

If we are agreed concerning Jesus Christ, how have we fallen short of our agreement?

For Catholics: do you sometimes in your devotions replace Jesus with the Virgin Mary or with the saints? Give reasons for your answer.

For Protestants: do you think your personal relationship with Christ would be incomplete if Mary, the saints and the other members of the Church were completely excluded from it? Give reasons for your answer.

For Orthodox: have you de-humanized Jesus and made him too remote and mystical? Give reasons for your answer. Has theological renewal in your Church given a new emphasis to the centrality of Jesus Christ in the Christian life?

Church, Bible and Tradition

The resource material for this dialogue states: "A second whole area of agreement among Christians centers around the bible: in itself, in its relation to the Church and to Tradition. We have far more in common on these points than was admitted by either 'side' of the dialogue. Now we are beginning to understand one another." As we have seen from the resource material, however, the bible must be viewed in its relation to both the Church and Tradition.

DISCUSSION QUESTIONS

What is the role of the bible in your Church? What does the bible mean to you personally? How has the study of the bible deepened our understanding of the Church in modern times? What are some of the biblical images of the Church? Are the Churches agreed on their interpretation of these images? What are some of the indications of renewed interest in the bible among Catholics?

Do Protestants interpret Scripture without reference to any other higher authority? Explain the correct idea of this matter. Do Catholics subject the bible to fallible human interpretation by allowing Church authorities to interpret it? Explain the correct idea of this matter.

What is the basic difference of opinion between Catholics and Protestants concerning the apostles passing on their authority to their successors? What is the generally held Catholic teaching today on the nature of Tradition? How does this differ from the teaching that there are two sources of revelation, Scripture and Tradition? What is the role of the layman in handing on Tradition? What is the area of agreement concerning the concept of Tradition? What are the implications of this for the Christian unity?

The Christian Life

"The area of general agreement concerning the Christian life is large, although obviously there may be wide ranges of difference in ways and practices of Christian living—and not only between denominations and Christian divisions, but also within any one group . . ." The resource material makes this important point for our consideration.

DISCUSSION QUESTIONS

What does your tradition believe concerning (a) the origin of the world and of man, (b) the nature of man, (c) man's sinfulness, (d) man's redemption, (e) the destiny of man, (f) life after death? What are the agreements and disagreements on these points?

What do you mean by the grace of God? How does the Holy Spirit relate to the life of grace? When does God give us his grace?

In what ways do you pray to God? by reading and meditating on Scripture? in your own informal, spontaneous manner? when contemplating God's creation? by reading and meditating on the events of Christ's life or of some saint?

What religious practice of another tradition most puzzles you? Can anyone explain the reasons for this practice? Why does the Christian life not have a stronger appeal to non-Christians? Where do we fail most in living out Christianity? How do our divisions affect this situation?

The Christian Community

There exist wide disagreements concerning the nature of the Church among Christians. Yet certain things concerning the Christian community run through all teachings on this subject.

DISCUSSION QUESTIONS

What do you mean by the Church as a community of the saving action of God? Granting the different teachings concerning the two sacraments to which all Christians adhere, is there any consensus concerning their main purposes? How does baptism establish a bond among all Christians? What does the doctrine of the priesthood of believers mean? Does your Church make a distinction between the priesthood of all believers and the priesthood of ordained ministers and priests? What is it?

SUMMARY

In the past, too little attention has been given the important things Christians hold in common. Our common Christian heritage extends to broader fields than most of us have realized. Through dialogue we gain for you a deeper knowledge of and love for our fellow Christians.

DISCUSSION QUESTIONS

List the three most important beliefs that Christians have in common? Why are they the most important?

As Christians have grown in understanding each other better in recent years, what major misunderstanding on your part has been cleared up?

Is there danger of taking ecumenical progress for granted by resting content with those thing we share now?

CLOSING PRAYER

O God of peace, who through your Son Jesus Christ did set forth one faith for the salvation of mankind, send forth your grace and heavenly blessing upon all Christian people who are striving to draw nearer to you, and to each other, in the unity of the Spirit and in the bond of peace. Give us penitence for our divisions, wisdom to know your truth, courage to do your will, love which will break down the barriers of pride and prejudice, and an unswerving loyalty to your holy name. Suffer us not to shrink from any endeavor which is in accordance with your will for the peace and unity of your Church. Give us the boldness to seek only your glory and the advancement of your kingdom. Unite us all in you, as you, O Father, with your Son and the Holy Spirit, are one God, world without end. Amen.

Our Common Christian Heritage

Clement Welsh
Wilfred F. Dewan, C.S.P.

INTRODUCTION

1. *"Heritage"*

It is probably not very safe to make any generalizations about Christians, but non-Christians may notice one obvious fact about us all: we take our past seriously. We cherish our inheritance. We talk about our history; we reverence our traditions and their roots in Scripture. It does not occur to us to be ashamed of our faith just because it was not invented recently. We are people with a past, and proud of it.

2. *"Christian"*

Furthermore, our sense of heritage is focused on an *event:* the life and activity of Jesus Christ. We call ourselves by his name. He did not simply give us some truths that we can now use without further thought of their origin. He, himself, is the important thing to us, and we are all characterized by our habit of looking back to the time when he came among us, to a moment in history that must forever be as important to us as the present moment in which we now live—or more so.

3. *"Common"*

It is no accident, therefore, that in spite of the plain fact that those who call themselves "Christians" now are found to be clustered in bodies that disagree on many matters, we all share in much that is common, and indeed experience a natural tendency to draw together in the common point of origin which we all take so seriously. If we were the kind of people who lived by the present, we might continue to drift apart. But we are kept together by the power of that concern for a moment in the past—a past which is, however, very much present to us. Our various Christian clusterings are like balloons on long strings, held together by one guiding hand.

4. *"Our"*

And finally, the first word of the title of this dialogue must be noted. No Christian, whatever Church he belongs to, would be so bold as to claim, except in a superficial sense, that this great Christian heritage is "his". He did not invent it, and does not really "possess" it. It comes to him from another, from God, and he receives it with reverence and submission. He speaks of it the way we quote a friend who is standing beside us: "John, here, was saying—and correct me if I am wrong, John—that . . ." The heritage is ours, but not as something to use as we will, or state as we will, or practice as we will. For what we are talking about is God himself, his coming among us, and his gift of self to us. We say, in a figure of speech, that "we make it our own" but God's it is and God's it remains, and we accept it as men ready to stand under his correction.

So we are people with a common Christian heritage, and when we talk together and discover how much we share in agreement, we experience, and rightly, an awakening of joy, a feeling of a sense of rightness, of having come home.

Let us explore together what we share in this way.

A Note on Procedure

The search for common beliefs runs into some natural hazards. Of these, one of the most obvious is that of ignoring those differences of belief that hedge and qualify the thing we agree on. These qualifications may make all the difference. Furthermore, we may be tripped up by a common terminology. Two people may say, "I believe in the Church as the Body of Christ," and later discover that they mean something quite different by that phrase. And it must be added that differences of language may *conceal* agreement; language must be closely watched and constantly interpreted.

Our method, here, will be to indicate more than verbal agreements, but rather to single out those great doctrines which all Christians have thought about and to indicate that their reflection of them has often started with a common aim or direction, a common set of first great promises. The more detailed theological thought about each of these may continue in common ways, or it may begin at once to diverge. One would hope that for each doctrine, we would begin to develop a sense of how each Christian community has approached it—some sense of the frame of mind that has governed its theological reflection. This kind of awareness should help each of us to understand what the other is saying and to "read between the lines" as he tries to expound his beliefs. Our task is to learn another theological *language,* and it is complicated by the odd fact that we often use the same *words!* By beginning together with the great doctrines—God, Christ, Scripture, Church, Man, Sin, Grace— we may listen with carefulness to each other, and with a sense of the greatness of the mysteries that each of our traditions has struggled to express.

I. AT THE CENTER: CHRIST

You might think that the first thing common to all Christians is a belief in God. We could, indeed, begin with that belief, but we might be startled to discover that other great groups of believers had suddenly joined us whom we had not expected: such as Jews and Mohammedans. Just behind them would be various groups designated as "Unitarians", together with assorted philosophers happy to be recognized as believing in God. We do share with many non-Christians the belief in a God who is "personal", who created the world and cares for it, and with whom man can be in communion. As Christians, we fit into the category which the textbooks in religion call "theist", and as such we have engaged in dialogue with those who cannot be sure about God (agnostics) or who deny that any such being exists (atheists) or who believe in God but define him in ways that differ sharply from the description of the theist (such as, for example, pantheists).

But Christians of all kinds find their common root not just in the sharing of a common idea of God but in a more specific point of unity: in Jesus Christ. The Christian is the man for whom all thoughts of God, however large and philosophical, are determined by Christ and the revelation of God that he has given. There was, of course, preparation for his coming, and there has been interpretation of him throughout the many years since the end of his earthly ministry, but what we believe about Christ himself is what must be set down first as the essential first point of agreement.

This is easily made clear if we consider how we differ from the many men of religious sensitivity who respect and honor Christ as a great man, a prophet, a religious teacher of unequalled importance, as indeed the greatest of men. They all, indeed, admire Christ, but it is the Christian who says something distinctively different about Christ. And he says it whether he be Protestant, Catholic, Orthodox, Anglican, or whatever, and because he says this distinctive thing he is a *Christian,* and deserves that technical designation in its strict sense. All others are "Christian" only in a general sense of the word, and in our discussion we must, to avoid confusion, avoid that general, often complimentary, usage.

What, then, is our common Christian understanding of Christ that makes all Christians "Christian"? Like any great truth, it is not easily expressed, and the New Testament and the early centuries of Christian thought present

the student with a history of the efforts of devout and
learned men to understand a mystery. In the course of that
history many partial and limited descriptions of Christ
were tried and rejected, but the great truth that emerged
under God's guidance in the Church has come down to
us as a core of belief that is held with astonishing unanimity. It might be said that no other complex idea has
had so long a history, and has been preserved with fidelity through so many changes of human culture.

1. *The God-Man*

The first thing that must be said about the common
Christian understanding of Christ is actually a twofold
truth: that Christ was a person who combined in himself
two natures. We could begin by speaking of him as God,
and in a following paragraph go on to speak of him as
man, and be quite right on both counts. The easy approach
(as the early heretics demonstrated) is to concentrate on
one clear aspect, and let the other slip. The hard matter
is to realize that *both* are true of one person, and so we
start with this great paradox, difficult though it is to grasp.
All Christians, of whatever traditions, are aware of the
importance of keeping this difficult "doubleness" in their
understanding of Christ, not stressing the divinity at the
expense of the humanity, or vice versa. For all Christians,
the norm for their description of Christ was stated by the
Council of Chalcedon in 451: "We all with one accord
teach the profession of faith in the one identical Son, our
Lord Jesus Christ. We declare that he is perfect both in
his divinity and in his humanity, truly God and truly man,
composed of body and rational soul; that he is of one substance with the Father in his divinity, and of one substance with us in his humanity, like to us in every respect
except for sin."

But we need not stop there. Christians are agreed that
it is misleading to say that "Christ was divine", as if he
were a heavenly being who briefly joined us on earth. He
is divine; for he lives in risen splendor with the Father.

He was, clearly, a man like us in his humanity. But his "divinity": this must be the presence in Christ of the one God, the creator, that is, God himself, and not just some "divine power" conferred on a human being. And so we have a common faith, in all sorts and types of Christians, that the God in Christ opens to us a knowledge of God himself, and that together with our knowledge of God as creator, we know him in Christ as redeemer. Thus this understanding of God, which at Pentecost was completed by the Holy Spirit coming into prominence, brings into our common heritage that great and difficult doctrine of the Trinity. It is worth noting that at its third Assembly in New Delphi (1961) The World Council of Churches expanded its "basis" for membership from acceptance of our Lord Jesus Christ as God and Savior to include a trinitarian statement: "The World Council of Churches is a fellowship of Churches which confess our Lord Jesus Christ as God and Savior according to the Scriptures and therefore seek to fulfill together their common calling to the glory of the one God, Father, Son and Holy Spirit."

We share this belief that it is indeed the true God who is in Christ, and not something less than God, in spite of many human temptations to think of Christ as a mere man with divine powers. But how can the fullness of God be present in a man on earth? This, the great mystery of *Christology,* has produced theological reflection in every age, but once again with a limit and norm: the fullness of God is found in a fully human being, like us in every way except for sin. The *Trinitarian God* (the Second Person, the Son, in Christ) and the *Incarnation* (very God and very Man); these two great mysteries of the faith, defying all our efforts at rational explication, are at the heart of the Christian faith, and it is worth noting that through the many stresses and strains of Christian disunity, we have all hewed to the difficult way of keeping before us the revealed fact in all its complexity: Christ, both God and Man, in perfect union.

All Christianity, then, must be Christocentric; it must all revolve around Christ as its heart and center. God came to us in Jesus Christ; we must find our way back to God in and through Jesus. Catholics have sometimes been accused of "leaving Christ out in the cold", of stressing peripheral doctrines instead. Whatever be the truth in this (certainly there was some, in practice at least), a huge renovation of theology is under way that puts Jesus Christ squarely in the middle. Pope Paul's words as he opened the second session of the Second Vatican Council should reassure many a Protestant: "Here and at this very hour we should proclaim Christ to ourselves and to the world around us: Christ our beginning, Christ our life and our guide, Christ our hope and our end . . ."

2. *The Works of Christ*

These difficult mysteries are accepted by all Christians but not without good reason. They are revealed in Scripture, which, with a wonderful frankness, gives the account of man's gradual awareness of the great truth. And this means that the coming of Christ is seen as the final event in God's creative purpose, of which the Old Testament gives the initial account and a history of what might be called man's adventures with the problem of salvation. The Incarnation is accepted by all Christians as an event like the creation itself: God acts by creating, and by coming into the creation (in Christ) and there and then doing all that man needs for his salvation. When seen as the saving event, this mysterious Incarnation is to some degree illuminated: it took the original creator God himself to save man, and to do it, he became man; therefore, all pseudo-incarnations, of half-gods, or semi-divine beings, or beings half God and half man, are seen to be ruled out, for it is *man* that must be saved, and only God can do it.

Christians may differ in the way they would explain further this saving action in Christ, but they would all agree that God took the initiative, he did what man could not do for himself, he did it by uniting to himself the manhood of a man like us in every way, and he did it once and for all for all men. We are redeemed by the passion, death and resurrection of Jesus (one total event). And Christians would all agree that the whole of the Christian life can be defined in terms of our appropriation of, or sharing in, that once-for-all saving event.

It would be easy (and impressive) to document this agreement by quoting from Christians in every age, and from every branch of our separated Churches. But it may be sufficient to note that among the many divisions within Protestantism, this ancient doctrine has met common acceptance. "At the beginning of the Faith and Order Movement, faith in the divine-human Lord and Savior tended to stand in a sort of splendid isolation, as the one clear point on which we were united . . ." So commented one of the study sections of the meeting of the Faith and Order Conference in 1957, concerning the beginnings in 1927. Discussions of the faith could begin there, even among theologians of widely differing points of view, for all had retained this difficult, complex, but essential doctrine of Christ's nature and work. All through the documents of the discussion of reunion among Protestants, Christ is announced as the common bond. The very Constitution of the World Council of Churches adopted at the First Assembly at Amsterdam in 1954 begins: "The World Council of Churches is a fellowship of Churches which confess our Lord Jesus Christ as God and Savior." And even as the difficult problems of disunity are brought forward for discussion, it is constantly asserted that Christian unity must be based on our common unity in Christ. This central emphasis of the ecumenical movement is noted in the Introduction to the Decree on Ecumenism of the Second Vatican Council: "This movement toward unity is called 'ecumenical.' Those belong to it who invoke the Triune God and confess Jesus as Lord and Savior . . ." The first chapter of the decree begins: "What has revealed the love of God among us is that the Father has sent into the world his only-begotten Son, so that, being made man, he might by his redemption give new life to the entire human race and unify it."

Our concern at the moment is the common ground of agreement among Christians, but it might be noted that the chief departures from this follow the pattern of the rejected heresies of the early centuries of Christian history, which the first four Councils dealt with: either an over-emphasis on the divinity at the expense of the humanity of Christ, or the opposite—humanity at the expense of divinity. The first of these often appears as a kind of exaggeration of devotional zeal. The worshipper, finding God in Christ, may speak as if his humanity were negligible. Its twin, stressing the humanity, has appeared in some Protestant thinkers who have moved in the direction of "humanism", a tendency not easily identified with any one denomination but which may be recognized by the way it speaks of the divinity of Christ as very nearly a quality of piety, or godliness, rather than that full presence of the Second Person of the Trinity in the God-man. But main line Protestantism has resisted strongly this humanizing tendency, and the Unitarian and Universalist Churches are not members of the National Council of the Churches of Christ in America, nor of the World Council of Churches.

It should be added that although there has been considerable discussion of the Virgin Birth among Protestants, adherence to this doctrine is also the rule rather than the exception, with vigorous insistence on the doctrine by all who may be classified as Biblical Fundamentalists. The Resurrection of Christ, however, is accepted by all Protestants (excepting only those who have departed from the central tradition in the direction of humanism).

II. THE CHURCH, THE BIBLE, AND TRADITION

A second whole area of agreement among Christians centers around the bible: in itself, in its relation to the Church, and to Tradition. We have far more in common on these points than was formerly admitted by either "side" of the dialogue. Now we are beginning to understand one another better. Let's look at the notion of the Church, first, and then come to the very important and central area of the bible. (Some might like to treat the bible first; our only reason for taking the Church first is that some notions concerning it will be helpful in the discussion of the bible in the life of the Christian community.)

1. *The Church*

First of all, the Church is a mystery. That is, though it is made up of a community of men on earth (even with some structure and law), it is first of all the presence of God's merciful action among men. In and through the visible community we encounter God himself, who declares his love and mercy over and over. We believe firmly that it is among and with our brothers in Christ that we encounter God's saving grace.

Too often the Church in the past has been taken for a legal society, an organization comparable to General Motors or Standard Oil, particularly by its critics. Maybe the presentation and image made by Christians was not too good. But today all Christians are going back to more biblical images, especially that of the Church as the *People of God*. Before Christ, God began his work of salvation by calling together a people unto himself, the Israelites. "I will be your God, and you will be my People," he said to them. By his favor, grace, and revelation he led them, formed them into a community (*kahal,* church) of believers, fiercely proud of their monotheism and favored position as sons of Yahweh.

With Christ came the perfection of God's plan, the inauguration of the *New* Israel. This new people of God was formed by Jesus Christ himself, made up of those who believed in him, and nourished by his continual presence and activity. From the very first, Christians have been a people, a fellowship (Acts 2, 42; 1 John 1, 3) gathered around their crucified and risen Lord. Whether praying, breaking bread together, preaching the good news of salvation, or living their daily lives, Christ was at the heart of everything—the creator of the fellowship, the center of worship, the giver of every gift.

This unity of the People of God has been disrupted by the sins and infidelity of many. We are a *pilgrim* people, still on the way to perfection and final union with God. So often we both individually and corporately have failed to live up to our calling. Thus, to admit failing and weaknesses in our Churches is not to dishonor God, but to see that the Church is holy in spite of our sins, and precisely because God is faithful. Penance and renewal must always be part of this pilgrim people of God.

Another wonderful image of the Church is the *Body of Christ*. St. Paul (from whom this doctrine is derived) had in mind the communion of life between the risen Lord and those who believed in him. Through baptism and faith we become one with Christ; we share in his life, in his obedience to the Father, in his death and resurrection. Basically, then, the mystical body (or body of Christ) is rooted in communion of life with Christ. Other biblical images deepen this conviction: the vine and branches, the bride and bridegroom, the building and the cornerstone.

So far, all Christians can pretty much agree on what has been said—and it is our desire to stress our *common* heritage. But how can all the different, and often conflicting, Christian bodies, be this *one* Church of Christ? Something is wrong. And this is the very reason for our ecumenical concern for reunion.

The understanding of Church, as we have indicated, is that of fellowship of men with Jesus: the union caused by Christ's presence through the Spirit in the midst of his People. (This is clear in the Second Vatican Council's important teaching on the Church). There is, therefore, a bond of union between all Christians who sincerely accept Jesus Christ as their Lord and Savor.

Who Belongs to the Church?

Many Christians (*e.g.,* Quakers, Baptists) insist that

the Church is fundamentally invisible, and transcends all sectarian barriers. Outward conformity to creeds, or formulas, or ways of worship should not be imposed as criteria for membership, they say.

Other Christian bodies see an obligation to adhere to confessions of faith and sacramental worship. Still others demand a certain obedience to external authority. But it is not always clear just how necessary these things are considered to be.

The Roman Church has long been considered very stand-offish and rigid in regard to membership in the Church. It saw the Mystical Body of Christ and the Catholic Church as exactly one and the same. Membership was co-extensive. Thus one could only be a member of the Church if he were baptized, participated in the same sacramental life of the Church, and adhered to the same authority.

However, the development seen in the Second Vatican Council's decree on the Church should be carefully noted. Life in Christ becomes the basis for membership; it is a much more personalist and interior approach. It carefully avoids identifying God's kingdom on earth with the Catholic Church. It says that while the Church of Christ "subsists" in the Catholic Church, many elements of sanctification and of truth are found outside of its visible structure.

This Constitution on the Church teaches that Catholics who possess the Holy Spirit (life of grace) are "fully" incorporated into the Church. Yet, since baptism is what initially incorporates, any baptized Christian already possesses an important relationship to the Church. And according as Christians have more of the other things which help to fully incorporate, namely, doctrinal, sacramental and hierarchical gifts, they, too, approach full membership. And even though the document does not treat it, Catholic theologians see a certain relationship to the Church for those who may not even be Christians, but are trying to follow their consciences and are actually living, however unconsciously, the true life of the Spirit.

Catholics are now saying to other Christians: "All of us Christians, however separated, are joined as brothers in Christ. We share with you the gift of the Spirit. We share with some, even many, of you elements which together build up the Church of the Lord. And while we believe that your Churches do not have the fullness of what Christ willed the Church to have, we acknowledge that, despite our separation, we do have real, even though limited, communion with you in the Holy Spirit."

But don't Catholics think their Church is the only true Church, that unity can only come about by others capitulating and joining them? Formerly the answer would be a simple yes. But today the Catholic Church humbly sees the great need to change itself. It realizes that, even though it retains all the essentials of Christ's Church, its present face is not all that Christ wills it to be. Much renewal and updating *(aggiornamento)* is necessary in order that it shine with the brilliance and attractiveness of the early Church. Catholics realize that they cannot dictate to God or even to other Christians the exact terms or time of unity. Nor can it predict the exact form of a re-united Church. So many changes have happened to her—which Catholics themselves several years ago would have called impossible—that no one is able to say what the future will bring. Certainly it would envision much more variety of worship, language, and even formulation of doctrine than in the past.

Churches in the Orthodox tradition have also held they are the one true Church, as, for example, in a statement made at the Second Assembly of the World Council of Churches in 1954: "In conclusion, we are bound to declare our profound conviction that the Holy Orthodox Church alone has preserved in full and intact 'the faith once delivered to the saints.' " (*Evanston Report,* p. 95.) Nevertheless, participation of Orthodox Churches in the

World Council has increased, and they are playing an important part in its ecumenical studies. All Churches come to the World Council with a deep sense of loyalty to the belief that they represent authentic embodiments of the faith, but the reports discussed and in general approved at the Council assemblies are characterized by many expressions of humility. At New Delhi, the Unity Report says: "The achievement of unity will involve nothing less than a death and rebirth of many forms of church life as we have known them. We believe that nothing less costly can finally suffice." (*The New Delhi Report*, p. 117.)

Thus, for all Christians the main objective in the ecumenical area is self-reformation. It is to live one's Christianity as fully and purely as possible, with a spirit of love, understanding, concern, helpfulness and cooperation toward all other Christians. And leave the rest to God. Well-known ecumenist Fr. Gustav Weigel, S.J., said: "The ecumenical movement is not an arena for the triumph of one Church over another. It is a fraternal confrontation of divided but brother Christians. . . . It is not the purpose of the ecumenical dialogue to make conversions. It is an effort of Christian love to give and receive witness to the Gospel."

2. *The Bible*

After fundamental commitment to Christ, reverence for and dependence upon the bible is what most unites us separated Christians. Since the Reformation, the sufficiency of Scripture has too often been the subject of bitter controversy. But today there is a most heart-warming measure of agreement.

Protestantism has always claimed to be the religion of the bible, and indeed nothing else is so characteristic of it. Scripture is not a "dead word" for them; rather, living Protestantism takes its life from its understanding of the bible, by understanding it in the light of the Spirit who gave it, and who inspired its authors. From this flows the living spirituality of the Protestant, and his desire to spread the bible to all men.

Protestant liturgy, too, has its roots in the Scriptures. Either the entire service or a great deal of it is bible reading, hymns and prayers inspired by the Word of God, culminating in a sermon designed to drive home the meaning and existential relevancy of the Word of God. Protestant worship is basically a hearing of the Word of God in an atmosphere of faith and adoration—a hearing meant to arouse the response of obedience, faith and love that radiates into the whole of life. Thus, Protestant spirituality is centered upon direct, familiar, heart to heart intercourse with God, created, upheld, ceaselessly nourished by the individual reading of the bible.

Roman Catholics, the Orthodox and Anglicans, who include sacramental practices in their worship, would heartily agree with all this. Indeed, their liturgies are filled with scriptural content. They, too, would assert that in the inspired words of Scripture we reach Christ the incarnate Word of God in a unique way. And this scriptural Word of God is alive, is an act of divine initiative, is even creative. It is continually challenging us, interrogating us on our whole existence. This is why it is "sharper than a two-edged sword", pushing us on to see that all of life must be dedicated to the glory of God.

This importance of Scripture in the ancient Church lay behind the careful preservation of texts and manuscripts, the meticulous re-copying of texts before the age of printing, and the exquisitely lovely and painstaking illumination of biblical texts. The great writers of the early Church, and even medieval theologians such as St. Thomas Aquinas, developed a theology which was deeply biblical in orientation. And one whole trend of spirituality from early Christian times hinged upon the personal reading of Scripture. God was present in this inspired Word, and spoke to them in the text. St. Jerome could say: "Ignorance of the Scriptures is ignorance of Christ."

Unfortunately, Catholics have to admit that in practice because of the "seige mentality" after the Reformation, there came about a sad neglect of the bible in the life of the average Catholic, distrust of direct study and personal reading. It was partly a result of the *"sola Scriptura"* controversy we shall mention further on. Some apologetic books even tried to explain how, since the oral teaching of the apostles preceded Scripture and continues on in the Church, Catholics could get along very nicely without the bible.

But today all this has been corrected. Karl Rahner even speaks of the bible as being a part of the very *essence* of the Church. And a simply incredible resurgence of biblical interest has swept the Church, from the deepest theological treatises, to first-grade catechisms, to the everyday liturgical worship. The restorations in Catholic worship have been largely motivated by the desire to restore to prominence the "liturgy of the Word" and the importance of preaching the Word of God. The whole first part of the Mass is now much more obviously a bible service.

Thus personal reading and study of Scripture and biblical renewal of theology are becoming increasingly common for all Christians. Interfaith cooperation of bible translations and study of manuscripts is today taken for granted. In England Protestants and Catholics now share a common bible. And interfaith study groups and ecumenical bible services for Christian unity are multiplying.

The Bible and the Authority of the Church

Catholics have long accused Protestants of gradually separating reading and interpretation of Scripture from the life and authority of the whole Church, thereby allowing too much subjective, individual, and often contradictory interpretation. Such individualism has aided the disintegration of Christianity into so many sects.

Protestants on the other hand often feel that in spite of Catholics' renewed love of Scripture, they still ultimately subject the inspired Word of God to the human and fallible judgment of Church authority. Such authority conceded to the Church detracts correspondingly from the authority of the Word of God in the bible. (Liberal Protestants add that such a method is also harmful to the individual religious conscience.)

Protestants themselves are not exactly agreed. The Reformers, even within their lifetime, saw the dangers of indiscriminate interpretation referred to by St. Peter (2 Peter 3, 16-17). They often asked for adherence to the views of a particular reformer, or to certain creeds and confessions. But they had to admit that each had the right to interpret according as the Spirit of God prompted him. And indeed, Protestants protest that their interpretations are *not* arbitrary; for no sincere believer is justified in basing his life upon any other interpretation of Scripture than that to which he is led in his personal life by the promptings of the Holy Spirit.

The Catholic answers: we don't mean to say the authority of Scripture can be limited by some other authority. But doesn't the Word of God—the message of Christ—come to us in both Scripture and the life of the divinely founded and protected Church? Can't we somehow come to a truer and fuller meaning of Scripture *in* and *through* the Church, so that the full authority of God's biblical word can be upheld in all its integrity?

A Certain Measure of Agreement.

Whatever be the place of the Church today in interpreting the bible, all Christians can perhaps agree on the intimate relationship of Church and bible. In the New Testament the apostles are aware of being sent by Christ to speak with his authority. The Word of God found in its final form in the New Testament is the collective preaching by the apostles of the "Good News" of salvation (the *kerygma*). The Word of God did not begin, then, as a written text, but as the living word of the apostles. The whole primitive Church recognized this special position of the apostles, how the Word of Christ was present in them with all its immediacy and power to help and save. Modern Protestant scholars, such as Oscar Cullmann, at least tend today toward the realization that the early Church acknowledged in the apostles a true doctrinal authority with regard to the Word of God.

Here the disagreement among Catholics and Protestants really takes over: was this original authority passed on to the successors of the apostles?

Protestants: No. The apostles are unique; they were founders. We today must simply abide in their doctrine; we preserve and accept; we do not judge.

Catholics: Agreed, the apostolic group was unique, and we only preserve and transmit its message. But this message of Christ lives on in the Church and must be proclaimed, and the Church has a duty and right to state authoritatively how it understands the Word of God living within her and expressed in her inspired writings.

It is not our aim to attempt any solution here, but simply point out the measure of agreement. The next section bears on this, too. Tradition has always been a terribly touchy point in Catholic-Protestant relationships. And though misunderstanding and disaccord still exist, a surprising measure of agreement and common heritage can now be detected.

3. *Tradition*

The very word conjures up the idea of a mysterious unwritten source of revelation which is distinct and complementary to that contained in the bible. Such an idea greatly disturbs Protestants. So they should be reassured that the Catholic Church nowhere teaches that such a secondary source of revelation exists. (Statements of the Council of Trent are the subject of heated debate.) Would Catholics then admit that all revelation is contained in Scripture? A growing number of Catholic theologians— indeed, a rapidly growing number, among whom are the most prominent of the Europeans—answer yes. What they mean is that, at least by the end of the apostolic era, the substance of the Christian message would have found its way into the inspired accounts of Scripture. Tradition, then, is not a second source of the Word of God. It is rather the living context, milieu, atmosphere, in which the Word of God lives in the Christian community. Its plus-value is not content, but interpretation.

Christian scholars, both Catholic and Protestant, are coming to a much broader and more meaningful notion of Tradition. If the Word of God *as given* to us is Revelation, then Tradition is this exact same Revelation *in its unceasing transmission* (being-handed-on) within the life of the total Church. In this sense Tradition can have no plural, since it is the one unchanging Christ-event (which means Christ in his total person, activity and message) ever present to the living Church, within whose bosom Scripture was written and preserved, and without which it cannot have its full meaning. In this sense no Christian should hesitate to admit that the Christian Church and Christian Tradition have the same birthday, and precede the formation of the New Testament.

The following may help to clarify the Catholic position —much of which will offend no Christian. The Gospel message is passed on not just by the action of pope and bishops (teaching church, or *magisterium*), but by the activity and life of the entire Church—by a lived and living transmission. This involves every baptized person, each being somehow a member of the Body of Christ. The Word of God, or message to be communicated to all, is not just a body of facts, a treasure to be guarded, but an experience to be lived and expressed ever more fully. One cannot be possessed and activated by the grace, life, and dynamism of Christ without being involved in this living transmission of the message. What is the role of pope and bishops, then? A Catholic will say that they are the divinely appointed official mouthpiece which alone can recognize infallibly and declare unerringly that such or such an expression of the message is valid and authentic. Catholics wish neither to exaggerate nor minimize the decisive role of their bishops and particularly the pope.

The Faith and Order Commission of the W.C.C. has recently made an intensive study of the subject. It puts it this way:

"The Tradition is the history in and by which all Christians live: the history of Emmanuel, the history of the Word made flesh in the Man of God's own choosing, the history of God in the history to which the Holy Scriptures bear witness and in which the Holy Spirit continues to bear witness . . . *The* Tradition, in this sense, is the living history of all history, gathering up the history of Israel, centering in the history of Jesus Christ, and continuing in the history of the Church, in *saecula saeculorum*

"These 'working definitions' reflect . . . substantial agreement as to the validity of the Reformation slogan, *sola Scriptura,* insofar as it asserts and identifies *the* Tradition as the prime datum of the New Testament. We are equally agreed that *sola Scriptura* is an inadequate catchword when it equates the New Testament and *the* Tradition without qualification, or when it rejects the evidence for *the* living Tradition in the Church throughout the ages."

The work of the American and European sections of this commission makes clear that within ecumenical Protestantism, as one of the theologians put it, "the search for the criterion which will determine which is the true Tradition cannot disregard either Scripture or the Church".

Markus Barth, prominent Protestant theologian insists that *sola Scriptura* is not a formula opposed to Tradition or the Church. "It is unwise in any form whatsoever to speak of the *absolute authority* of the Bible."

Let us remember Tradition, then, as the total life of the Church, the vital context in which the Word of God, the scriptural message, lives today. It is a dynamic force continually activating and reactualizing the once-for-all revelation of Christ, and impelling each new Christian generation to a new awareness of the biblical message in terms of its own times.

On the other hand, we ought not be surprised if some Christians take exception to what has been said here. For example, in the Baptist Church the bible alone is held to be "the supreme standard by which all human conduct, creeds, and opinions should be tried". The absolute authority of Scripture as the guide to Christian living is the deepest bond of unity in this otherwise loosely knit Church.

III. THE CHRISTIAN LIFE

In the Westminster Shorter Catechism of 1647, a Presbyterian document widely used by other Protestants also, the questions and answers begin: "What is the chief end of man? *Ans.:* Man's chief end is to glorify God, and to enjoy him forever." At the heart of all Christian ideas as to the meaning and purpose of life, some such notion as this could be found. That God made us for himself, and that our true happiness is to be found in our turning to him: this would be a matter of general agreement.

1. *Man: His Nature and Sinfulness*

The area of general agreement concerning the Christian life is large, although obviously there might be wide ranges of difference in ways and practices of Christian living—and not only between denominations and Christian divisions, but also within any one group. Clearly one might find wide divergencies, for example, between Quakers and Greek Orthodox, in the working out of the details of the Christian life, but the basic theological agreements are remarkably large.

First: all would agree about man's origin, as a creature made by God in his image, to live in the world God created and to return to God in a future life. All would also agree that man has fallen away from God's purpose; that he is a sinner, in need of redemption. All would agree, finally, that God has provided means of grace for the redemption of man, that the Church and the sacraments constitute the community of the Holy Spirit, and that this community has a mission to the world. Within this framework one could find many variations of doctrine, but the framework itself is worth noting, for it has served to keep Christian reflection among separated Churches within certain limits.

The definition of man as a *creature of God's* creative work has survived the advancing secular studies of man which, from time to time, have seemed to threaten it. Christians may still be troubled by the idea of human evolution, but such ideas are now usually taken as specifying the details of God's creative act rather than as suggesting some alternative origin for man. For many, the idea of evolution has indeed underlined the notion that the universe has a history and a destiny. Christians would all part company from those who would say that man is merely a highly developed animal doomed to be wiped out in the final destruction of the world.

Immortality

Modern studies of man have, however, raised for some Christians a question as to whether it is necessary to continue to assert the existence in man of a "soul"; yet whatever debate there may be about the word, Christians would be found in agreement about man's uniqueness among God's creatures, his creation "in God's image" as meaning, in part, his fitness to be in communion with God, and especially his destiny for a future life beyond death. Again, details concerning all these ideas would reveal variations of emphasis and interpretation. Popular among discussions now is the assertion that the idea of the "immortality of the soul" is a Greek idea not completely agreeable to Christian belief, for Christians have inherited the Jewish conception of the resurrection of the body; for the Christian, therefore, the "soul" may be the resurrected (and spiritual) body and all its higher functions rather than a disembodied spirit.

Sin

Concerning sin, again it can be said: a doctrine of man's sinfulness is common to all Christians. Agreement would center on the definition of sin as that which separates man from God, and on the remedy for sin as God's saving action, rather than man's unaided efforts. We can look back on a long history of theological controversy as to whether the sinner is completely helpless or not. Yet in spite of much discussion concerning how much man can contribute to his own salvation, there seems to be no doubt that without the saving action of Christ, man would not be redeemed. The great word, to be found in all Christian traditions, is "obedience", and the great theologian who has explored these questions of man's freedom, his bondage to sin, and the action of God's redeeming grace, is St. Augustine of Hippo to whom all Western Christians, whether Catholic or Protestant, turn. "To follow Christ", "imitation of Christ", these are phrases that are found in all our Christian manuals on the Christian life.

Concerning "original sin": the main Christian traditions have commonly stressed this disorientation of man from God because of the sin of Adam, the head of the race. But there are varying degrees of pessimism or optimism concerning man's abilities, as a sinner, to do anything that is good. At least it can be said that there would be widespread acceptance of the idea that there remains in man a "tendency" toward sin (concupiscence) as if it were an inherited susceptibility; in short, something more than causes arising from each's man individual shortcomings. The effort to locate the source of sin in mankind itself characterizes all theories of original sin. It has had a notable revival in Protestantism in what is called "neo-orthodoxy", which is really a return to Reformation Protestantism after a period of optimism (*e.g.,* original sin is only bad example) concerning man, in the early years of this century. Again, we could separate from the mainstream of Catholic and Protestant thought on this matter those Protestant groups who remain strongly influenced by contemporary humanistic theories of man stressing his ability, the psychological roots of his mistakes, the residue in him of animal nature as a result of human evolution, and other non-theological explanations of man's tendency toward self-centeredness.

Grace

If we turn to the doctrine of grace, we can discern a common inheritance of Christian ideas, and also many expressions of it and interpretations of its manifestation in the life of the Christian. Essentially, it is the idea that God not only has created but cares for man; grace is the word that describes God's loving attitude toward his children, and since God is a living and acting being, the word includes an overtone of God's benevolent pressure on man to turn toward and continually respond to his initiative. Therefore, grace is found, or at least is present, throughout the whole creation. At this point it may be noted that a major point for theological discussion has been whether or not man as sinner still enjoys the gifts of God's grace, or whether he must receive the saving action of Christ's life, death and resurrection first. On such matters, a man's sense of his own sinfulness often determines his point of view, and Christian history gives us many examples of the paradox that it is the saints who claim the least for themselves, yet who seem to demonstrate the most grace in their lives. We are aware, then, of the importance of the work of Christ as the source of redemptive life, the life of grace; in all Christian traditions it has special place as essential and crucial. But part of the life of grace is the action of the Holy Spirit upon the Christian. All believers acknowledge this important reality, whether it be called the indwelling of the Spirit, inspiration, or interior direction and guidance. No Christian can ignore this personalism in his spiritual life—as if all divine guidance came through external intermediaries. (For the Pentecostal type it becomes all-important.)

The Communal Aspect

The life of the Christian community is of special importance to all Christians. All have some doctrine of the Church, sacraments, prayer and worship, of right belief, and of the application of belief to practice in life. In the midst of many disagreements in these areas one might not notice the common concern that lies behind the variety of formulations. It is the conviction that through Christ God is working in a way that is, one might say, superior to his working elsewhere in his creation, and further, that this special saving action of God through Christ is mediated to his people through the Church, as its source and as its continuing agent.

Therefore, in spite of important differences of doctrine, all Christians share a veneration for two sacraments: Baptism, the sacrament of initiation into the Christian community, and Holy Communion, the sacrament of nourishment in that community. The differences of doctrine concerning these sacraments are indeed difficult problems (and are considered elsewhere in this series). But we note, as a matter of significance not to be lost sight of, a common concern of Christians in all traditions that each person stand in the true inheritance from Christ and that he be truly in communion with him. Quite apart from natural human pride, there is a rightness in the claim each Christian makes to "belong to the *true Church*". He understands, rightly, that this is a proper and essential concern for a Christian. Theologians working on unity problems among Protestants find not only a variety of doctrines of the Church, making this one of the hardest of the doctrines to deal with, but also a high seriousness about the importance of the doctrine. Both Catholics and Protestants are careful to avoid any superficial glossing over of the real theological problems that must be faced when the Church is the subject of discussion, and especially when the ministry is being considered.

Response in Faith

Moving from the part the Church and sacraments play in the Christian life to an examination of the interior life of faith, the response, that is, of the Christian to God in private and corporate worship, the subject becomes vague and diffuse. But it is no doubt safe to say that Catholics and Protestants share much more than the variety of the devotional practices might suggest. A Catholic at high Mass and a Quaker at a silent meeting may both experience the presence of God, and it may be respectfully said that only God knows how to evaluate their experiences and responses. Christians in all traditions have used the same language in describing their devotional life, deriving it often from the bible, but this common language may conceal both similarities and differences of religious experience. The wisest generalization to make may be that each tradition includes the same broad spectrum of devotional life, from the indifferent person to the saint, from the person dependent on "externals" to the person whose communion with God tends toward private meditation. One can say that dialogue between Catholic and Protestant may produce, in this matter, much helpful understanding that our separate worshipping may not have permitted.

The doctrine of the universal priesthood of all Christians must not be overlooked in this response of faith. Whether in offering corporate worship, or in private communing with God, every baptized follower of Christ shares in his one priesthood and is enabled truly to offer God the Father his prayers of adoration, thanksgiving and sorrow. He can, indeed, make a meaningful offering of his whole being, his whole life. Whatever be the complicated problems regarding the special nature of ordained priests, it should not take away from the profound area of agreement found in our common sharing in the priesthood of all believers.

The Christian in the World

Christians, even before the era of "dialogue", had much in common in working for the betterment of the world. All agreed that the Christian layman had a ministry in the world; there was even remarkable unanimity about the shape it should take. Promotion of peace, social justice, war on poverty, illiteracy and oppression must be all part of the Christian heritage from long ago.

The Second Vatican Council *Decree On Ecumenism* says: "The faith by which Christians believe in Christ bears fruit in praise and thanksgiving for the benefits received from the hand of God. Joined to it is a lively sense of justice and a true charity toward others. This active faith has been responsible for many organizations for the relief of spiritual and material distress, the furtherance of the education of youth, the improvement of the social conditions of life, and the promotion of peace throughout the world."

But too often our efforts have lacked a genuine family spirit, fraternal trust and cooperation. Things are better now but have still far to go. The same decree on Ecumenism ends on a challenging note: "If in moral matters there are many Christians who do not always understand the Gospel in the same way as Catholics, and do not admit the same solutions for the more difficult problems of modern society, they nevertheless want to cling to Christ's Word as the source of Christian virtue and to obey the command of the Apostle: "Whatever you do in word or in work, do all in the name of the Lord Jesus, giving thanks to God the Father through him" (Col. 3, 17). Hence, the ecumenical dialogue could start with the moral application of the Gospel."

DIALOGUE NO. 5
Renewal of God's People

Resource Readings

Reform—An Essential Element in the Church (pp. 145–159)
Julius Cardinal Döpfner
The Way of Renewal (pp. 160–174)
W. A. Visser 't Hooft

Suggested Readings

Cox, Harvey. *The Secular City*. New York: Macmillan, 1964.

Döpfner, Julius. *The Questioning Church*. Westminster, Md.: Newman Press, 1964.

Küng, Hans, Congar, Yves and O'Hanlon, Daniel (editors). *Council Speeches of Vatican II*. New York: Paulist Press, 1964.

Küng, Hans. *The Council, Reform and Reunion*. New York: Sheed and Ward, 1963.

Schutz, Roger. *Living Today for God*. Baltimore, Md.: Helicon, 1962.

Visser 't Hooft, W. A. *The Renewal of the Church*. London: S.C.M. Press, 1956.

Wolf, William J. (editor). *Protestant Churches and Reform Today*. New York: The Seabury Press, 1965.

Tavard, George. *The Church Tomorrow*. New York: Herder and Herder, 1965.

CHRISTIAN DIALOGUE
Renewal of God's People

OPENING PRAYER

Leader: Come, Holy Spirit, fill the hearts of your faithful.
All:　　Enkindle in them the fire of your love.
Leader: Pour forth your spirit, and they shall be created.
All:　　And they shall renew the face of the earth.
Leader: For our failure to open our minds and hearts to the pouring forth of the Holy Spirit.
All:　　Forgive us, O Lord.
Leader: For our failure to live according to the precepts of your Gospel.
All:　　Forgive us, O Lord.
Leader: For being Christians in name only, failing to renew our personal lives in your justice and charity.
All:　　Forgive us, O Lord.
Leader: Glory be to the Father, and to the Son and to the Holy Spirit.
All:　　As it was in the beginning, is now and ever shall be, world without end. Amen.

BIBLE READING

Therefore, if any one is in Christ, he is a new creation; the old has passed away, behold, the new has come (2 Cor. 5, 17).

I appeal to you therefore, brethren, by the mercies of God, to present your bodies as a living sacrifice, holy and acceptable to God, which is your spiritual worship. Do not be conformed to this world but be transformed by the renewal of your mind, that you may prove what is

138

the will of God, what is good and acceptable and perfect (Rom. 12, 1-2).

So each of us shall give account of himself to God. Then let us no more pass judgment on one another, but rather decide never to put a stumbling block or hindrance in the way of a brother (Romans 14, 12-13).

So, whether you eat or drink, or whatever you do, do all to the glory of God. Give no offense to Jews or to Greeks or to the Church of God, just as I try to please all men in everything I do, not seeking my own advantage, but that of many, that they may be saved. Be imitators of me, as I am of Christ (1 Cor. 10, 31-32).

MEDITATION

Lord, at our baptism we died to sin and were raised up in you as Christians, new creatures. . . . Bless us with an abiding awareness of the dignity and destiny of the baptized. . . . Up to now most of our time and talents have been used to conform to this world. . . . From now on we desire only the good and acceptable and perfect will of God. . . . Up to now through our sins we have been stumbling blocks and a hindrance to the Church of God. . . . From now on we desire to present our bodies as a sacrifice, living, holy, pleasing to God, so that we may lead our brothers to full Christian unity.

BIBLE READING

I therefore, a prisoner for the Lord, beg you to lead a life worthy of the calling to which you have been called, with all lowliness and meekness, with patience, forbearing one another in love, eager to maintain the unity of the Spirit in the bond of peace. . . . Now this I affirm and testify in the Lord, that you must no longer live as the Gentiles do, in the futility of their minds; they are darkened in their understanding, alienated from the life of God because of the ignorance that is in them, due to their hardness of heart. . . . You did not so learn Christ!— assuming that you have heard about him and were taught in him, as the truth is in Jesus. Put off your old nature which belongs to your former manner of life and is corrupt through deceitful lusts, and be renewed in the spirit of your minds, and put on the new nature, created after the likeness of God in true righteousness and holiness. . . . (Eph. 4) for once you were darkness, but now you are light in the Lord; walk as children of light (for the fruit of light is found in all that is good and right and true), and try to learn what is pleasing to the Lord. Take no part in the unfruitful works of darkness, but instead expose them (Eph. 5, 8-12).

MEDITATION

Lord, these words of St. Paul to the Ephesians apply to us today. . . . Help us to see that the chief obstacle to the union of all men in you is still the failure of Christians to renew their personal lives according to the truth as it is in Jesus. . . . Impress upon us the importance of helping each other to live richer Christian lives through our *Living Room Dialogues*. . . . We are so likely to walk with the modern Gentiles, in the futility of their minds, clouding our minds with their darkness. . . . Give us the strength to put on the new man, to walk as children of light, to expose the darkness around us with all goodness and justice and truth.

Christian Dialogue

Introduction

One aspect of Protestant belief has been described by Dr. Robert MacAfee Brown as "an openness to the judging and renewing activity of God made known in Jesus Christ . . . it is in this constant renewal at the hand of God that Protestants conceive the life of the Church to exist."

In the *Decree on Ecumenism* of Vatican Council II we read the Catholic view on renewal: "Christ summons the Church to continual reformation as she sojourns here on earth. The Church is always in need of this, insofar as she is an institution of men here on earth."

Tonight we wish to look at the present-day renewal as it affects Christian Churches and their twofold effort to witness to Christ and to seek unity.

Motives for Renewal

In one sense the Church does not change and in another, it constantly changes. Modern theologians have stressed anew the dynamic element in the Church. They point out how renewal and reform are essential if the Church is to fulfill its mission.

DISCUSSION QUESTIONS

Why must the Church constantly renew and reform itself? What are the motives of such renewal? What is the relationship between renewal and the Church's mission to proclaim Christ to all men?

Does the condition of the world today call for renewal more insistently than in other ages? Why?

Catholics and Protestants differ in their understanding of "the sinful Church". What do you think this phrase means? How can the Church be holy and still contain sinners? Who are the people who have done most to renew and reform your Church? What have they done?

The Cause of Renewal

Some people view renewal in the Church only in human terms. The Church is after all, they seem to say, an institution like all others. Every so often it has to be revitalized.

DISCUSSION QUESTIONS

Why is such a human view of Church renewal incomplete and incorrect?

Who causes renewal in the Church? Why is Pope John XXIII's phrase "a new Pentecost" an apt description of renewal in the Church?

Where in the Acts of the Apostles do you see the Holy Spirit guiding and renewing the early Christian Church? Why should Christians pray fervently for the Holy Spirit to renew the face of the earth?

Reform in Your Church

In an earlier dialogue we discussed renewal of public worship in our Churches. Yet this is only one dimension of the vast work of renewal going on in the Churches. Other areas of Church life are being reformed or stand in need of it.

DISCUSSION QUESTIONS

What reforms has your Church undertaken in recent years? What have been their goals? Have they succeeded? Why? Are members of your congregation anxious to co-operate with these changes? Has there been resistance? What are the reasons? Why from a psychological point of view do some people fear change? How can those opposed to reform be made to understand its value?

What aspects of the Christian community most need renewal? Why?

Personal Renewal

When we talk about renewing the Church we are tempted to think of the Church as an entity separate from ourselves. But the hard truth is I am the Church and renewal means the reformation of me! As one of God's people, I must first of all renew my own life.

DISCUSSION QUESTIONS

What secular influence in your life has most de-Christianized you? How could you meet this challenge in a more Christian way?

What is *your* attitude toward changes in your Church? Have you entered into the spirit of these changes? Why?

To what kind of service is God calling individual Christians—people like those in this dialogue group—in today's world? How does this service differ from what God asked of us before?

Renewal and Ecumenism

All agree that progress in Christian unity will be in proportion to the renewal within the Churches. This does not mean Christians must be unfaithful to their understanding of the Gospel or what they hold in conscience to be the truth. It does mean, however, that in those matters where they know renewal is needed and possible, an effort is made to reform. It means also that the Churches need one another's help in renewal.

DISCUSSION QUESTIONS

Why is renewal the key to progress in Christian unity? What reforms in other Churches have most impressed you? In a spirit of Christian charity and candor, what reforms do you think should be undertaken in other Churches? Since reform comes about slowly, what is the great temptation to those concerned with Christian unity? What virtue do they most need? Why?

Renewal and Mission

Renewal touches the most profound work of the Church: its mission to witness to Christ in the world. In a world where the proportion of Christians is decreasing we are urged by the Holy Spirit to reach out anew, to reevaluate all we are doing in the Church to show men Christ.

DISCUSSION QUESTIONS

In the resource reading Richard Schaull describes the Church in the modern diaspora. Do you feel that Christians in your community are dispersed, scattered, in diaspora? Is this an appropriate description of the modern situation? Why? Do you agree that new forms of Church life are necessary to meet the new situation? Why? What forms should these new structures take? What must remain as basic to the Church and what may be changed?

What is the best way to renew the Church's mission to the poor and oppressed in the great urban-suburban areas of the world?

Where will Christians, busy with family problems and earning a living, become engaged in this phase of Church renewal? Have any interesting experiments or projects been undertaken by your Church to preach the Gospel to modern man? Describe them.

CLOSING PRAYER

O Lord, in the beginning your all-powerful Word created the world. Over the ages you have spoken through your heralds and have made known your truth to us. When time reached its fullness, your eternal Word, Jesus the Lord, came and revealed your love for men. Through him arises our present hope in you for time and eternity. And yet, we to whom your Word was spoken are divided in way and opinion, and our division compromises your holy tidings to mankind. It is your will that faith be one even as truth is one. Make us grieve over so much confusion. Let us feel the power of your truth that we may be of one mind in him whom you have sent us, Jesus Christ our Lord. Teach us to respect one another. Let your grace be mightier than all the scandal we have given. Help us to overcome what separates us. Amen.

Reform—An Essential Element in the Church

Julius Cardinal Döpfner

1. The Need for Reform as Incentive for the Council

The exceptional developments and events of our century have long given rise to an unmistakable call for reform within the Church. Countless numbers of the faithful have been lost, some lapsed, just drifting away, others driven by the pressure of totalitarian régimes. Many see the Church as an institution enslaving freedom and inhibiting progress, or else as a venerable but none the less obsolete memento of a bygone age. For many, too, the devastating wars, started by so-called Christian peoples, have robbed the Christian message of peace of its credibility. Modern communications are bringing the nations of the world ever closer together, yet the number and diversity of the Christian denominations, often so contradictory, have only served to weaken the power of the *one* Gospel to enlighten mankind.

On the other hand, movements for renewal have long shown quite clearly that life is quickening in the womb of the Church: the liturgical movement, the strivings for a re-appraisal and deeper appreciation of Holy Scripture, the ecumenical movement, to name only a few. In the course of the past few decades these movements have changed the face of the Church in many countries; but in some instances the final clarification and recognition of their work by supreme authority prevented their fruitful expansion throughout the world. Their position was ambiguous: they were either tolerated or else regarded as extravagances of uncertain worth.

On the one hand, then, we have the—at least apparent—failure of the Church in the modern world; on the other, young and vigorous reform movements, still, so to speak, in process of fermentation. In this complex situation the question was asked with growing concern: Surely the Church is in need of radical renewal?

Here I would mention some of the observations current nowadays—and voiced often enough by the Council fathers themselves. Of course not everything is included, nor should such statements be judged out of context. I merely wish to indicate the general atmosphere in the Church.

The Church, it is said, is not close enough to the people; she often speaks to them in a foreign language, not only in the liturgy where so much which is intrinsically venerable has become incomprehensible to people today, but above all in her preaching and teaching in which the abstract or time-worn phrases often used are wholly out of touch with life. The Church, it is further argued, is far too restricted by one particular civilization—the Roman and Western. The episcopal office is often exercised much too legalistically; the love of the Good Shepherd is hardly discernible. Instead of permeating the world like leaven, the Church is shut up in a ghetto, trying to build up her own small world apart from the great world outside. Instead of encouraging a movement of the whole people of God, the hierarchy and clergy too often claim the exclusive right to all activity and initiative, while the layman is treated, by and large, as what Fr. Karl Rahner has called "an object in a clerical sanatorium for the cure of souls".

The concern is often voiced that in a changed world the Church is still too tied to antiquated forms, and has not really moved with the times. That she has failed to adapt herself sufficiently to the ideological pluralism which does in fact exist. That she has still not come to terms with democracy and its manifold consequences.

That the Church still lags behind the developments of modern technology, particularly in mass communications media which have often formed a man's mind before the voice of the Church reaches him at all.

All this has led to the Second Vatican Council. Realization of the discrepancy between the modern way of life and the form and functioning of the Church was what led Pope John XXIII to summon the Council. This man, trained in traditional theology and altogether steeped in tradition, had retained in his simple faith and obedient search for the will of God a sensitive perception for the needs of our day.

"Should the Mystical Ship of Christ remain at the mercy of the waves and drift, or is it not from her that the world expects not only a new warning but also the light of a great example?" Those were some of Pope John's words to Cardinal Tardini, his Secretary of State, during the conversation in January 1959 in which the idea of the Council was first raised.

This "light of a great example" is what the Church must give the world. The Pope believed the Church capable of this on account of her inherent vitality. But, to quote from the Bull convening the Council, this latent force must first be activated: "Faced with the double spectacle contrasting the great spiritual need of mankind with the flourishing vitality of the Church of Christ, We have, from the beginning of our pontificate, felt it to be a solemn duty of our apostolic office to call together our Sons in order to give the Church the opportunity to contribute more efficiently to the solution of the problems of this modern age."

Reform, then, is the specific aim of this Council which indeed can most appositely be called "the Reform Council". Resolutions involving reform were, of course, made at all councils, but these were concerned either with deepening, clarifying or defining a point of dogma (the Christological issues of the fourth and fifth centuries, Protestant doctrine at Trent, infallibility and primacy at

the First Vatican Council) or with specific points of ecclesiastical discipline (investiture, celibacy, simony, and
reception of the sacraments at the Lateran Council). By
contrast, the present Council, by far the largest in history,
has no one definite theme. Its purpose is to consider on a
wide front the problems with which the modern Church
is confronted. From these deliberations should emerge the
new form suited to a contemporary Church. The central
feature of the Council is reform as such, *aggiornamento,*
adjustment to present-day conditions.

2. *Reform as an Inherent Element in the Church's Structure*

The convening of an ecumenical council aiming at
the general renewal and adjustment of the Church expresses more than just an insight into the specific situation of the Church in the present time. The truth of
Ecclesia semper reformanda, the inherent and therefore
constantly recurring need of reform, also comes to light.

This need of reform, conditioned by the very nature
of the Church, is mainly rooted in *three essential characteristics of the Church,* namely in her *humanity,* in her
historicity, and in her involvement in the *sinfulness* of her
members. It is common to all theology today to understand the Church principally as the People of God and
the Mystical Body of Christ. Both concepts stress the immersion of the Church in the createdness and bodiliness
of the world. Both imply limitations. The Church can never
at one time express the whole fullness of the life conferred
upon her by God. If the human community, in which the
Church expresses herself, is the visible *medium* of divine
intervention, it is also that which limits the scope of this
intervention.

Anyone who thinks seriously about the mystery of the
Incarnation will not be surprised at this. Just as the Son
of God assumed a concrete human nature and entered
history as a true man, so the continuation of Christ's
work of salvation is, in the Church, also bound to the

human. The *inconfuse* and the *nusquam sublata differentia naturarum propter unitionem magisque salva proprietate utriusque naturae* of Chalcedon are correspondingly valid for the Church.

As a result of the incarnational nature of the Church, two points relevant to our theme arise, the first of which is immediately clear from what has just been said: since no concrete form that the Church may take can ever completely express the fullness of the divine life working in her, she must of necessity be able to alter this form if she is to realize her true nature.

The second point requires more detailed interpretation. So far we have been considering rather the limitations, the "bodiliness" of the Church. Now let us turn to the inner structure which sustains and animates the bodily form. Here, too, Chalcedon shows the way; the definition deals simultaneously with the *inconfuse* and the *inseparabiliter,* in other words with the concepts of distinctness and inseparability.

Just as the divine and human natures of Christ are inseparable in the unity of his Person, so too are the divine and human elements in the Church inseparable, though there is a different kind of unity. This means that the divine life, which is the immutable essence of the Church, is always really present and active, no matter how inadequate the bodily forms may be. Since, however, this life is full of vigor, it is ever seeking new forms of embodiment. It lies in the nature of the Church not only that she should assume different forms of expression, but also that she should constantly seek new forms.

The *historicity* of the Church, the second basic reason for the phrase *semper reformanda,* is in fact no new factor, but rather the natural development of what has already been said.

It is the continuous tension between the infinite fullness of Christianity and its actual realization at any given moment that occasions changes in the Church.

Since the form she takes is necessarily limited, the Church needs to progress in time and space so that she may in the course of history more nearly express what Christ conferred upon her.

The various forms of expression which the *Ecclesia semper reformanda* assumes in the course of history cannot, therefore, necessarily be contrasted as good and bad or right and wrong; in their multiplicity they convey something of the wealth of revelation. The longer the Church moves through history and the nearer she leads mankind towards its final goal, the more clearly will her nature be manifest to mankind, the fuller will be her image.

A further basic reason for the Church's need of reform cannot be overlooked if a grave misunderstanding is to be avoided. Renewal in this sense is inherent in the nature of the Church as a human and historical institution; it implies nothing imperfect or to be deplored; it is a mark—in earthly terms, of course—of her inner riches.

Renewal is necessary in the form of conversion, as cleansing from guilt, as correction of false developments. This is the point beyond which the mystery of the Incarnation can no longer be applied to the Church. The God-Man was free from all sin, but he confided the continuation of his work to frail and sinful men. This is why not everything in the Church is unswerving evolution towards perfection: there are culpable shortcomings in meeting God's wishes. The presentation of Christ's love can be defective if the Church, say, works through power rather than humility, through compulsion rather than service. In short, the Church can fall culpably short of what God wishes for her at any time due to indolence, selfishness, lust for power, sloth, etc.

True, the Church has the promise that the gates of hell shall never prevail against her, that the divine life founded within her will never die. She is and will always remain, therefore, the *holy* Church, and it would be contrary to the Catholic concept of the Church to refer to the Church as such as being sinful. Nevertheless this changes nothing of what has been said. It follows from this that renewal in the Church can become a duty whose fulfillment or non-fulfillment means quite simply the salvation or not of mankind.

Let us now consider the marks the necessary reform must bear as criteria for distinguishing valid and invalid moves for reform.

Let us start with one which is very closely connected with what we have been saying about the sinfulness of the Church. True reform can be brought about only in a spirit of repentance, of *metanoia*. The Church is aware that she is a community of sinners, acknowledging her guilt daily in the *Confiteor*. But this spirit of repentance must also be put into practice. It is quite rightly expected of the clergy that they lead the way by good example.

And today we indeed encounter instances almost unprecedented in the history of the Church. The admission of guilt by Pope Adrian VI blazes the trail for modern Church history. In the instructions he gave to Chieregati, his nuncio to the German Reichstag in Nuremberg in 1522, this pope spoke with startling frankness about the corruption of the Church. But even this noble papal declaration could not heal the breach. And how often has Adrian's example been forgotten in our own ranks where so often undue emphasis is laid on the defence of rights and the combat of heresy.

Now Vatican II has brought about a change. The spirit of *metanoia* is already discernible in the Council's Message to Mankind issued on October 20, 1962: "In the course of our meetings, under the guidance of the Holy Spirit, we intend to seek the most efficacious ways of renewing ourselves and of becoming the ever more faithful witnesses of the Gospel of Christ. . . . But we who are followers of Christ are still far from freeing ourselves sufficiently from earthly concerns to allow faith, hope and the love of Christ to impel us to serve our brothers and so to follow the example of our divine Master. . . ."

But above all there is the admission of possible guilt

by Pope Paul VI at the beginning of the second session of the Council. Addressing the representatives of the separated Christian Churches and communities, he said: "If we are in any way to blame for that separation, we humbly beg God's forgiveness and ask pardon, too, of our brethren who feel themselves to have been injured by us. For our part we willingly forgive the injuries which the Catholic Church has suffered, and forget the grief endured during the long series of dissensions and separations. May our heavenly Father graciously accept this our declaration."

The same spirit informed the speeches of many of the Council fathers which were noticeably free from any note of triumph or self-glorification.

A further mark of true reform is *consideration of essentials*. In all our efforts for reform the unchanging essentials must always be borne in mind. In concrete terms this means thinking back to Christ who is the Head of the Church, to his message, and to the core of historical tradition whose sustaining function must not be overlooked in the search for something new.

In this connection let us listen once more to the words of Paul VI who places Christ in a unique way in the centre of all the Council's strivings for reform. "Christ is our starting point. Christ is our leader and our way. Christ is our hope and our goal. May this Ecumenical Council be fully aware of this bond, single yet complex, stable yet dynamic, mysterious yet manifest, compelling yet at the same time gratifying, which unites us to Jesus Christ. . . . Let no other light be shed on this Council but Christ, the Light of the world; let no other truth be of interest to our minds but the words of the Lord, our only master. . . ."

Looking to Christ means at the same time looking to his message as it is contained in the words of Holy Scripture. Here the Church has the Word of God in concrete form in her hands, as the apostles and disciples of the Lord received and transmitted it. This Word must be proclaimed today in such a way that "the men of our time . . . may understand it and accept it freely" (the Council's Message to Mankind). In effect the daily enthronement of the Book of the Gospels was no empty ceremony. The Constitution on the Sacred Liturgy shows that in future—in the liturgy first and foremost—the life of the Church should bear the stamp of God's Word much more deeply impressed. Thus, for example, we find: "Sacred Scripture is of the greatest importance in the celebration of the liturgy. . . . Thus to achieve the restoration, progress and adaptation of the sacred liturgy, it is essential to promote that warm and living love for Scripture to which the venerable tradition of both eastern and western rites gives testimony" (n. 24).

Finally, in the consideration of essentials, historical tradition cannot be ignored. Renewal in the Church does not simply mean renovation, nor does it mean revolution. If, as we have seen, the Church in the course of her history has assumed a variety of legitimate forms, then each new form can and must take over what is permanently valid from the earlier form, so that the renewal is, in fact, essentially an evolution, taking place in what Paul VI called "the honoring of tradition". It should not, as he says, "be thought that in its desire for reform the Council wishes radically to change the present life of the Church, or to break with what is essential and worthy of veneration, but rather to honor tradition by discarding obsolete and inappropriate forms, to bring out what is good and fruitful".

On the other hand the eyes of the Church in her self-renewal must be wholly turned to the present time and its special demands. For, after all, only through contact with life can the new form be found if it is to be truly modern. This sets a most difficult task, for Christianity is so infinitely rich that possible future developments cannot all be envisaged. How the form of the Church will change is unforseeable.

How often has it been thought—all throughout the history of the Church—that what was new would exceed the bounds of what was Christian and would therefore have to be rejected. Think, for example, of the Jews' transition to a gentile Church with all the difficulties involved, illustrated by the attitude of Peter in Antioch, or James's intervention in the Apostles' council (Acts 15), difficulties which could only be overcome by a radical return to the Gospel, effected principally by Paul. We find further examples in the history of religious orders, the rise of the Franciscan Order and ideal of piety, for instance, and the founding of new orders in the sixteenth century.

We are no less in danger of resisting ideas, forms and possibilities to which perhaps the future belongs; and we too may think much impossible today that will yet prove to be a legitimate form of Christianity.

This danger applies even to dogma which, though a permanent and valid expression of the truth, does not and cannot reveal the mystery of divine truth, but only its infallible but human expression. Even dogma can give only incomplete expression to the riches of divine truth, because it is knowledge perceived in human terms; the reality, being a mystery, is incommunicable. And so in the evolution of dogma—as elsewhere in the renewal of the Church—it is not only a question of new formulations of truths already known, but also of truths not as yet realized in their full light and vigor.

You may well ask whether the Council is prepared to conform to the needs of our day, to deal realistically with contemporary problems, seeking new ways of helping modern man.

Forecasts about the Council certainly predicted no revolutionary innovations. But surely we have already witnessed a unique spectacle of how matters, once set in motion with goodwill, genuine readiness for reform and a broadminded outlook, developed quite naturally, and compelled, of themselves, solutions which one would scarcely have dared to think of a few years ago. Some aspects of liturgical reform, for instance, have been finally agreed and solemnly promulgated. There is to be a more extended use of the mother tongue in the liturgy, the liturgy of the word is to be restored to its proper place; Communion under both kinds will once more be possible, at least in principle; so too will concelebration on certain occasions. Think of the arguments, mostly in extremely dry apologetics, once assembled to defend Latin in the Mass, for instance, or the Council of Trent's prohibition of the Chalice for the laity.

In the draft constitution on the Church, several of the first promising beginnings indicate important steps forward, many of them unexpected.

As a first example, let us consider the relationship of the Church to individual non-Catholic Christians and other Christian Churches and communities. The starting point is the doctrine, already defined by the Fourth Lateran Council, of the necessity of the Church for salvation. Now, for the first time in the history of the Church, an ecumenical council is tackling in a positive manner the situation of those separated from the Church.

Various dogmatic questions, the solution of which is essential to any useful work in the field of reunion, were until now without clarification. Misunderstandings arising mainly from the phrase *extra Ecclesiam nulla salus*— "outside the Church there is no salvation"—must be cleared up. This is one field in which we shall see that it is possible without abandoning essentials to express the truth in such a manner that those who do not share our belief are not only not offended by it, but are also brought to understand what it really means. The Church cannot delete the phrase without relinquishing her claim to be the true Church of Christ. She is bound to the will of the Lord who desired his work to be carried on by a visible institution; but today we recognize that the word and grace of God are active among men in many ways and varying degrees outside the Catholic Church as well. The specific recognition of this in a statement by the highest teaching authority is undoubtedly an innovation which in earlier times, when people of other faiths were almost

exclusively regarded in the light of formal heresy, would
have been inconceivable. But the recognition of the manifold working of the Spirit outside the Catholic Church
has many concrete consequences. For then there is an
inner connection, a link binding us to our separated
brothers. For then what God has done among them is
significant for us too. For then there is a common basis
on which to start honest, brotherly, patient discussion to
clarify what still divides us. Here we see the first step on
the road on which God can at last bring us together. Naturally what lies ahead is still uncertain, for many questions still remain open in which both sides, in allegiance
to the Lord's word and in good conscience, hold different
opinions.

A further example of a legitimate reform is the relationship between the Pope and the episcopate. In this
matter the Council will make important dogmatic statements and significant changes. From the new view of the
episcopal office, both the collegial character of the hierarchy and the primacy of the Pope will gain a far greater
practical significance than in the past. Collegiality is, of
course, nothing fundamentally new. Anyone acquainted
with Church history knows how significant the provin-
cial synods were right up to the Middle Ages for the development of doctrine alone, doctrine concerning the Trinity and grace, for instance. After the definition of papal
infallibility and the jurisdictional primacy of the Pope,
the collaboration of the bishops in the government of the
Church as a whole seemed to many people inconceivable
or at any rate superfluous, but here too the Council has
brought about an undreamed-of change. The Constitution
on the Sacred Liturgy is already making a beginning by
placing important decisions—such as the introduction of
the vernacular—within the competence of national or re-
gional bishops' conferences. Further important changes in
this direction are: the central commission to be sum-
moned by the Pope so that the bishops of the world may
directly participate in the government of the universal

Church; and the reforms announced for the Curia and for canon law.

We can hope for other promising developments resulting directly or indirectly from the Council: in a deeper appreciation of the laity in the Church, in the re-evaluation and renewal of the religious state, in the training of priests, in the vital matter of religious freedom, to mention only a few.

All this is, of course, encouraging, but even for the Council the axiom *Ecclesia semper reformanda* is valid. Here too we find the human element, inadequacy, even guilt. Moreover, whatever it may achieve, the Council can only be the impulse and beginning of reform. More it cannot achieve. Whether reform will then really bear fruit depends on the response of the whole Church, hence on our *readiness* for reform as well.

3. Our Response in the True Spirit of Reform

All of us, clergy, laity and religious communities alike, are called upon to continue the work begun in Rome and to bring it to a fruitful conclusion.

This applies particularly to the active forces of the Church, the spiritual and intellectual centres and groups and the Catholic press. Surely it is *these* circles, and lay people active in Catholic life today, who must feel especially encouraged to new exertions now that the course they have been following and their work to date have been crowned and confirmed by the Council!

What attitude must we adopt for the future?

First of all, a wholehearted assent to the Church, a sense of commitment. This means readiness to immerse oneself as a Christian utterly and personally in the Church, living, thinking and feeling wholly in her. *Sentire in Ecclesia* has always been the primary basic condition for genuine and lasting reform. The Church is a living reality; only if you have known her from within can you really contribute personally towards the organic, sound development of her life. Surely what is wrong with much that is said or written today about reform in the Church is that it comes from *outside*.

Only such immersion in the stream of the Church's life can save us from making utopian demands for reform in the Church. For no mere concept of the Church, however nicely thought out, can be the criterion of reform; only the Church of the incarnate Word and of the Spirit, which cannot be adequately expressed in abstract concepts, can be the real yardstick.

Such commitment within the Church supposes readiness to preserve continuity, for bygone forms were also relevant in their day, and the new must grow organically out of the old. Certainly, rapid changes are occasionally possible and even necessary. But we must not forget that *the Church can never change into something different,* but only into another form of herself, for her mission, ultimately, is always one and the same: to enact the living presence of her glorified Lord in the world.

Continuity can only be preserved in a spirit of great patience and selflessness. We must patiently examine and distinguish between what is enduring and what is a product of its time and therefore subject to change. Even when only talking about reform we must exercise patience if we are not to scandalize our weaker brethren. Even Paul, bold as he was, called for this patience when, during the period of transition from the law of the Old Dispensation, he insisted that those who no longer observed the Jewish rules about food should be considerate towards those who still felt obliged to follow them (Rom. 14, 1).

Genuine readiness for reform always begins, as all the great saints in the history of the Church have shown, with self-reform. For each of us is that part of the Church where he can begin reform at once and persevere in it, so that the life of Christ is made manifest through him.

The last and unshakable basis of all reform is *absolute faith* in Christ, Lord of the Church. Only faith can sense the innermost mystery of the life of the Church. Since faith is primarily open to God's Word and it is faith that opens our hearts to his working, since faith leaves all guidance to God, only faith can lead us surely to our goal. The Christian examines all human plans for reform in the light of God's plan for salvation disclosed to him by revelation and known by him to be at work throughout the events of history. Only the Christian has that sensitive instinct which distinguishes unfailingly the genuine from the spurious, the true from the false, and the practicable from the utopian. And only the man of faith has the courage to make the personal decision demanded by every new call God makes upon him. God uses no conventions and stereotyped patterns in the guidance of his Church. That is why we need the courage of faith which does not at once fear for the Church as soon as something unfamiliar appears, but which at the same time embarks surely on whatever course is predetermined by God, even if it perhaps seems less popular, less open to the needs of our day, less progressive.

Such a faith inspired Pope John XXIII, the father of the Second Vatican Council. In his third Christmas message in 1960 he told us: "The humble successor of St. Peter has not so far been tempted to lose courage. We feel ourselves to be strong in faith and, at Jesus' side, we can cross not only the little lake in Galilee" (he is referring to St. Matthew's account of the storm on the lake —Matt. 14, 22) "but all the oceans of the world. The Word of Jesus is enough for deliverance and victory." The word of Jesus is enough.

The Way of Renewal

W. A. Visser 't Hooft

We can group the various attitudes to and conceptions of renewal of the Church under six heads. All of these appear in different Churches and in different periods of history

The first is that the very concept of renewal of the Church must be rejected. Renewal has only to do with individual piety and morality. For the Church as such is a perfect society which in the nature of the case cannot be changed, improved or renewed. The life of the Church must therefore be wholly guided by the criterion of antiquity.

A most interesting example of this obsession by the argument of antiquity is the position of the great Bossuet. The basic argument of his famous *History of the Variations of the Protestant Churches* is that the difference between truth and heresy is the same as that between unchangeableness and novelty. According to him the Church never varies in its teaching. In fact "the catholic truth, which comes from God, has its perfection from the very beginning".[1] Antiquity is therefore a conclusive and sufficient criterion.

Now it is a curious and rather tragic fact that Bossuet's own life illustrates so clearly that even his own Roman Catholic Church did not in fact maintain this principle. In the great conflict between the French Church and the Papacy Bossuet became the defender of the "Gallican Declaration" which stated that the Gallican privileges must

[1] 'a d'abord sa perfection', *Oeuvres complètes*, 1864, Tom., VII, 5 and several times repeated on p. 364.

be respected "since the greatness of the Holy See requires that the laws and customs established with its consent and that of the Church remain invariable" and that a "decision (of the Pope) is not unalterable unless the consent of the Church is given". Bossuet's impressive and voluminous defense of this declaration is wholly based on the principle which he had used against the Protestants and on the basis of this principle his case is unanswerable. But the declaration was indignantly rejected by the Vatican. And Bossuet's defense was not published until long after his death. Thus the great defender of the unchangeable nature of the Church against the Protestants found his own basic apologetic principle rejected by his own Church.

The second attitude is that there is renewal in the life of the Church, but only in the sense of development. The principle of antiquity is not given up, but it is completed and relativized by the notion of growth, of increasing realization of the inherent law of the living body. This is the governing concept of the new Roman Catholic ecclesiology as it arose under the influence of romanticism in the early nineteenth century. J. A. Moehler introduced at that time the conception of doctrinal development. For him and his many followers until our day the key to the understanding of the Church is "the growth of the life of the Church". One of his most faithful interpreters summarizes his position in these words: "If the Church and its doctrine were in every respect immutable they would have no history. There must therefore be changeable (variables) elements together with an absolutely immutable foundation".[2]

It is not difficult to see that this concept of renewal provides new opportunities for Christian apologetics in that the "biological" categories which are used, seem to be in harmony with the concepts of modern science and culture and that the problem of justifying new doctrinal formulations (which Bossuet could not solve) can thus

[2] Ranft in *L'Église est Une. Hommage à Moehler*, p. 123.

be restated. But the difficulty is that this conception of the Church isolates the image of the "Body of Christ" from all other images concerning the Church. A true interpretation of that image must surely take into consideration that the Church is also the people of God and the fold of the Shepherd. And if that wider context is taken seriously, it cannot be maintained that the Church has its law of life within itself, for it is then seen that it receives its life ever anew from the God to whom it belongs, that it must ever be gathered by the Shepherd and that the Body is directed by him who is its Head.

The third position with regard to the changing and unchanging elements in the life of the Church is that of the modernist movements which we find in practically all confessions. Their claim is that the renewal of the Church must take the form of an adaptation to the new cultural developments and that not merely at the level of formulation and structural patterns, but at the level of the content of the faith. The *Protestantenverein* in Germany, founded in 1863 in order to gather together the liberal forces in the German Protestant Churches, declared in the first article of its constitution that it stood for "a renewal of the Protestant Church in the spirit of evangelical freedom and in harmony with the whole cultural development of our time". For our generation which has witnessed great conflicts between the Church and the ideologies, it is not difficult to realize that this type of renewal tends to lead to a complete self-annihilation of the Church as it adopts a criterion of renewal which is external and foreign to its own life. But it remains surprising that Christian theologians could forget the eschatological context of newness in the New Testament to such an extent, that they replaced it by its exact opposite, namely conformity to this world.

In the fourth place we have the position of those who take the eschatological nature of renewal seriously, but whose eschatology is exclusively futurist. In their view real renewal can only take place when the present dispensation is wholly replaced by the new dispensation. In the meantime there is only the newness which we receive in faith but this newness has nothing to do with renewal on the historical plane. This has been the teaching of Protestant orthodoxy in various forms. Its result has generally been that the Churches accepted their status as Churches composed of justified sinners in such a complacent manner that they became defenseless in their dealing with the world.

The very worldliness of the Churches has produced a fifth position according to which renewal means the immediate realization here on earth of the "Church without spot or wrinkle". The first of the long series of sects which have taken this position, the Montanist movement which described itself as "the new prophecy", had already all the main characteristics which appear again and again in the sects of later periods of history. It reacted against the increasing worldliness of the official Church, it sought to create a fellowship of awakened Christians,[3] it believed in special revelation over and above the biblical revelation, it proclaimed a *novissima lex* to be followed. And it did all this on the basis of an apocalyptic type of eschatology. It is at this last point that its weakness can best be shown. For in this respect it breaks the balance between the "not yet" and the "already" which we found to be the New Testament perspective. It is not the task of the Church to act as if the new age had wholly replaced the old age. The "angelic fallacy" of the apocalyptic sect is a challenge in that it reminds the Church of the constant danger of worldliness, but, in spite of its impressive insistence on genuine renewal of life, it must not tempt us to think that renewal once for all, perfected renewal such as will characterize the "Church without spot or wrinkle", can be attained in this world.

The sixth position is that which we try to develop in these lectures.

---

[3] According to Epiphanius, Montanus said, "Men sleep, I awaken them".

Luther once described the pilgrimage of the Church in the following concentrated formula: "It is not yet done and accomplished, but it is going on. It is not the end, but the way. It is not all glistening and shining, but it is all being swept."[4] We must now try to describe that way of renewal and that process of cleansing.

The starting point is that the renewal of the Church is the work of God and not of man by himself. That is not meant as a pious reminder that we need the help of God in all that we undertake. It is meant in a much more radical sense. All that we have found in the Old and New Testament confirms that the renewal of the Church means first of all the creative work of God among his people, the victories won by the new age over the old age. The Church does not renew itself: it is the object of God's work of renewal. "Be ye renewed" does not mean: "Get busy and find some different and better method of Christian action." It means: "Expose yourself to the life-giving work of God. Pray that he may make the dry bones come to life. Expect great things from him. And get ready to do what he commands."

This is a very practical truth. For it implies that the renewal of the Church does not begin with more or less solemn decisions of synods, conferences or committees, but with an encounter between God and men, in which God takes hold of the situation and empowers them to serve as his instruments of renewal.

Must we then always wait for God before taking any action for the renewal of the Church? Yes, but our waiting must be waiting in the biblical sense. "As the eyes of servants look unto the hand of their masters and as the eyes of a maiden unto the hands of her mistress, *so* our eyes wait upon the Lord our God" (Ps. 123, 2). We know that he is the living God, who makes all things new. We know that he desires his Church to be the center of new life in an old and passing world. So we must be

[4] Martin Luther, *Ausgewählte Werke. Calwer Ausgabe,* 5, 154.

continually on the watch for the initiatives which he will take. It is inevitable that the Church living within a world which knows no real renewal, falls again and again into the worldly way of just "going through the motions" of Church life and thus becomes part of the world. But it is equally inevitable that the Lord who has created the Church and given it newness of life rescues it continually from its worldliness. The Church must be renewed, because it has been renewed. We have therefore sure ground for our hope that God will not leave the Church alone in our day and generation. And we have good reason to expect him to give us clear guidance as to the specific task which he desires us to accomplish for the renewal of the Church today.

But how and where do we discover what renewal according to God's will means? Every true renewal of the Church is based on the hearing anew of the Word of God as it comes to us in the bible. This seems at first sight impossible. How can the new result from a return to the old? There have therefore been many who have sought the renewal of the Church by breaking away from the bible or by adding to and improving upon the bible. But we must maintain this simple truth that outside the Word of God there is in this world no true source of renewal. Why is that so? Because the bible is the authentic record of the only radically new event that has ever taken place in the world. All other newness is either borrowed from that event or it is only newness in appearance. If the Church which seeks to renew itself takes its lead from some new religious or cultural development or some new technique, it remains in fact within the closed circle of the old world. If it turns for inspiration to some period of its own past it is not directly in touch with the source. It can only break out of the old world and enter into living touch with the new world by submitting itself to the judgment and inspiration of God's revelation itself and that revelation is given to us through the Holy Scriptures. Here alone a true dialogue can take place between the Church and its Lord. Here the Church discovers that it needs renewal and what renewal means. This "orientation to the center" (Cullmann) has been and is the great life-giving force in the Church and this is the true return to the source. In saying this we do not forget the work of the Holy Spirit. As we have seen, the New Testament teaches with the greatest clarity that there is no renewal except through the Holy Spirit. The bible is a dead letter if the Spirit does not make it the living Word of God for us. But it is wholly unbiblical to oppose the Spirit and the Word of God or to separate them from each other. The Spirit does not speak "on its own authority" but speaks "whatever he hears". He "takes what is mine", says Jesus (John 16, 13-14). And all appeals to the Spirit which seek to by-pass the historical record of the actual work of the Lord are therefore appeals to the spirit of man rather than to the Holy Spirit.

Karl Barth says: "Since the Church has been called into being by the Word of the new birth and the new creation, it cannot maintain its life except through this Word. What is the use of all natural vitality even if it is so great that it enables the Church to win the whole world? In that way the Church can maintain some kind of life as one of the institutions which are hastening to their death. But as the Church of truth and of eternal life it is dead, right in the midst of the most flourishing development, if the word of truth withdraws itself from it."[5] And we can also put this the other way round. A Church which has nothing but the living Word, a Church which is attacked on all sides but has this one defender, is a Church which need not fear for its life, for its youth is renewed like the eagle's (Ps. 103, 5). It is in listening to the Word of God in the Scriptures that the Church discovers again and again what God's design is and what its own place is in that design. Where else can it find out about the total plan of God and come to know what particular mission he has as-

[5] *Kirchliche Dogmatik*, I, 2,772.

signed to the Church? Where else can it come to realize the full content of its own life and come to understand its own past and its own future?

It is through the bible and the bible alone that the Church can and must recover the eschatological dimension of its own existence. A Church in which the bible has the last word is bound to be forcefully reminded of its very *raison d'être* as a first fruit of the new age and will therefore be saved from conforming itself to the world. And a Church in which the bible has the last word will never be able to forget that it is not the Kingdom of God, and that it lives under the constant judgment of the Kingdom of God. Thus it will be saved from the solitude and self-centeredness of a sterile monologue. And thus it will be driven to constant self-criticism.

The tragedy of a Church which does not give to the bible the decisive place in its life is that it loses the eschatological perspective, that it becomes increasingly tempted to consider its own existence as an aim in itself and that it thus loses the capacity for radical self-criticism and renewal of life. This is illustrated in the story of the medieval Church and especially in the use it made of St. Augustine's conception of the Church. In *De Civitate Dei* St. Augustine had made the crucial affirmation: "So the Church now on earth is both the Kingdom of Christ and the Kingdom of Heaven."[6]

Now St. Augustine was far too profound a theologian to maintain that identification without qualification. And so we find in his writings strong tension between the conception of the Church as the Kingdom (or at least as part of it)[7] and the eschatological affirmation that the Church in this world is still a Church of strangers and pilgrims. Thus he affirms: "The whole Church says: Forgive us our sins. She has therefore spots and wrinkles. But in the confession of sins the spots are washed away, the

[6] *De Civitate Dei,* Book XX, ch. 9.
[7] *De Civitate Dei,* Book XIX, ch. 17; cf. Harnack, *Dogmengeschichte,* III, p. 136.

wrinkles taken away."[8] Now the medieval Church did
not follow St. Augustine in his eschatological emphasis, but
embraced his teaching concerning the identity of the
Church and the Kingdom. And on the basis of this so-
called "Augustinianism" the Church became that proud
institution living its own autonomous life which found its
full expression in the medieval papacy.

Now it is a curious fact that even in the Reformation
this erroneous identification of the Church with the Kingdom of God was at first maintained. Martin Bucer says
quite definitely that the Kingdom of God is the Church of
Christ.[9] Beza did not speak otherwise. So whatever we
may think of his real motives, Thomas Hobbes had a real
point when in his *Leviathan* he accused both the Roman
Catholics and the Protestants of identifying the Church
and the Kingdom and of thus confusing promise and ful-
filment.[10]

What William Temple has said of the Roman Catholic
Church is to a certain extent true of other Churches too.
He says: "All the doctrinal errors of Rome come from
the direct identification of the Church as an organized institution, taking its part in the process of history with the
Kingdom of God."[11] The Church needs to remember all
the time that, in the excellent phrase of an Anglo-Catholic
theologian, it "is the body, alike of sin and of glory, at
once the object and the instrument of the judgment and
salvation of God".[12]

There can therefore be no renewal without repentance.

All great renewals in the history of the Church have
been movements of *repentance*. This is inevitable because

[8] *Serm.* 181.7. Quoted by Grosche, *Pilgernde Kirche,* p. 67.

[9] Courvoisier, *La Notion de l'Église chez Bucer,* p. 70.

[10] *Leviathan* (1651), pp. 334, 341, 385.

[11] Iremonger, *William Temple,* p. 420; cf. the Encyclical *Quas
Primas* of 1925: 'The Church is precisely this Kingdom of Christ
destined to cover the whole world.'

[12] Dom Gregory Dix, quoted in *Catholicism To-day* (The Times),
p. 39.

renewal presupposes a break with the old world. We have
noticed that the restoration of the Covenant in Israel was
conditional upon true repentance. In the New Testament
repentance is the burden of the message of Jesus; it is the
climax of St. Peter's preaching at Pentecost; it is the key-
word of the letters to the seven Churches of Asia in the
Book of Revelation. Thus Martin Luther went straight to
the center, when in the first of his theses which he nailed
to the church door in Wittenberg in 1517 he said: "When
our Lord and Master Jesus Christ says Repent, he means
that the whole life of the faithful is to be a life of repentance."

What does this mean? For Luther repentance is the
dynamic element in the Christian life. Where there is no
repentance, there can only be the static, old existence
which is tantamount to death. In his Commentary on
Romans of 1515-16 (on Rom. 12, 2) he explains that life
is not to stand still but to move on. The Christian moves
from sickness to health. His life is a passage from sin
(which is non-being) through repentance (which is becoming) to righteousness (which is being). The Christian
is always *in fieri*, in process of becoming, and repentance
or the new birth is the transition from sin to righteousness.
This conception corresponds to the dialectic between the
old and the new man in the epistles of St. Paul. And it
is just as true of the Church as it is of the individual
Christian.

We must then not think of repentance as a quietistic
and introverted preoccupation with the sins of the Church.
On the contrary we must think of it as the opening of the
doors of the cage in which the squirrel can only go through
the vain repetition of the same monotonous movements.
Repentance is turning from the old world to the new, from
the past to the future, from the closed world to the open
heaven, from egocentricity and Church-centeredness to
God's Kingdom. Since repentance implies a rupture with
the old, it means the concrete liberation of the Church
from the various forms of enslavement and imprisonment

to which it has submitted itself. We shall have to come back to this point when we discuss the renewal of the Church in its relation to the world. But we must say in this connection that the recovery of the total independence of the Church is an essential condition of all renewal. For the chief characteristic of the old, unrenewed condition of the Church is precisely its dependence upon and imitation of the ways of the present age. All through the history of Israel the great temptation is to follow the example of the other peoples, to cease being "different". And for the New Testament the temptation is to be conformed to this world which (according to Rom. 12, 2) is the exact opposite of renewal in Christ. For this world is, as Calvin puts it: the *scopus veteris hominis*, that is, the field of activity of the old man.

The liberation of the Church does not mean that it turns its back upon the world, but that it becomes again wholly dependent upon its Lord, does not listen to the voice of strangers and is in the midst of this world the spokesman of the Word of God which is not fettered (2 Tim. 2, 9). Thus every renewal of the Church is in one sense a movement of withdrawal from the world and from entangling alliances in the political, social, cultural or philosophical realms. But that withdrawal is never an aim itself. It is a withdrawal with the purpose of returning to the attack.

Church-renewal also means *re-edification* of the Church. In the New Testament edification is not used in the subjective sense of intensification and nurture of personal piety. It means the action of the Holy Spirit by which he creates the people of God and gives shape to its life. In Ephesians ch. 4 *oikodome* is the upbuilding of the Body of Christ. In 1 Peter, ch. 2 *oikodomein* is the building of the spiritual house or house of the Spirit. And this reference to the Church as the work of God is included whenever the expression "edification" is used. "The object of edification is not in the first place the individual, but the whole, the Church", says Karl Ludwig Schmidt.[13]

In one sense the Church *has* been built; but in another sense it is constantly being built and rebuilt.[14] The task of men is to "let themselves be built up", but it is also to participate in the work of the Holy Spirit and to build up or edify each other.

What does this mean concretely? It means to make the Church what it is in essence, to realize its destiny, to make it manifest in the world as the holy nation, as God's own people (1 Peter 2, 9). Karl Ludwig Schmidt has called attention to the relationship between *oikos* (house) and *oikodomein* on the one hand and *paroikia* on the other.[15] Now this word *paroikia*, from which our word "parish" (*paroisse*) is derived, really refers to the fact that Christians live in this world as people who have no abiding city in this world (Heb. 13, 14), but who have their commonwealth (or citizenship) in heaven (Phil. 3, 20). They live in this world as strangers and pilgrims (1 Peter 2, 11). To build the Church is therefore not to build up a solid institution which is wholly at home in the world and uses the methods of the world. It is rather to organize a band of pilgrims who are on the way to a new and better country and who must therefore not adapt themselves to their temporary surroundings.

It would seem that this New Testament conception of Churches which are by their very nature Churches in exile cannot possibly have any relevance for our congregations which have become so firmly rooted in the world and which often pride themselves on the fact that, so far from being exiles, they are the most stable element of the

---

[13] K. L. Schmidt in *Wesen und Aufgabe der Kirche in der Welt,* 1946, p. 20.
[14] 'Die immer neu zu vollziehende, sich vollziehende Konstitution, die *creatio continua* der Kirche' (Vielhauer cited by Bornkamm, *Das Ende des Gesetzes,* p. 117).
[15] K. L. Schmidt, loc. cit., p. 26.

society in which they live. But that only shows how badly we need to hear the New Testament message of renewal with its all-pervading eschatological perspective. And is it not true that the degeneration of much of our Church life comes precisely from the fact that it has lost its "otherness" in relation to the world and that men no longer see any noticeable difference between the Church and any other society which is concerned with spiritual or moral uplift? Our congregations can only be built up and renewed, if we recover the sense of the unique place of the Church in God's plan and history and show the world that it is precisely because of this uniqueness that the Church has a word of hope for the life of the world.

The building up of the Church means at the same time the restoration of true *fellowship* in our congregations. For the New Testament *koinonia* belongs to the very nature of the Church. And what does this mean? It means partnership in a common calling, sharing in the same spiritual gifts and above all common participation in the Body of Christ. This is most simply expressed in the formula the "*koinonia* (fellowship) of the Holy Spirit", for that means, really, participation in the Holy Spirit. This fellowship cannot be created, where there is nothing to participate in except human sentiments. And the renewal of this fellowship depends on the re-entry of the Church into the realm of the new creation. Where that happens a congregation ceases to be an amorphous mass of people, becomes a true family of God and fulfills its function of showing the world how God desires men to live together.

In one sense the Church is definitely an otherwordly Church, for it knows that it belongs to the new world, which is indeed another world in relation to the old world. But that "otherworldliness" has nothing to do with an egotistic enjoyment of the blessings of individual salvation or with indifference concerning the life of the present world. For the *raison d'être* of the Church is to announce the good news of the new creation in Christ. It is not a refuge for saved souls; it is a band of messengers or, to use a very typically biblical word, of "heralds" who proclaim the good news of the Kingdom and of the entrance of that Kingdom in this world in the person of Jesus Christ. These heralds are not self-appointed; they are commissioned by Christ. They do not invent a message of their own. They speak of what they have seen and heard (Acts 4, 20).

The renewal of the Church implies therefore also that the Church rediscovers its *apostolic*, missionary character. This will express itself first of all in that its witness to its own members becomes again a true *kerugma*, that is to say the proclamation of the great deeds of God and the events through which he has intervened in the world for the salvation of men. And thus the witness itself will become an event. For true preaching is not talking about God and even less talking about our own experiences and ideals. It is (to use a magnificent phrase of Bernard Lord Manning) "a manifestation of the Incarnate Word, from the written word, by the spoken word".[16] As P. T. Forsyth put it—many years before Karl Barth began to hammer on this truth—"God's living word reproduces itself as a living act". And the question is: "Does the Gospel preach itself through us with power? Are our sermons deeds, action-sermons?"[17]

But renewal means at the same time that the evangelistic and missionary task is seen as the normal task of the whole Church. Evangelism and missions, not as a peculiar and somewhat peripheral concern of a special group of church members, not as one of many activities to which one contributes one's gifts of money, but as the inevitable expression of the understanding which the Church has of its own nature and calling. This can only come through the work of the Holy Spirit. But the gift is precisely

[16] Bernard Lord Manning, *A Layman in the Ministry*, p. 138.
[17] P. T. Forsyth, *Positive Preaching and the Modern Mind*, 1949 (first edition in 1907), pp. 55 and 57.

promised to the Church for this purpose. "You shall receive power when the Holy Spirit has come upon you and you shall be my witnesses in Jerusalem and in all Judea and Samaria and to the end of the earth" (Acts 1, 8).

We have seen that the renewal of the Church is in a very literal sense a superhuman task. The old world seems always to have the advantage of the conflict. Every intervention of the Holy Spirit appears as a partial intervention and all true newness in the Church seems to lead a precarious existence. Every time the work of renewal has to be begun all over again. There is in the life of the Church in history no definitive renewal, no renewal which is not threatened by relapse into old ways, no reformation which is not followed by some form of deformation. But if we conclude that therefore the situation of the Church is hopeless we are wholly at variance with the biblical view.

According to the Old and New Testament, the people of God live in the dangerous, insecure situation that nothing in their own life is ever a definitive, finished achievement. The Church is not itself the new creation; and it needs constantly to be renewed by judgment and repentance. But this is not a reason for despair. For the miracle is the miracle of God's grace, of his patience and forgiveness. The miracle is the faithfulness of God who does not leave his people alone, but continues to work at their salvation. The miracle for which we can never be grateful enough, is that the Holy Spirit continues to plead with the Church "Be transformed by the renewal of your mind" and that through him the Church is actually renewed.

DIALOGUE NO. 6
Our Common Christian Witness

Resource Readings

Report of the Section on Witness (pp. 183–199)
Third Assembly of the W.C.C., New Delhi, Nov. 18—
Dec. 6, 1961
The Nature of Christian Witness
Philip Berrigan, S.S.J.

Suggested Readings

Barnes, Roswell P. *Under Orders: The Churches and Public Affairs.* Toronto: Doubleday, 1961.

Berrigan, Philip, S.S.J. *No More Strangers.* New York: Macmillan, 1965.

Duff, Edward, S.J. *The Social Thought of the World Council of Churches.* New York: Association Press, 1956.

Gremillion, Joseph. *The Other Dialogue.* New York: Doubleday, 1965.

Hastings, Adrian. *Mission: The Church's #1 Problem.* New York: Paulist Press, 1965.

Orchard, Roland K. (editor). *Witness in Six Continents.* London: Edinburgh House Press, 1964. Available: New York: Friendship Press.

Schutz, Roger. *Unity: Man's Tomorrow.* Baltimore, Md.: Helicon, 1964.

Seven Great Encyclicals. New York: Paulist Press, 1963.

CHRISTIAN DIALOGUE

Our Common Christian Witness

Leader: Christ, our Savior, who desire the salvation of all men,

All: Hear our prayers and grant our petitions.

Leader: That we may be the instruments to restore Christian unity and to lead all unbelievers to the light of the Gospel,

All: We beg you to hear us, O Lord.

Leader: For the bad example of our lives which have hindered or prevented the workings of grace in the souls of those around us,

All: We beg your forgiveness, O Lord.

Leader: Let us pray.

All: God, who desire that all men should be saved and that all should come to know your truth, we pray you, send us as united laborers to your harvest so that your teaching may be received with honor throughout the world and all nations may acknowledge you, the true and only God, and him whom you have sent, Jesus Christ, your Son, our Lord. Amen.

BIBLE READING

Holy Father, keep them in thy name, which thou hast given me, that they may be one, even as we are one (John 17, 11).

I do not pray for these only, but also for those who believe in me through their word, that they may all be one; even as thou, Father, art in me, and I in thee, that they

176

also may be in us, so that the world may believe that thou
hast sent me (John 17, 20-21).

So we are ambassadors for Christ, God making his
appeal through us . . . Working together with him, then,
we entreat you not to accept the grace of God in vain
. . . Behold, now is the acceptable time; behold, now is
the day of salvation (2 Cor. 5, 20-6, 1-2).

MEDITATION

Lord, we offer our Christian dialogue to you. . . .
We stand before you divided in belief and worship. . . .
The vast majority of the men in the world do not believe in
you because we speak to them in conflicting voices. . . .
But through your grace we still share many gifts of your
Redemption. . . . Do not allow us to continue to share
these gifts in vain. . . . Help us, by working together with
you, to build a common Christian witness upon them. . . .
Impress upon us that now is the acceptable time, now is
the day of salvation.

BIBLE READING

You are the salt of the earth; but if salt has lost its
taste, how shall its saltness be restored? It is no longer
good for anything except to be thrown out and trodden
under foot by men.

You are the light of the world. A city set on a hill cannot be hid. Nor do men light a lamp and put it under a
bushel, but on a stand, and it gives light to all in the house.
Let your light so shine before men, that they may see your
good works and give glory to your Father who is in heaven
(Matt. 5, 13-16).

Blessed are those who hunger and thirst for righteousness, for they shall be satisfied. . . . Blessed are the
peacemakers, for they shall be called sons of God (Matt.
5, 6-9).

Meditation

Lord, as Christians you tell us that we must be the salt
of the earth and the light of the world. . . . Up to
now, because of our divisions, the earth has been weakly

salted with the message of your salvation. . . . Our light
has been removed from the lamp-stand, it does not
give light to all in the house. . . . Help us to hunger and
thirst for justice together. . . . Teach us how to unite in
a common witness of social justice and charity. . . . Once
we begin to perform good works together we shall once
again be called peacemakers and children of God. . . . As
we continue to witness together for you, we pray our
desire for full unity in your will shall be satisfied.

Christian Dialogue

Introduction

In this evening's dialogue we hope to explore the nature of the imperative, which affects each one of us, to
witness to Christ who is at work in his world. Contemporary conditions challenge the Christian as never before to
relate his beliefs to the world about him. Even though
the Christian people live in today's world severed by
denominationalism and doctrinal disagreement, we must
strive anew to make Christ known to all men.

The Need for Witness Today

Ours is a world riddled with strife and hostility. Crime
and savagery, born out of sub-human living conditions, are
rampant on our city streets. Nuclear destruction hangs
over our heads, war seethes in several sections of our
world, two-thirds of the world's population are hungry,
racial conflicts trouble men all over the globe. Christians believe that Christ has brought new life to men and
changed their whole order of existence. But Christ does
not seem to be present in the struggles of mankind today.
Is it because the Christian people do not proclaim him
there?

DISCUSSION QUESTIONS

Do you agree that Christian witness is necessary today
not because of the desperate problems of our times but

rather because the Gospel of Christ must be proclaimed in every age?

Rather than bemoaning the contemporary situation, how can the Christian find even greater potential for the proclamation of Christ in our troubled times? What does the New Delhi report mean when it says that "the opportunities for witnessing patiently and faithfully to the deed of God in Christ are as many and as great as the difficulties we face"?

What forms might Christian witness take in your neighborhood? Why does true Christian charity demand that the Christian be conscious of the needs of his brothers? Have you ever seen any situations in which you felt strong Christian witness was given? Do you think it is too late for the Church to begin to offer witness in your area?

What Makes A Witness

The New Delhi report insists that it is not the Christian who bears witness in the world but God who witnesses to himself in the world—it is not we who take Christ to men, but Christ himself who gives us to them as the agents of his own work amongst them. It is not we who save the world, but Christ. The Christian who will truly offer witness to his fellow men, must understand clearly his relationship to Christ ever present in the world, ever witnessing to men.

DISCUSSION QUESTIONS

If Jesus offers his own witness in the world, why does he need us to witness to him? Have you seen Christians who seemed to consider themselves saviors of the world rather than Jesus? How does this approach hurt their witness?

Can we witness to men we do not love? Must the witness share the concerns of men, sympathize with their aspirations, and learn their language? Is the command to witness given to individuals as well as to the whole Church?

What are some of the opportunities in your neighborhood for individual witness? What is the place of small witnessing groups or cells of Christians in addition to the witness given by a whole congregation? Along what lines or interests might small witnessing cells be organized? How does Christian witness relate to the individual's growth in Christ? In what way is Christ's life the model of Christian witness?

Church Structures and Christian Witness

The New Delhi report states that the Christian witnesses to Christ, not to Christianity. It is sometimes maintained today that conventional Church structures confine the Christian and emasculate his witness in the world. Separation among Christians is seen as a scandal which compromises much Christian witness in the eyes of nonbelievers. The renewal of Church structures and life as well as the ecumenical movement among Christians relate very deeply to the impact of Christian witness.

DISCUSSION QUESTIONS

How does the Church as manifested by the local congregation exhibit and how does it obscure the witness of Christ in the world? Have you ever seen instances of Christian disunity affecting Christian witness in your neighborhood? How can the parish or local Church serve as a center for the formation of Christian witnesses? Does your parish or church form witnesses? If not, why not?

Witness and Ecumenism

Cooperative witness among separated Christians on religious-social problems such as civil rights has already taken place in many cities. There is a wide enough consensus among Christians so that such co-operation is possible on many issues without violating conscientiously held beliefs. Such collaboration not only draws the participating groups closer together and places the unity Christians already have in a clearer light, but it also multiplies many times over the effectiveness of the witness.

DISCUSSION QUESTIONS

What areas of social concern offer opportunity for collaborative witness in your community? Civil rights? The poor? Juvenile delinquents? Addicts of drugs or alcohol? Beautifying the community? Care of the aged? Scouting and youth work?

In what ways would your combined efforts increase the fruits of your labor?

Have any such cooperative works been undertaken in your community? Why have they, or why have they not, succeeded?

Why have Christians in stress situations like the concentration camps in World War II found it easier to collaborate than those in more comfortable circumstances? Does our collaboration lead us to a clearer perception of the meaning of our baptism and common life in Christ?

Politics and Witness

The political sphere offers thorny problems for the conscientious Christian. Some feel that the Church must confine itself to laying down ethical norms by which the Christian will come to sound political decisions. The Church as such, they say, has no role in the midst of the fray. Others hold that the Church on certain political issues with direct moral and religious overtones must engage directly in political action.

DISCUSSION QUESTIONS

Do you think the Churches should engage in direct political action or merely offer principles of action? What is your opinion of ministers, priests and nuns who participate in public demonstrations? What is the value of this kind of witness?

Should the Churches speak out concerning the moral aspects of nuclear warfare? Should they engage in any direct political action on this question?

CLOSING PRAYER

O God, our Father, good beyond all that is good, fair beyond all that is fair, in whom is calmness, peace and concord: reconcile we pray you your servants separated one from another by dissension, and lead us back into a unity of love which will bear some likeness to your sublime nature. And as you are above all things, grant that we may be united in generosity of spirit; that by the bonds of love and ties of affection we may become spiritually one, within ourselves as well as with each other. Through that peace of yours which makes all things peaceful in the grace, mercy and pity of your beloved Son. Amen.

Report of the Section on Witness

We live in critical times, but it is not because of the desperate nature of the problems of our age that the task of witness to the Gospel of Christ is urgent today. The urgency of the Church's evangelistic task arises from the Gospel itself, because it is the Gospel of Jesus Christ. Christ loves the world, which he died to save. He is already the light of the world, of which he is Lord, and his light has preceded the bearers of the good news into the darkest places. The task of Christian witness is to point to him as the true light, which is already shining. In Christ was life, and the life was the light of men, the light that enlightens every man. The work of evangelism is necessary in this and in every age in order that the blind eyes may be opened to the splendor of light.

Nevertheless, the urgency of the predicament in which our age finds itself should underline for Christians their duty and their opportunity. The whole world has become for the first time in history an interdependent world, in which the peoples of all lands either must solve their problems of living together in peace or must perish together. We live in an age of revolution, in which immense changes are taking place in every sphere of human life. Christians know that God is the Lord of history and that therefore the critical issues of our times have not arisen outside his loving purpose and are not beyond his control. Hence for them times of crisis will become opportunities for witnessing to the Lord. Conscious of their

own impotence in a world of apparently blind and un-
controlled forces, they will nevertheless go forth with joyful confidence, knowing that the Holy Spirit will lead
them to where Christ already is, and will enable them to
bear their witness in every place to the light shining in the
darkness, which the darkness cannot overcome.

Today the task of evangelism must be performed in
new situations and therefore in new ways. The Church in
every land is aware that new situations require new
strategies and new methods, an adventuring into new
forms of human social relationships with appropriately
new ways of approach and understanding, a renewed sympathy with all men in their aspirations and sufferings and
a fresh determination to speak to men the truth of the
Gospel in the actual situation of their lives.

But the Church knows also that the outcome of her
mission depends solely upon God and not upon her own
cleverness or adaptability in the struggle for co-existence
with other ideologies, scientific, technological, nationalistic, political or religious. She knows that she can witness
faithfully to the true light only in penitence and in humble
obedience to the voice of the Living God. She knows also,
that though the strategies and techniques of evangelism
must change from age to age, the Gospel which she proclaims is still the changeless Gospel of God's saving love,
in the redemption of the world by our Lord Jesus Christ,
made known to us through the power of his Holy Spirit.

The considerations which are here offered upon the
theme of Witness are not complete in themselves; they
must be read in connection with the other two themes of
the New Delhi Assembly. The question of the Church's
Unity is of vital importance, since the Bible teaches us that
the Gospel cannot be authoritatively proclaimed to the
world by a disunited Church. The question of the Service
of Christians to the world in which men suffer is also of
essential importance in the matter of Christian Witness, for
the world will not listen to a Church which professes
Christ as Lord but does not do what he has commanded.

The three themes of Unity, Witness and Service are in the last resort not three, but one.

Jesus Christ:
The Saviour of the World

Jesus of Nazareth, the Christ, is the universal Lord and Saviour. This is our common faith, and it has been confirmed in us by our worship and study together in the Third Assembly of the World Council of Churches. As we have reflected on his Lordship we have realized afresh that the whole world is the continuing concern of the Father's love. It was for the sake of all men that the Son of God became man. The mighty acts of his ministry, death and resurrection and ascension were the outworking of a single purpose, the redemption of the world.

We say these words about Christ, not about ourselves. We are not the world's saviour. We are called to witness to him as the Saviour and Lord of all. We cannot bear his name without coming under the searching light of his judgment on all men, beginning with us. This means asking some practical questions in our churches: whether we love men enough to be able to witness to them; whether we are sensitive to the ceaseless work of the Holy Spirit among men; whether we think and act as though Christ died for all men and not just for us. But we acknowledge our blindness and faithlessness and accepting our forgiveness we can testify that Christ never has forsaken his Church; by his spirit its life is sustained and many are brought by him into its faith and fellowship.

I

God is his own witness; that is to say, God has been and is at work authenticating his own message to men. When we speak of witness we mean testimony to the whole activity of God in the creation and preservation of the world, but especially in his mighty acts in Israel's history and in the redemption of the world by Jesus Christ. To this testimony the Holy Spirit in the Church bears witness.

God continues to bear witness to the Son, as the only Lord and Saviour of all men. In the apostolic witness, coming to us in Scripture in the Spirit-filled Church, God gives us the foundation of all subsequent witness. In the sacraments of baptism and the eucharist, God down the ages of the Church has drawn near to men in Jesus Christ and borne witness to his own faithfulness. In the faithful preaching of his Word, God himself bears testimony to the truth. In the very existence of the Church, there is a constant witness—in silence as it were—to the reality of God's dealing with men in Jesus Christ.

We stand today in this long tradition of the Church's witness, having its origin in God himself, repeating itself constantly in the life of the Church. Therefore, we have confidence and enter with joy into the task of witness which has been laid upon us. We can speak as those who know in our own lives that 'he who believes in the Son of God has this testimony in his own heart.' We are convinced that Jesus is the risen, living Lord, victorious over sin and death. Of him and of the restored fellowship with God which he has worked for us and for all men, we would speak to our brothers for whom Christ died.

Today men fear death, not so much, as formerly, because of the sanctions of judgment and hell, as because it brings a total end to their enjoyment of this world, apart from which they know of no other life. The Church in preaching Christ's death proclaims victory over the power of death itself and the reality of a fuller and richer life than this world knows. Baptism signifies passing through the waters of death and entering here and now upon the life of the age to come.

II

In Jesus Christ, God has shown man his true nature and destiny. Through faith in Christ men receive power to become the sons of God. Christ has taken our manhood into God and 'our real life is hid with Christ in

God.' So we look forward with eager longing to the glorious consummation of all things, when we shall share the fullness of the life of God. Nothing less than this can be the measure of what it means to be human, the fullness of the stature of Christ.

Because God in Christ has reconciled the world to himself, we may no longer judge our brother man by ordinarily accepted standards. God has not condemned us; we may not condemn any man. Only the rebellious will of man stands between us men and the realization of our true humanity and our eternal destiny. Joyfully we affirm our solidarity with all men, for our Lord has joined himself to us all by becoming man. Solidarity with all men of every nation, class, color and faith without distinction in our common manhood is a starting point of the renewal of the life and witness of our churches by the Holy Spirit.

In Christ, the promise of God that man should have dominion over the created world is confirmed and demonstrated. The witness of Christ is that the full responsibility for ordering life in this world is with men, and that grace and truth for this task are available to them in him. He sets men free to know that the uncreated God alone is Lord over men, and that all created things are made to serve man in him. The new knowledge and enhanced power of modern man call aloud for a majestic witness to Christ in the fullness of his Lordship over nature and history, so that man may be able to accept the forgiveness of sins and find peace, wisdom and courage to handle the events of our time.

III

The gathering of the Church by Jesus Christ in every age demonstrates the loving purpose of God to draw men out of isolation and sinful separation into a community of brothers with a common Father, God himself. In Christ there is no place for pride in race, language, authority or sex. All are made equal with the humblest that all may share the glory of the Son. By the Spirit the Church is moved to the service of neighbor without distinction or discrimination. Through his Church God witnesses to his purpose to gather all nations, peoples and tongues, all sorts and conditions of men into his city. The story of God's dealing with Israel is the clue for our understanding of God's will for all nations and his present work among them.

In a time of rapid social change men find liberation from the constriction of old forms of community, but are demoralized because they do not find true community in their new surroundings. God calls the churches to witness in a life of humble interdependence and mutual service so that the will and imagination of men may be made strong to work for new and just relationships among nations, races and classes, and between the generations and the sexes.

Above all else, the Spirit stirs up the Church to proclaim Christ as Lord and Saviour to all the nations and in all spheres of life. The Church is sent, knowing that God has not left himself without witness even among men who do not yet know Christ, and knowing also that the reconciliation wrought through Christ embraces all creation and the whole of mankind. We are aware that this great truth has deep implications when we go out to meet men of other faiths. But there are differences of opinion amongst us when we attempt to define the relation and response of such men to the activity of God amongst them. We are glad to note that the study of this question will be a main concern in the continuing study on 'The Word of God and the Living Faiths of Men.' We would stress the urgency of this study. In the churches, we have but little understanding of the wisdom, love and power which God has given to men of other faiths and of no faith, or of the changes wrought in other faiths by their long encounter with Christianity. We must take up the conversations about Christ with them, knowing that Christ addresses them through us and us through them.

Communicating the Gospel

The good news about Christ is relevant to all ages, but, since every age differs from other ages, so must its ways and forms of communicating the Gospel. In every age the Holy Spirit makes possible the communication of the truth, but often the new ways in which he seeks to lead Christ's witnesses seem strange and dangerous to those who are accustomed to traditional methods. Nevertheless, if some kind of a break-through is to be made, the surmounting of obstacles and the seizing of opportunities must be attempted, so that we may confront the real situation of today and thus discover that through the power of the Spirit many apparent impossibilities have become possibilities and that the word of proclamation has still its ancient power. In our discussion we have been concerned chiefly with what seem to us the most important factors in the new situation of our days, which call for a new approach.

I

To communicate the Gospel involves the willingness and the ability of the evangelist to identify himself with those whom he addresses. To get alongside our hearer, to sit where he sits, is the essential condition upon which alone we may claim the right to be heard. By such sympathetic identification, in which the love of Christ is reflected, the Christian witness shows that he is not proclaiming his own message or superior gifts, but the truth of Christ; it is as though one beggar is telling another where the bread of life may be obtained. There are certain areas of life today where this kind of sympathetic identification is particularly needful and in which it is especially important that the witness should himself be first of all a listener. Amongst these areas may be mentioned the spheres of youth, the worker and the intellectual. If they are to be won, we must share their concerns, sympathize with their aspirations and learn their language. Otherwise they will translate our words into their own terms and they will not understand what we are saying. The evangelist must study the milieu in which his message is to be proclaimed. The resurgence of ancient faiths under the stimulus of nationalism is an example of the kind of challenge which demands from us a sympathetic and patient understanding, if we are to convince their adherents that in the universal Christ is to be found the answer to the desire of all nations. Or again, on the other hand, the view of many intellectuals in our technological society that all religious language, including Christian language, is a using of words that have no meaning at all, is an expression of disillusionment which demands from us a patient study and a sincere attempt to understand its deep causes. Only if we enter the world of our hearers will they be able or willing to listen to us. Instead of dismissing men's negative reactions to our message, we should take upon ourselves the burden of their unbelief.

We must search for a common language in which we and our hearers may understand each other. The truth of the Bible can be conveyed in twentieth-century words and idioms. This does not imply 'popularizing' the Gospel, but rather flexibility in translating our familiar words and images into a new medium. Since we cannot expect men to understand the vocabulary of the Bible until they have learned its language, we must mold our own speech into the vernacular of everyday language.

II

Christian witnesses must be prepared to be tested by the Gospel which they proclaim. Communication involves much more than speaking, and our message will have to be embodied in our life. We must be ready to be judged by the awful standard of the Christ whom we preach. If we are affluent in the midst of poverty or indifferent amidst injustice or suffering, our speaking will avail less than our silence. The Church as manifested by the local congregation will exhibit or obscure the presence of Christ, and onlookers will judge by what they see. The service, unity and common life of the churches are powerful factors in evangelism. Our message has not been truly proclaimed until it has been lived in real life. This sober reflection throws us back upon the mystery that God can and does use us in all our inadequacy to make manifest the truth which our imperfect works conceal. It is Christ, not Christianity, which is to be proclaimed as the truth, as it is God's power and not ours which brings men to accept it.

III

Dialogue is a form of evangelism which is often effective today. Many experiments are being made in this direction. This is not the place to express judgments upon their value, but rather to rejoice in the encouragement which they give to those who see the urgent need for new approaches to the task of evangelism in the twentieth century. There are, for example, the vigorous work of the Evangelical Academies, the leaderless face-to-face exposure of 'group dynamics,' the dialogue sermon, the study group, the experiments in corporate Bible study, the 'parish meeting,' and so on. They all emphasize the point that the communication of the Gospel today consists in listening first and then in showing how the Gospel meets the need of the times as we have learned to understand it.

Small groups have often been found to be a valuable method of encouraging true dialogue. There is much evidence of the way in which church life has been revitalized through the meeting of such groups for study, prayer, action or worship. The less obvious but not less real fellowship of persons who have thus willingly learned from one another has been a means of rediscovering the meaning of Christian community and of the realization that Christians are not units of an organization, but members of the body of Christ. Many who have been drawn into such groups have learned for the first time the true character of personal life within the Church.

IV

We can hardly mention Christian communication in the modern world without raising the question of the so-called mass-media of radio, television and the press. At first sight they may seem to have little to do with personal dialogue, but if we look more closely it will be apparent that in each of these media forms of intimate address take place, which identify and engage the individual listener, viewer or reader. Religious broadcasting and television are still only beginning to explore the possibilities of these new instruments of communication, and it is to be hoped that still more daring and imaginative use will be made of them.

It is often said, as we have said, that we are living in revolutionary times; as Christians we believe that God is at work in all the great changes which are taking place in our age. Christian communication has to be effected within the orbit of these changes. It is not enough to detect the judgment of God upon the status quo, which is being destroyed in an age of revolution. Times of revolution are precisely times when, if opportunities are seized, the judgments of God can be made plain and his purpose proclaimed to a world which will be shaken out of its complacency by the events of the day. Though we must resist the temptation to see the hand of God in the particular movements of history of which we personally approve, or to claim his blessing for every cause which seems righteous at the moment, we may nevertheless proclaim in such situations the lordship of Christ over the whole process which is changing the aspect of our world. But we must firmly reject all those revolutionary movements in all parts of the world which claim a half-religious sanction for a political or nationalistic end, and which pretend to a 'messianic' significance that justifies even their excesses. No earthly kingdom can set itself up as the kingdom of God on earth, and no political ambition is wholly conformed to the divine purpose. We must not be blind to the truth that our hope is in God alone, and we must read the signs of the times in the light of his historical dealings with men and with nations as we have learnt about them in the Bible.

In all these areas of concern there is both danger and opportunity. We believe that in our present moment of history Christ still stands at the door and knocks. Our communication of the Gospel is, we believe, Christ's own knocking at the door. A door may be a point of entry or of exclusion. We must continue to knock in the name of Jesus at the very doors which are shut against him and against the claims of humanity. To our fellow Christians we would speak this word of encouragement: The opportunities for witnessing patiently and faithfully to the deed of God in Christ are as many and as great as the difficulties which we face. We must grasp the opportunities, knowing that in them the Holy Spirit of God witnesses with us.

Reshaping the Witnessing Community

The command to witness to Christ is given to every member of his Church. It is a commission given to the whole Church to take the whole Gospel to the whole world. When the Church recognizes that it exists for the world, there arises a passionate concern that the blessings of the Gospel of Christ should be brought to every land and to every man and woman. These blessings include the alleviation of poverty, disease and hunger, and the creating of a true fellowship that relieves the loneliness of modern mass society. Christian evangelism is therefore a joyful privilege, being sustained by the knowledge that all the world is the object of God's love and is even now under the lordship of Christ. It is not we who take Christ to men, but Christ himself who gives us to them as the agents of his own work amongst them. The evangelistic task of the Church is to give the whole Gospel to the world, not merely those parts of it which we find congenial; for the unity of the Church itself is bound up with the unity of the Gospel, and neither must be divided into separated or merely partial expressions of the whole. We must be especially careful to note those elements in the Gospel which challenge the bases of the society in which we live and the social configuration of the Churches within it, so that under the merciful judgment of God the Church as the witnessing community may be continually reshaped to the pattern of the Gospel that is preached.

I

To proclaim the whole Gospel must mean to take seriously the secular causes of men's inability to hear or respond to our preaching. Those who are enslaved to the gods of this age, race, wealth, power and privilege, are likely to be deaf to the preaching; and also those who are oppressed by the burdens of poverty and drudgery and racial discrimination will be like the Israelites who 'hearkened not for anguish of soul and cruel bondage.' Witness to the Gospel must therefore be prepared to engage in the struggle for social justice and for peace; it will have to take the form of humble service and of a practical ministry of reconciliation amidst the actual conflicts of our times. The wholeness of the Gospel demands a corporate expression, since it concerns every aspect of men's lives. Healing and the relief of distress, the attack upon social abuses and reconciliation, as well as preaching, Christian fellowship and worship, are all bound together in the message that is proclaimed.

Within this whole enterprise of corporate witness, every individual Christian will play his own unique part according to the gifts of the Spirit with which he is endowed. Each stands in his own special place: the missionary in a country that is not his own; the pioneer in new fields of service; the Christian worker in his factory or office or home—each will be conscious that his witness is a part of the one ministry within the whole mission of the Church and that he is the representative of the whole Church. In the exercise of his vocation he will rely upon the care and prayer of all, and he will acknowledge that he owes to all a reciprocal care and prayer.

The Church whose members are thus to be the commissioned witnesses of Christ to the world is made up, for much the greatest part, of those who earn their living in the various forms of secular employment. In everyday English usage they are called 'laymen,' and indeed rightly so, for they are members of the *Laos,* or People of God. It is obvious that, if the Christian witness is to penetrate into all those areas where the work of the world is carried on, it must be carried there by laymen. They alone can bring Christian judgment to bear upon all the issues of life in the spheres of industry and commerce, scientific research and social organization, and all the other activities which make up the work-a-day world. Their meeting points in the secular world can become real opportunities for the witness of a living Church in the midst of the busy world's life.

To be truly effective, lay testimony must proceed from a thorough understanding of the Gospel, so that it may be clearly and forcefully articulated in language which the hearers can readily comprehend and which they will at once recognize to be relevant to their personal and social conditions. Only laymen can speak to their fellows in terms of their common involvement in the work upon which they are engaged, and can demonstrate that the Gospel of Christ is highly relevant to this actual situation and not merely to some remote 'church' sphere or afterlife. The layman who acknowledges his own personal responsibility for evangelism in his daily life will therefore welcome such training as he may be able to get in the matter of the understanding and defence of Christian truth. He will be anxious to clarify his own mind, to remove his own perplexities about the Bible or doctrine or ethics, so that he may the more confidently and convincingly speak to others about his faith. The lay institute in which such preparation for the evangelistic task may be adequately undertaken is needed as much in the churches of Asia and Africa as in those of Europe and America. But for the majority the proper place of training will be the local church. It is possible to set up very helpful courses in lay witness and leadership in many local churches and areas, and many week-end courses have been held with useful practical results. Situations vary widely, and it is not possible here to specify courses suitable for them all. But the need is urgent, and the possibilities are unlimited.

The ordained minister can be of great help in the work of preparation for such evangelism. Not only can he assist in such matters as the understanding of the Bible and of doctrine, but he can enter into discussion with laymen and listen to them as they speak of the actual situation in which their witness is to be borne. Together the laymen and the pastors may thus come to a fruitful appreciation of the relevance of the Gospel in the life of the secular world today. The pastor will not attempt to tell the layman how to bear his witness or to do his job, for only the layman can understand its real nature; but there are many ways in which the mutual discussion of the common problem will help to clarify the issues and to stimulate zeal according to knowledge. The pastor and the layman must learn to work as a team, each recognizing that the other has an essential ministry and gift of grace for his own special task in the one Body of Christ. There is an urgent need for all church members to recover the true meaning of certain words; to learn that the laity is really the *Laos,* that is, the whole People of God in the world, including, of course, those who have been ordained; to learn that ministry means any kind of service by which a Christian, exercising his particular skill and gift, however humble, helps his fellow Christians or his fellow men in the name of Christ. A far richer fellowship and team spirit is bound to appear as soon as the whole Church comes to realize its function as the People of God, which God himself has provided with many kinds of ministry, in which one special kind of ministry, that of the ordained clergy, is set apart to strengthen and teach, to encourage and unite all the several witnesses in their various callings whose ministry is set in the heart of the secular world's manifold activity.

II

If this penetration of the world by the lay witness is an essential part of God's plan for his Church, we must examine the conventional structures of our churches in order to see whether they assist or hinder the work of evangelism. We must not think of the 'Church' as primarily a building nor as an enterprise run by ministers to which people come or are scolded for not coming. We must ask whether we do not too easily fall into the habit of thinking of the Church as the Sunday congregation rather than as the laity scattered abroad in every department of daily life. We must inquire of ourselves whether our present structures do not preserve our divisions in a fossilized way, instead of enhancing the unity of the witnessing community. The scandal that renders the Gospel insignificant in the eyes of the unbelieving world and turns away genuine inquirers and potential converts is not the true scandal of the Gospel, Christ crucified, but rather the false scandals of our own practices and structures which prevent the message of the Gospel from challenging the world.

The situations by which the Church is confronted in different parts of the world today are so varied that it is impossible here to make recommendations which will be equally suitable for all areas. In certain places, especially those in which the Church faces active hostility and organized opposition, it is important to strengthen the local parish, or congregation, in every way possible, to hold it together and tend it as a shepherd gathers and feeds his flock. The pastoral task of the minister and his helpers is quite different in its expression, though not in its spirit and purpose, from its expression in other places, such as,

for instance, those in which the local congregation has lost
its sense of mission to the world and is happily content to
regard its primary function as that of keeping itself alive
as a prosperous, going concern. Or again, in many ur-
banized or industrialized areas in the West, the Church
has lost contact with the masses of the people, who do
not feel at home in our churches or understand the
language that is spoken in them.

In such places, it may be that the local church
should seek to penetrate into the unevangelized population by the setting up of 'cells' or local Christian community groups: a handful of typists and salesgirls in a big
store, a dozen or so workers on the various floors of a
factory; eight research workers and their wives in a big
chemical plant; a few Christian teachers on the staff of a
big school; a little congregation gathered from two or
three streets, meeting as a house-church in the home of
one of their number. They will try to be the Church, the
People of God, in their own particular context. There
are obvious difficulties in such attempted new forms of
Christian fellowship. There is the obvious danger of
fragmentation. But here the ordained ministry may rediscover its function as a traveling apostolate and as a
focus of unity. Just because the ordained minister is somewhat detached from secular groupings, he ought to be
able to enter into many different milieus. But if his ministry is to be effective in areas such as those where denominations are irrelevant, he must be ready to recognize
the ministers of other confessions as his fellow workers and
to work with them as a team. What already operates in
many universities, schools and hospitals must be practiced
in towns and neighborhoods. Eventually the local church
buildings might function as the centers to which all these
groups might come, not destroying their fellowship or their
own way of witness, as a 'congregation of congregations,'
witnessing to the reality of the whole Church to which they
all belong and the Lord of all life in whom all human
categories and classes are made one.

III

Different situations from those which we have taken as examples will undoubtedly demand different patterns of reshaping. The Assembly wishes only to urge that those who know themselves to be called to the responsibility of Christian witness in their own locality should examine afresh the structures of their church life with a view to meeting the challenge and opportunity of a new day. In a spirit of penitence and of willingness to be led by the Spirit of God into new ways of witness, the whole Church must recognize that her divine mission calls for the most dynamic and costly flexibility. We have discussed many situations and the different problems of different areas. We have mentioned only a few examples. We are aware that far-reaching changes are taking place, especially in the traditionally 'missionary' lands of Africa, Asia and Latin America. The way in which the challenge of Christian witness is met in those areas will be an example to us all. The relation of missions to churches is already being greatly modified in some lands, although in some areas progress is slow. Nevertheless, in other areas the process is being carried forward courageously and trustfully, so that the churches are carrying increasing responsibility for their own life and witness. In other areas more vigorous action is still awaited. A reappraisal of the patterns of church organization and institutions inherited by the younger churches must be attempted, so that outdated forms which belonged to an era that is rapidly passing away may be replaced by strong and relevant ways of evangelism. This is only one illustration, but an important one, of how the Church may become the Pilgrim Church, which goes forth boldly as Abraham did into the unknown future, not afraid to leave behind the securities of its conventional structures, glad to dwell in the tent of perpetual adaptation, looking to the city whose builder and maker is God.

The Nature of Christian Witness

Philip Berrigan, S.S.J.

Christians receive from Christ and his Church the essential role of witness. Following the Resurrection, the mandate Christ gave to the Twelve was that of witness. ". . . you shall be witnesses for me in Jerusalem, and in all Judea and Samaria and even to the very ends of the earth" (Acts 1, 8). That they understood him very well is proved by the repeated use that John and Paul made of the same expression of "witness" in their writings as evidence that they looked upon the role of witness as standing at the heart of Christian existence. Finally, the apostles drew attention to Jesus by the testimony of their blood, for they regarded martyrdom to be the supreme evidence of their Lord, the first martyr.

The theological roots of "witness" go deep into the Trinitarian Life, and to the very existence of God. In creation, God bore witness to himself, to his thought and to his love, because of his desire to communicate the limitless goodness that is himself. The reality of man is a witness to his maker, insofar as human nature is a created expression of the divine nature, and of the Three Persons in man's power of thought and word and love. Again, the Redemption is a witness to God, showing once more the paramount concern of the divine for the human; showing that God did not shrink from embracing the human condition to prove this concern; showing finally, that God would even die to testify that his own death to sin would break the power of death if man would recognize him as the Life.

The Church bears witness to God in that she is the prolongation of Christ; more than this, the Church is the witness of God, because she is Christ in his members. Lastly, the eucharist bears witness to all of the above, since it creates anew, announces the Redemption, gives life to the Church, and feeds the Christian; all for one purpose, to witness to the death and resurrection of Christ as salvation and everlasting life.

Christian Witness Today

What is the quality of Christian witness today, and what forms best characterize it? As might be expected, it has taken a wide variety of expression, ranging from the heroic to the safe. In lay circles (it is with the layman that we are most concerned) the reality of life commitment grows, both at home and abroad. There are those who have pledged themselves to the interests of the Church in action outside of the Church structure. These are men and women who are helping to revitalize the extra-parochial and parish apostolates. There are in average parishes the Catholic masses who, in matters of a positive Christian witness, have yet to be heard from. Finally, there are those who are on the move in different stages of decision and development. And though the Christian apostolate is as diversified and complex as life itself, it is no less true that those who are lapsed and uncommitted often present the greatest challenge to the reality of Christian witness. Among these can be found not only the poor and the racially ostracized, but victims of all kinds, whose shackles may include wealth, psuedo-intellectualism, status-seeking, and neuroticism. It is simply not possible to reach these people in depth with the saving message of the Gospel unless a far broader apostolic base is established, unless the layman is given his work and the freedom and training necessary to pursue it.

Judging from the sobering absence of significant num-

bers of lay apostles in the Church, there is also a decided confusion as to how Christian witnesses are to be
formed. This confusion is marked and widespread, plainly
visible on all levels of Church education—in the caliber
of liturgical participation and preaching, in the choice and
number of parish lay organizations, and in the quality of
apostolic training. It is possible that general embarrass-
ment would follow any inquiry on the parish level as
to what is being done to produce the authentic layman.
The history of most American parishes speaks of many
things, but particularly of a fearful dearth of motivation,
awareness, and sophistication in the kind of social experience that will move the lay Christian from apathy to interest, from inactivity to initiative. Without being aware of
it, our parishes have very often supported an apostolate
that is no apostolate at all, because it possesses so little
of the essential quality of evangelism. Without being aware
of it, we have been supporting one of the most powerful forms of social control, simply because our conception
of religion has caused a neutrality of conformism. And
we have never gauged what this might mean to our neighbor, or to one larger community.

What must be done, therefore, to realize the aim of
Christian formation, which is, as Yves de Montcheuil
calls it, the "obtaining of free acts from men"? What is
needed to convince the lay Christian, of whatever age or
condition, that he stands between God and the world as
Christ's ambassador, that his mind and heart and hands
are Christ's, and that his essential gift is himself as a
force of peace and reconciliation? What is needed to discipline the Christian mind and heart that service of
neighbor becomes a *sine qua non* of life, a central and
integrating principle? What is needed to instill in the
Christian that rare type of intelligence and love which con-
sistently attacks personal egoism, thereby making charity a
form of consciousness? To a dangerous degree, our parishes are incapable of answering these questions, either
academically or structurally. In fact, they are often not

able to diagnose why they are not centers of formation for a witness of this kind.

Witness and Growth in Christ

The question of Christian witness is, largely speaking, a question of man's growth in Christ. This crucial matter has often been neglected, or if it is dealt with at all, it is treated in an unrealistic and impractical manner. There is no point in glossing over the difficulty here. Human growth, even in the best of situations, is a painful business, and great care must be taken that the person is not overwhelmed by prospects that seem unmanageable or impossible. Growth in Christ must therefore be presented as a normal condition of life, one analogous to physical maturation. Moreover, it should be spoken of as the essential way toward a fully human life, as the necessary qualification for personal mastery, and above all, as a true sign of adulthood in Christ's Kingdom. Conversely, moral stagnation, or any sort of leveling off in one's relationship with God, should be exposed as a source of fallacy and illusion, including a crystallized ego, emotional immaturity, vulnerability to error and myth, impotence of will, social myopia, superficiality of friendship, and escapism. It is the experience of priests who are profoundly engaged with laymen that any appeal to legitimate self-interest, any presentation of the way toward true freedom, engages the lay imagination, enkindles hope of betterment, and creates an interior expansion favorable to the action of the Holy Spirit.

Perhaps two things are accomplished by this initial discussion of human consciousness as a seedbed of growth: the person gets both a taste of what he is, and a promise of what he can be. By it, the distinction between self and egoism is clarified, and soil has been prepared for an enlightened and beneficial choice.

It is quite impossible to expect the growth of man to truly human stature without reference to our Lord. For the Christian, humanity must mean Christ, both in growth and in the realization of adulthood. In the Redemption, Christ took our life to himself, and if the single task of life is responsive and loving reaction to that act, man must now put on Christ. In this view our Lord becomes the first and final definition of the human, the Holy One who creates, saves and awaits us, who would, in the process, give us new life and liberty. We must all reach out toward him through faith and love, recognize and serve him in the lives of his brothers, pass through him in death. There is no other way to the Father. His humanity, perfect and unstained, through which the Word of God has entered history and sworn himself to the human lot, would be the unifying energy in man's nature, once divided within itself, the victim of its own violent fears and divisions. As St. Augustine wrote: "We who were sundered and at enmity, by reason of our sensuality and the diverse desires and uncleanness of our sins, being cleansed by the Mediator, should set out together (with him) toward that same blessedness, and being forged together into one mind by the fire of love, are united, not in our common nature alone, but by the bond of a common love."

Christ Lived the Life of Man

In his human life he took us up, the burden of his loving kindness; he lived the common life of man, at the same time transcending our life by way of the promise of immortality, the sign of what he could make of us. He was "made like unto men . . . appearing in the form of man" (Philippians 2, 7), yet no man ever spoke as this man, no man served as he, no man died as he died. Blaise Pascal wrote of Christ: "Without possessions and having produced nothing which could be called science, he is of the order of saintliness. He made no invention; he did not reign; but he was humble, patient, saintly— saintly before God, terrible in the eyes of demons, sinless." He who was God became man; every word or act of his life spoke of his love for us. Finally, whatever else could be said of his passion and death, it came upon him because he was willing to pay the price of heroic love, willing to embrace us as we were, willing to expose himself to the attacks of a nature so at variance with itself that it had become a force of destruction, both of itself and of any man who would unmask its futility and waste.

Gethsemane was Christ's first experience in a total identification with the rebellious humanity of every age, and the confrontation would so unnerve him that he would plead for release. From it, Calvary was the summit of his self-denial, the last and most excellent example of a love that would prove his undoing by impelling him to death, the woeful and glorious moment of his final union with sinful man, who would kill him, and in turn, die to sin through the Savior's blood. The men who caused his death, then, were those he took to death with him, and they became those who rose with him. From that point on, everything in human life, whether in time or in eternity, would rest upon the reply to that question of his: "What think you of the Christ?" Perhaps the tragedy of today is not precisely that men answer wrongly to this question. It is rather that they do not know how to answer, or that they are so seldom asked.

Christ, then, was witness to God, but he was also witness to man. To emphasize a series of truisms (neglected because they are so true): He became man and universal man, because in the economy of Redemption, *he was now man*. He stood for absolute fidelity to the contract made with man, that is, with himself. For it was the hope of Christ, a hope that in his Resurrection became a reality, that when God had proved his fidelity to man, then man would see the possibility of fidelity to God. The implications for ourselves are clear. It is that Christian witness incarnates and projects the mediatorship of Christ, his obedience to his Father, and his commitment to man. Our witness must introduce into the human order the truth of Christ's present existence, his present Law, and his present Redemption in such a way that no man need feel alone, without guidance or hope. Witness means standing for Christ in the midst of human pain, perplexity, and inertia in such a way that alleviation becomes real, understanding is relished, and spiritual growth becomes imperative. The Christian witness, if he knows what he is about, is one who can preserve a healthy tension between the stature of his own person and the hesitant gropings of another, even while preserving in the other the necessary ingredient of hope. So it is that he can extend compassion without paternalism, and service without self-righteousness or didacticism.

Witness Is for the sake of Man

It would seem that honesty requires one to underscore (at the risk of protesting the obvious) that the object of witness is man. Without man and his fallen state, there would be no reason for God's present order of things, for the Incarnation, or for Christ's redemptive plan. In spite of our theoretical acceptance of this truth, we often subscribe to a persistent and paradoxical Christian heresy which takes as the point of departure a witness to God without witness to man, which attempts to live Christian truth without communicating it, which claims love of God, but fears love of man. It is a heresy which has long cloaked itself as a religious and moral system, but which is, in reality, a selfish and pragmatic ethic. Its emphasis upon worship at the expense of the works of mercy (Emmanuel Cardinal Suhard observes that this is a criterion of religious decline) is evidence that we unconsciously seek in religion a divine sanction for personal pride, a climate suitable for sentiment, a philosophy that will pad and cushion one from the demands of life, or allow us to deal with only its more palatable forms, justifying a contact with life that is peculiarly detached and contemptuous.

Such an outlook has bred a system in which the following facts stand out. The institution supersedes the person, because it offers tools for ready communication with

God, while proposing at the same time a simple, unde-
manding code to cover association with men. Principles
assume a convenient vagueness and can be promptly denied or adroitly rationalized when they do not fit personal desires. Subjectivism is regarded as invulnerable to
proof or experience, ready to be projected into the community under the force of precept, or even counsel. Rules
are central, but such a mentality will ignore their underlying spirit, for to such an outlook, issues must be kept
black or white—the browns and grays are dismissed as
nonexistent, or as conspiracies of the far left. Change
is received with apprehension and suspicion, for there
is an assumption operating that the personal world is the
best possible world—one to be kept as immovable as the
personal pattern of life. One's approach to the human
community will be unilateral to the degree that judgment
as to its course and aspirations becomes very nearly ob-
sessive, as the groping attempts of others to accept and
improve life are met with fear and castigation. God and
other men are pressed into service of the self; and life
becomes a recital of proving to others how unenlightened
they are. Finally, men committed to such a system often
espouse a religiously and politically right position which
tends to contradict the hopes of man, his human rights,
human liberty, human needs, and even on occasion, the
magisterium of the Church, the Gospels themselves. For
one's self and one's possessions must be protected at all
costs, or the agencies which protect one's self and one's
possessions must be preserved.

By way of contrast, the Christian witness will not seek
for himself the dangerous luxury of any appraisal of
Christ that Christ himself has not taught. The Gospels and
the Church speak too strongly to him for that. Nor should
his worship detract from service of neighbor—it rather
prepares him for such service. He sees Christian institutions as helpful and effective as long as they are well
used; but he is not wedded to them as absolutes which
are above evaluation and, in some cases, above replace-

ment. The Law he views as a thing of mighty importance, as indeed Christ viewed it; yet the Christian knows that unless legality has a base in love and is interpreted by love it can become a weapon to club and cripple people, instead of encouraging them and supplying guidelines for conscience. The world may challenge his values, indict his life, cause him suffering, demand from him unceasingly his time, effort, and money, but he still loves it as the matrix of his humanity, the preserve of his Church, the home where he is born into life and into God. So he will take from the world with gratitude and give to it with largess of spirit, knowing that even as he nourishes his being on its elements, he must renew it by the gift of his spirit.

Again, the labels of right or center or left will acquire meaning and command the adherence of Christians only as they meet the test of the Gospels, the mind of the Church, and the requirements of mankind. God is his Father whom he serves in other sons; history is a charge and stewardship which must be administered through dependence upon his Father and through faithful bonds with other men. The Christian witness is the man, finally, who sees his life as a redemptive fact, as a definition which God himself has made:

"That man is a Catholic (Christian) who opens himself to all and allows the universal love of the Lord to resound in his heart. He is a Catholic who, when he remembers the mercy of Christ toward him, becomes merciful, that is to say, overwhelmed with distress, whatever form that distress may take. He is a Catholic who instinctively rejects everything that is a source of division, who cannot meet anyone without tirelessly seeking out an area of agreement. He is a Catholic who sees in each man not the social category to which he belongs, not the label which is applied to him, of unbeliever or Protestant or Jew or Communist, but the brother for whom Christ died and who has been placed in his path in order to receive his love. He is a Catholic who, through humility, has made himself poor in spirit and is always ready to welcome those who are deprived, whether it be of material goods or the light of faith."*

The Formation of Christian Witness

The formation of Christian witness is a task as long as life itself, a task which implies many avenues of initiative and influence. But generally, its aim is a developed view of the historical Christ, of his unbreakable link with contemporary man as he builds up Christ's Body. The formation must begin with the awareness that within time, our Lord achieved an effect which surpasses time. Through the Church, Christ's death, resurrection, and ascension are the *fact* of every age, injected into history through Word, sacrament, and man. There are presently among us diverse epiphanies of Christ: the Word of Truth that teaches us within the Church; the birth, nourishment, and healing that He accomplishes through the sacraments; the degree of fullness or deprivation of himself that he shows us in the face of our neighbor. The first virtue must necessarily be one of faith; it must be the hard and ennobling struggle to look upon the world of Church and man as God sees it—in the all-encompassing glance which accepts the realities of human nobility and degradation, contrast and paradox. ". . . We suffer tribulation, but we are not distressed; we are sore pressed, but we are not destitute; we endure persecution, but we are not forsaken; we are cast down, but we do not perish; always bearing about in our body the dying Jesus, so that the life also of Jesus may be made manifest in our bodily frame" (2 Cor. 4, 8-10).

This faculty of active faith makes the Christian witness the indispensable leaven and benign catalyst in society. In the divine plan, it is both his role and capability to direct the hopes of mankind, mature its adolescence, and temper

* Bishop Gérard Huyghe, Bishop of Arras, Pastoral Letter, May 14, 1962.

its violence. Therefore, both his intellectual and instinctual resources will help him to perceive issues which thinking men everywhere are perceiving: the classical alternatives to the Bomb, the therapeutic and providential struggle of the Negro, the challenging and reproachful presence of the Marxist, the reforming contributions of Protestants and Orthodox. He will support, with rationality and articulate explanation, the need for international and world government; and he will be impressed with the damaging irrelevancy of nationalism. He will be pained by the inequities of wealth and poverty; he will work for a political and economic system which will place limits on the greed of the rich while eliminating the distress of the poor. He will regard responsibility of leadership as the greatest need of his community, and will toil tirelessly in the molding of others of like conviction. He will be a good citizen, but his primary allegiance will be to God and world; and when he reflects upon patriotism, it will be in these terms. Apostolate, movement, neighborhood, and job: these are the areas where he meets the world, while his prayer, effort, and suffering invigorate all men, circling the globe and penetrating every life within it.

DIALOGUE NO. 7

Why We Don't Break Bread Together

Resource Readings

Why We Don't Break Bread Together (pp. 219–255)
Wilfred F. Dewan, C.S.P.
Clement W. Welsh

Suggested Readings

Aulen, Gustaf. *Eucharist and Sacrifice.* Philadelphia: Muhlenberg Press, 1958.

Cullmann, Oscar. *Early Christian Worship.* London: S.C.M. Press, 1953.

Cullmann, Oscar and Leenhardt, F.J. *Essays on the Lord's Supper.* Richmond, Va.: John Knox Press, 1958.

Higgins, A.J.B. *The Lord's Supper in the New Testament.* New York: Henry R. Regnery Co., 1952.

Jungmann, J.A. *The Mass of the Roman Rite.* New York: Benziger, 1964.

Kilmartin, Edward. *The Sacrificial Meal of the New Covenant.* New York: Paulist Press, 1965.

Martimort, Aime G. *The Signs of the New Covenant.* Collegeville: Liturgical Press, 1963.

Nicolas, Marie-Joseph. *A New Look at the Eucharist.* New York: Paulist Press, 1964.

CHRISTIAN DIALOGUE

Why We Don't Break Bread Together

OPENING PRAYER

Leader: We thank you, Father, for the life and knowledge which you have granted us through Jesus, your Son and our brother.

All: Glory be to you for ever and ever.

Leader: We thank you, Father, for the benefits which you grant us in the ecumenical movement.

All: Glory be to you for ever and ever.

Leader: For our lack of humility and our unwillingness to learn from one another.

All: Forgive us, O Lord.

Leader: For our lack of love and failure to pray for one another.

All: Forgive us, O Lord.

Leader: For hindering the course of the Gospel by our divisions and for our lack of zeal.

All: Forgive us, O Lord.

Leader: Glory be to the Father and to the Son and to the Holy Spirit.

All: As it was in the beginning, is now and ever shall be, world without end. Amen.

BIBLE READING

That very day two of them were going to a village named Emmaus, about seven miles from Jerusalem, and talking with each other about all these things that had happened. While they were talking and discussing together, Jesus himself drew near and went with them. But their eyes were kept from recognizing him. . . .

So they drew near to the village to which they were going. He appeared to be going further, but they constrained him, saying, "Stay with us, for it is toward evening and the day is now far spent." So he went in to stay with them. When he was at table with them, he took the bread and blessed, and broke it, and gave it to them. And their eyes were opened and they recognized him; and he vanished out of their sight. They said to each other, "Did not our hearts burn within us while he talked to us on the road, while he opened to us the Scriptures?" And they rose that same hour and returned to Jerusalem; and they found the eleven gathered together and those who were with them, who said, "The Lord has risen indeed, and has appeared to Simon!" Then they told what had happened on the road, and how he was known to them in the breaking of the bread (Luke 24, 13-35).

Meditation

Lord, how often have we failed to recognize you in one another . . . . How often have our eyes remained closed at your visitations among us . . . When we do recognize you in the breaking of the bread, how distressingly are we reminded of our divided fellowship and our separation . . . . How can we invite others to join us at the Lord's Supper, that banquet of brotherhood and unity, when our daily lives proclaim our division? . . . Lord, lead us surely and swiftly to that day when all of us who proclaim you as Lord and Savior may gather in fellowship at the same table to celebrate the Lord's Supper . . . . Give us the strength and courage honestly and openly to seek the accomplishment of your will for the unity of your Church.

BIBLE READING

The cup of blessing which we bless, is it not a participation in the blood of Christ? The bread which we break, is it not a participation in the body of Christ? Because there is one bread, we who are many are one body, for we all partake of the one bread (1 Cor. 10, 16-18).

For I received from the Lord what I also delivered to you, that the Lord Jesus on the night when he was betrayed took bread, and when he had given thanks, he broke it, and said, "This is my body which is for you. Do this in remembrance of me." In the same way also the cup, after supper, saying, "This cup is the new covenant in my blood. Do this, as often as you drink it, in remembrance of me." For as often as you eat this bread and drink the cup, you proclaim the Lord's death until he comes (1 Cor. 11, 22-26).

And they devoted themselves to the apostles' teaching and fellowship, to the breaking of bread and the prayers (Acts 2, 42).

And day by day, attending the temple together and breaking bread in their homes, they partook of food with glad and generous hearts, praising God and having favor with all the people. And the Lord added to their number day by day those who were being saved (Acts 2, 46-47).

Meditation

Lord, tonight we have gathered here to share our beliefs on the Lord's Supper. . . . We grieve because your words to us in the Scriptures have come to mean many clashing things to us. . . . We pray that you will send your Spirit to open our hearts and minds to know the meaning of your words. . . . Our bread is not one; we are not one body. . . . We yearn to continue steadfastly in "the communion of the breaking of the bread and in the prayers". . . . May our common praise of you this evening—our common searching and our love one for another lead us to be of one heart and mind in all things. . . . Not until we break the one bread in unity of faith will our company grow and your name be praised with one voice. . . . Begin to lead us tonight, Lord, to the common table of brotherhood.

Christian Dialogue

Introduction

Every Christian Church has some teaching on the Lord's Supper. Some call it the Table of the Lord; others call it the Breaking of the Bread or the Eucharist or the Sacrament of the Altar. In this discussion we hope to look at our own beliefs about the Lord's Supper and to share them with each other. In this way we will shed light on our different understandings of the eucharist and the reasons for our not going together to the Lord's Table.

What Happens at the Lord's Supper?

"Men break bread together. They share wine together. They claim that as they do so the risen Christ is in their midst. This has been true ever since two men, walking along a dusty road, invited a stranger home for supper and then recognized who the stranger was. How did they know him? 'He was known to them in the breaking of the bread'. When 'he took the bread and blessed and broke it, and gave it to them . . . their eyes were opened and they recognized him'. As other men have broken bread together and shared the cup, they have found that Christ is present" (Robert McAfee Brown, *The Spirit of Protestantism*).

DISCUSSION QUESTIONS

Everyone briefly tell how your Church celebrates the Lord's Supper. Is the ceremony carried out around a table? Do the members of the congregation actually eat and drink the bread and wine? When you participate in a celebration of the Lord's Supper, what does it mean to you?

Why the Symbolism of a Meal?

To celebrate a great event such as the inauguration of a President or the retirement of a beloved school teacher, we often have a festive banquet. On Thanksgiving Day the family unites from far and wide around the dinner table. Their thanksgiving to God for his many gifts becomes at the same time a deepening and a renewal of family bonds of love and loyalty. The table has traditionally been the place of friendship and sharing. Jesus chose to mark his farewell to his apostles with a meal.

DISCUSSION QUESTIONS

Can anyone think of a particular meal or banquet that greatly impressed him? Describe it. Why did Jesus choose a meal as his farewell gathering with his disciples?

Why does a meal make all present feel closer to one another?

Why do eating the same bread and drinking from the same cup create a sense of community? When you worship do you feel you are part of a community of believers or are you more conscious of your individual relationship to Jesus?

What effect do you think this common sharing of the same bread should have on our daily life with one another?

What Do the Scriptures Tell Us about the Lord's Supper?

Read again: Luke 22, 1-23 and John 6, 22-65. Maybe someone would like to read one of these passages to the group.

DISCUSSION QUESTIONS

What did this meal which Jesus and his friends ate mean to the Jewish people? What do you think Jesus meant when he said, "This is My Body"? How do you think the Apostles understood him?

Did the Apostles have any idea what was going to happen to Jesus on the following day? Do you think he might have chosen the actions of this meal to help them understand what was going to happen?

Word and Sacrament

Roman Catholics center their worship around the Mass or re-presentation of the Lord's Supper, wherein they recall the great things God has done for his people, especially in sending his Son to be their salvation. Other Christians maintain that Christian worship is primarily a proclamation of the Word of God found in the Scriptures. When the Scriptures are expounded to the Christian people, Christ becomes present in a special way to them. Today in all the Churches there is a new appreciation of the significance and close relationship of both these aspects of Christian worship. The Roman Catholic liturgical reforms have laid great stress on the restoration of the Liturgy of the Word; and Protestant liturgists call for more frequent celebration of the eucharist.

DISCUSSION QUESTIONS

How do you think the hearing of the Word of God in the Scriptures relates to the receiving of the Word of God at the Lord's Supper?

What do you think about a Protestant service that does not end in a celebration of the Lord's Supper? What do you think of a Catholic Mass where the Liturgy of the Word is hastily proclaimed and no sermon or homily is given?

How can the sermon be a bridge between the liturgy of the Word and the Lord's Supper?

The Manner of Presence of Jesus in the Lord's Supper

In a report following the meeting of the Faith and Order Conference of the World Council of Churches at Lund, Sweden in 1952, the delegates said that the main question about the eucharist is the real bodily presence of the crucified and risen Lord and our receiving of his body and blood.

DISCUSSION QUESTIONS

Is Jesus present in the Lord's Supper? How do you think he is present? Do you think it is not necessary to say how he is present? Should we be content to call his presence mysterious?

Why do you think the Catholic Church has insisted upon the doctrine of transubstantiation? Why have other Churches denied it?

The Lord's Supper and the Death of Jesus

St. Paul says, "For as often as you eat this bread and drink the cup, you proclaim the Lord's death until he comes" (1 Cor. 11, 26). St. Paul sees the Lord's Supper as a proclaiming of the death of Jesus whereby we are saved. The offering of the bread and wine to God our Father during the Lord's Supper is seen by some Christians as a sign of Jesus' offering of himself to his Father on the cross. They view their participation in the Lord's Supper by eating the bread and drinking the wine as a sign of their participation in the saving grace of Jesus, our Brother.

DISCUSSION QUESTIONS

Do you think the Lord's Supper is a "sacrificial meal"? What are your reasons for this answer? Was there need for sacrifice on the part of Jesus? Does St. Paul see any relationship between the Lord's Supper and the death of Jesus? Why do we proclaim it?

The Lord's Supper and Christian Unity

"The eucharist is and must be the sacrament of unity. Yet the variety and exclusivity of communion services have made it an apparent sign of division among Christians, no longer united as were the first Christians 'in the fellowship of the breaking of the bread' (Acts 2, 42).

DISCUSSION QUESTIONS

Why is the eucharist called the Sacrament of Unity? Do you think the present situation in which so many Churches celebrate the Lord's Supper, while excluding other Christians, is a scandal? Is a common celebration of the Lord's Supper immediately the answer? Why?

CLOSING PRAYER

O Christ our God, who at all times and in every hour, in heaven and on earth, are worshipped and glorified, who are long-suffering, merciful and compassionate, who love the just and show mercy upon the sinner, who call all to salvation through the promise of blessings to come: O Lord, receive our supplications and direct our lives according to your commandments. Sanctify our souls, hallow our bodies, correct our thoughts, cleanse our minds, deliver us from all tribulation, evil and distress. Encompass us with your holy angels, that guided and guarded by them, we may attain to the unity of the faith and to the knowledge of your unapproachable glory, for you are blessed until the end of time. Amen.

Why We Don't Break Bread Together

Wilfred F. Dewan, C.S.P.
Clement W. Welsh

Nearly all Christians consider the Lord's Supper as the very heart of worship. The bread and wine are the sacramental signs through which Christ and his saving grace are offered to us in the most striking way. Yet is is a shocking fact that Christians have been terribly divided over the meaning of this central reality. What should be the great means and expression of their unity has become divisive.

This treatment will attempt (I) a brief biblical background, (II) an outline history of the eucharist, pointing out where and why division crept in, and (III) present trends of eucharistic thought among Christians. We wish neither to gloss over true differences, nor to perpetuate confessional rigidity if it is no longer demanded. It is hoped that the historical perspective will serve to create more understanding of individual beliefs.

Lord's Supper, Table of the Lord, Breaking of the Bread, Sacrament of the Altar, Blessed Sacrament, Eucharist, Mass, Holy Communion—all are ancient and honored terms. Eucharist comes from the Greek, meaning thanksgiving, because Christ our Lord offered a prayer of thanksgiving and blessing over the bread and wine at the Last Supper. The Christian sacrament of the Lord's Supper is obviously a continuation of the Last Supper which Christ had with his apostles. It is therefore a sacred meal somehow involving Christ's presence and has a vital connection with his sacrifice.

I.   BIBLICAL BACKGROUND

Some acquaintance with the scriptural evidence of the Lord's Supper is absolutely necessary in order to discuss it intelligently. To begin with, three Old Testament events are brought to fulfillment by Christ:

OLD TESTAMENT

(1) *The First Passover* (Read Chapter 12 of Exodus). God prepares the final blow to make the Egyptians release the enslaved Israelites. Every firstborn is to be slain. The Jews are told to sacrifice a lamb, sprinkle its blood on the doorpost, and consume the lamb. By doing so, they are saved and the Egyptians are punished, while the Lord "passes over" the Israelite homes (Passover). Their salvation has begun.

The first Christians were quick to see the final acts of Jesus as fulfillment of the paschal lamb theme. The Christian era is begun when Jesus, "the lamb of God" (John 1, 29) is slain, when "Christ, our paschal lamb, has been sacrificed" (1 Cor. 5, 7).

(2) *The manna.* During the years in the desert food was scarce. Said God, "I will now rain down bread from heaven for you", and a breadlike substance was divinely given to nourish the pilgrim Israelites. (See how) Jesus later perfects this by giving his flesh as the true bread from heaven, bread which will give eternal life to the Christian pilgrim (John 6, 48-52).

(3) *The blood of the covenant.* The culmination of the first great saving events was God's agreement with the Israelite people ("I will be your God, and you will be my people") at Mount Sinai. It was ratified by a sacrifice of blood, a most solemn manner of sealing a pact. (cf. Exodus 24). At the Last Supper Jesus perfects this by the ratification of the new Christian dispensation: "This is my blood of the new covenant" (Matt. 26, 28). And the author of Hebrews vividly points out how much more worthwhile is the blood of Christ than that of goats and bulls (Matt. 9, 11-15).

The first Passover was not only the inauguration of this one great saving event, culminating at Sinai, but also the sacred meal and ritual by which all later generations were to enter into this great act of God. The yearly paschal sacrifice had a threefold significance: to make real and actual the event of the past—making it possible for each to be drawn into the great saving act of Yahweh; here and now, to bring about deeper union with God and with the other members of the People of God; and it was a promise of the future messianic banquet, symbol of the final and glorious messianic era.

NEW TESTAMENT

The New Testament emphasis on the Lord's Supper is most impressive, as Christ brings to perfection the things foreshadowed in the Old. All Christians agree that we are saved by the passion, death and resurrection of Jesus—and that the Last Supper and every eucharistic meal must be treated with this in mind. In no way can we pretend that the Lord's Supper repeats or fills up the once-for-all sacrifice of our Savior.

The Institution

It is at a Passover meal that Jesus begins his passion, begins the definitive saving events that end in his death and resurrection. At the start of the meal the head of the family takes bread, blesses, breaks and shares with all. At the end, the principal blessing is given over a cup of wine, which is passed to all. We believe that Christ used these two ceremonies, which framed the actual eating of the Paschal lamb, to institute the eucharist.

And he took bread, and when he had given thanks he broke it and gave it to them, saying, "This is my body which is given for you. Do this in remembrance of me". And likewise the cup after supper, saying, "This cup which is poured out for you is the new covenant in my blood" (Luke 22, 19-20).

Like the first Passover meal, then, the Last Supper was an explanation-in-advance of the saving works about

to happen. Indeed, this was the solemn beginning of the
passion. Christ offers himself to the Father in heaven
under the form of bread and wine in a way unmistakably
connected to his sacrificial death. (The exact relationship
of the supper to the sacrifice is very mysterious, and
theology has no one absolute answer.) But as long as we
insist upon the close connection of the Last Supper with
the sacrifice of Jesus, then the apostles are already entering into the saving grace of Christ when they receive the
eucharistic food. And so at this sacred meal, Jesus has not
only initiated his final act of total self-giving to the Father,
and made clear what it leads to (sacrificial death), but he
has also graciously given to us the sacred act which will
be our memorial of his sacrifice ("Do this . . . ."), the
sacred meal by which we can partake of the saving
victim and his grace.

The First Christian Eucharistic Meals

These are recorded by St. Paul. The Christians were
surely aware they were receiving the true body and blood
of Jesus. "The cup of blessing which we bless, is it not
a participation in the blood of Christ? The bread which
we break, is it not a participation in the body of Christ?"
(1 Cor. 10, 16). Only this belief could justify the severity
of Paul's warning, "Whoever, therefore, eats the bread
or drinks the cup of the Lord in an unworthy manner will
be guilty of profaning the body and blood of the Lord"
(1 Cor. 11, 27).

The sacrificial aspect of the eucharistic meal is made
clear when Paul compares the Christian sacrificial meal to
those of the Jews and pagans. Both Jew and pagan offered real sacrificial victims and then ate of the sacrificial
food, believing that they were thereby united to divinity.
The Christian, says Paul, must not participate in these
other sacrifices because he already has the one true and
acceptable sacrifice, that of Christ himself. Through the
consecrated bread and wine he can partake of the victim
sacrificed once-for-all, Christ the new Pasch (1 Cor. 10,
14-21).

Chapter Six of St. John's Gospel

The sixth chapter of St. John's Gospel cannot be over-looked in any discussion of the eucharist. Written about 90 A.D., its realism is aimed at refuting the Docetists, who denied the reality of Christ's human body. After the miracle of feeding 5,000 with a few loaves and fishes, Jesus is besieged by the crowd seeking more wonders. He promises them not the ancient manna which perishes, but the new manna—himself. Verses 35-47 point out how we must partake of this life-giving food of Christ and his doctrines by living and personal faith. "Truly, truly, I say to you, he who believes has eternal life" (John 6, 47).

But Jesus then speaks of another way of obtaining divine life. Verses 50-60 identify the new bread from heaven with Christ's very flesh and blood: "I am the bread of life. Your fathers ate the manna in the wilderness, and they died. This is the bread which comes down from heaven, that a man may eat of it and not die. I am the living bread which came down from heaven; if any one eats of this bread, he will live for ever; and the bread which I shall give for the life of the world is my flesh" (John 6, 48-51).

The text is clearly one about sacrifice. The Jews were shocked at the idea of human sacrifice and by the further demand to drink his blood, consuming of blood having been especially forbidden (Lev. 3, 17). But Jesus took nothing back; in fact he repeated the same doctrine several times again (John 6, 54-60).

Those Christians who tend to hold the symbolic or dynamic presence of Jesus in the eucharist maintain that this section of St. John does not add anything to the earlier—the whole thing can be interpreted in terms of the doctrine and person of Christ accepted in faith—verse 63 indicating exactly this, when it says: "It is the spirit that gives life, the flesh is of no avail; the words that I have spoken to you are spirit and life."

Those who hold the true bodily presence of Christ in

the eucharist say that Jesus was in no way attenuating his strong words just spoken. Thus verse 62 implies that when they see Jesus' glorious ascension into heaven with his visible body, they would realize that the eucharist meal would not be a cannibalistic eating. Verse 63, on the other hand, points up the necessity of faith; mere outward and carnal partaking of the body and blood must not be seen as a magical rite or mere physical act. There must also be true internal and spiritual communion, according to the spirit of faith already stressed in verses 35-47.

II.   HISTORICAL APPRECIATION

Testimony of Early Writers

Anyone studying the meaning of the Lord's Supper cannot ignore how it was understood by the early Church as expressed through its writers. The aspects of the sacred meal, memorial of Christ's death and resurrection, sacrament, and sacrifice are all present. Without commenting on the exact meaning of each author, the following is a sample. "On the Lord's own day (Sunday), assemble in common to break bread and offer thanks; but first confess your sins, so that your sacrifice may be pure" (Didache, ca. 75-100). St. Ignatius of Antioch criticized those who "hold aloof from the eucharist and prayer because they do not believe that the eucharist is the flesh of our Savior, Jesus Christ" (Letter to the Smyrneans, ca. 110). Justin Martyr explained to Emperor Pius the Christian belief in the eucharist: the Christians receive the bread and wine not as common bread and common drink but as "the food over which thanksgiving has been made by the utterance in prayer of his Word, and which nourishes our flesh and blood by assimilation in the flesh and blood of that Jesus who was made flesh" (Apology, ca. 150). St. Cyril of Jerusalem's realism is typical: "He [Christ] once changed water into wine . . . Shall we not therefore believe when he changes wine into blood? We consume these with perfect certainty that they are the body and blood of

Christ, since under the appearance of the wine" (*Mystagogical Catechesis,* ca. 348). Many, such as Justin Martyr see the Lord's Supper as the pure and pleasing sacrifice which God foretold would be offered daily to his name (Malachy 1, 10-12). Great saints such as Chrysostom and Augustine insisted upon the sacrificial nature of the daily eucharistic celebration; they saw it as the means by which the Church could enter into the one sacrifice of Christ.

Catholics and Orthodox have always held firmly to the sacrificial nature of the eucharist because of the scriptural indications, supported by long-standing belief of the early Church. Perhaps it was because of exaggerations arising in the Middle Ages, that the Reformers reacted so strongly, stressing exclusively the words of Hebrews 10, 12. 14: "But when Christ had offered for all time a single sacrifice for sin, he sat down at the right hand of God. . . . By a single offering he has perfected for all time those who are sanctified." After all, the Reformers said, didn't Justin Martyr go on to insist "that prayers and thanksgiving offered by worthy persons are the only perfect and acceptable sacrifice to God"? (Dialogue with Trypho). As we shall see, the ecumenical movement, and contemporary study of Scripture and the Fathers is bringing about more agreement and more balanced expressions regarding the sacrificial aspect of the Lord's Supper.

Brief History of Eucharistic Service

A more balanced and sympathetic view can be had on all sides by even a cursory understanding of how the Lord's Supper was celebrated, first in the early Church, then in the pre-Reformation days.

In the early Church there were originally two parts to the public worship. The first was held on Sunday morning, and centered upon reading from the Old and New Testaments, with prayers and homily. The other part was the eucharistic worship, seen as a re-presentation of the Lord's Supper, and celebrated in conjunction with a sacred fellowship meal on Sunday evening. The local bishop presided as head of the community around an altar-table. At first the service was very simple: the words of institution and a few other prayers. Before long an offertory was added, during which the gifts were brought to the altar.

At the start of the 3rd century the two services of the Word and of the Sacrament were joined into one—usually on Sunday morning. (Due to abuses [cf. 1 Cor. 11, 20-34] the accompanying meal was discontinued. What remained was only the sacred meal consisting of the consecrated elements.) The bishop presided, the deacon read the lessons, and all responded. Then after the scriptural part came the properly eucharistic section at the altar-table. It was quite a simple form of *offering* of the gifts, *thanksgiving* (*i.e.,* consecration, using the words of institution), *communion,* and *dismissal.* The mother tongue of the people was used (whether Greek, Latin, Syriac, etc.). All was said aloud, and everyone present had a role. There was a true sense of unity and family spirit. It was taken for granted that the participants would receive communion. There gradually emerged a standardization of the texts and rubrics, but generally all in the best sense.

Problems Created by the Conditions of the Middle Ages.

Between the ideal of the early centuries and the deplorable conditions of eucharistic practice in the 15th century, what happened? Without taking strongly partisan views, the following may help to understand what happened. (Anglican specialist Gregory Dix admits that it was almost inevitably brought about by circumstances.) During the barbarian invasions destroying much of the civilization of Europe, the monasteries became islands of culture and education. When the reconquests started, the missionaries made Latin the uniform language of worship. A few of the most intelligent converts were formed into choirs and trained to answer. For the others the Mass became something to see and hear, rather than take part in. The clergy gradually took over all the prayers that other parts of the congregation had formerly contributed. Indeed, the Mass was often looked upon as a miracle play, a sacred pageant somehow reenacting the passion of Christ (each move of the priest symbolic of various steps of the passion).

Again, too many "extras" tended to obscure the sacred meal aspect. As bric-a-brac piled up on the altar (relics, expensive candlesticks, ornaments) the altar-table lost its table quality, and in fact the priest could no longer be seen easily across all the decorations. So the altar was turned around. Unfortunately this left the priest with his back to the people, reducing their sense of participation still further.

Added to this a new emphasis on sacred mystery and the value of silence during the more solemn parts came to be extolled. The people tended to fill the silences with their own private prayers and devotions. So much was the "mystery" element predominant in some places, it was thought better almost to shut off the altar and choir sections from the rest of the church by means of rood screens and enclosures. This only added to the view that one need only be physically present during this rite (particularly when the consecrated bread and chalice were held up for all to see) in order somehow to benefit. This, in turn, tended to obscure the true meaning of sacramental efficacy, and all too often resulted in the notion of the Mass as an occasion of the automatic dispensing of grace.

Again, there arose in the Middle Ages a great devotion to the humanity of Christ, and the physical aspects of his passion and death. And even though good theologians knew the risen Christ could no longer be injured, the realistic presentations of the sacrificial aspects of the Mass seemed to assert the presence of the dying Christ, and some kind of new immolation or equivalent death in each Mass. And, without denying the central and all-important quality of Christ's sacrifice on Calvary, each sacrifice of the Mass had its own value. Hence the understandable desire to multiply Masses—particularly in order to help the souls in purgatory. This practice was inevitably not without abuses connected with money.

But probably the most tragic loss was that people no longer received Holy Communion. The Lord's Supper was not seen as a sacred meal in which all were to participate. Conditions became so bad that the Church had to establish a law, during the 13th century, requiring Communion at least once a year! Suspension of Communion to the people under the form of wine (just now being re-introduced by Roman Catholics) only made it all the harder to appreciate the banquet involved in the eucharistic service.

Reactions of the Reformers

Nothing in the basic Church doctrine of the eucharist as sacrament of the Lord's Supper, as real and sacrificial presence, had changed. But the new conditions left much room for criticism and reform. Unfortunately the reaction was sometimes extreme in the other direction: tending to obscure certain elements of basic Christian Tradition. But then, doesn't violent debate always produce one-sided views? As we will see, both Roman Catholic and Protestant debaters adopted unnecessarily (though understandably) rigid viewpoints.

The Reformers reacted strongly against abuses of the sacraments as well as external practices such as indulgences and the rosary. They feared that Roman Catholics were trying to imprison God in external formulas and rites, making the sacraments into levers to force God to give grace. Actually, when Catholics say that the sacraments act by themselves (*ex opere operato*), it really means that they owe nothing to us men; they remain the Word and action of God in Christ. So it is not magic at all, or a trick to compel God. (Unfortunately, Catholic *practice* sometimes creates difficulty—expectation of quasi-automatic additions of holiness by frequent communion, evidence of a sort of *quid pro quo* with God.)

Luther's Teaching

Luther's *Small Catechism* gives us the following summary: the sacrament of the altar "is the true Body and Blood of our Lord Jesus Christ, under the bread and wine, given to us Christians to eat and drink, as it was instituted by Christ himself"; communion brings about the remission of sins, life and salvation; these effects are produced by the words "given and shed for you for the remission of sins," for besides the bodily eating and drinking, these words are the chief thing in the sacrament. He who believes them has what they say and declare, namely the remission of sins.

Unlike some of the other Reformers, Luther held firmly to the true bodily presence of Jesus in the eucharist, as did the Roman Catholic Church. But he strongly objected to the doctrine of transubstantiation: namely that the very substance (inner reality) of bread and wine are *changed into* the substance of the body and blood of Christ. He held that this explanation destroyed the nature of the sacrament in that it involved the destruction of the reality of the bread and wine. Luther held to a doctrine of consubstantiation, namely that Christ is present *along with* the reality of the bread and wine.

Actually, Luther objected to saying (as Zwingli did) that Christ's risen body is in one place, namely, in heaven. Rather, because of its glorification it partakes of the omnipresence (ubiquity) of God himself; it is therefore independent of space and time. But through the words of institution Christ wills to connect his presence in a very special way with the bread and wine.

Martin Luther's great contributions were (1) his insistence on the importance of Scripture, thus bringing into prominence again the liturgy of the Word. He restressed St. Augustine's idea that the sacrament is a "visible word", a mysterious event in which the Word touches us directly, not only to enlighten, but also to act within us, and change us; and (2) his desire that all should receive communion at the eucharistic service each Sunday, a practice that had fallen upon bad times.

Some of the Reformers thought that Luther had not

gone far enough. *Ulrich Zwingli* was one such. He denied any kind of presence of Jesus in the eucharist. The bread and wine were but symbols and signs to remind us what Christ had done. He thought Luther too much concerned with the individual gift of Christ to each communicant. Rather, it was precisely in the eucharist that the People of God should become conscious of its spiritual oneness. The celebration of the Lord's Supper is a feast of the whole Church community gathered together in common faith in the resurrection of him who was dead, but is now living forever. This communal note was completely in line with the best understanding of the early Church, which saw the eucharist as the common worship of the faithful and the bond of unity, as well as the gift of Christ to us individually.

Still another view of the eucharistic presence of Christ was held by *John Calvin* at Geneva—a position between that of Luther and Zwingli. He thought that Catholics and Luther (real, substantial presence) demanded too much, and Zwingli (symbolic presence only) demanded too little. Calvin taught that Jesus is present according to power or dynamism. So even though there is no bodily presence of Christ in the eucharist, when the believer receives, his mind is lifted up to heaven by Christ, and Christ gives himself in a sort of psychological presence to the communicant. Christ can be called spiritually present in the Lord's Supper.

There was much disagreement then among the Reformers about the presence of Christ in the eucharist. But in their rejection of the Lord's Supper as a sacrifice, they were unanimous. All too frequently in the Middle Ages it seemed as if the Mass were regarded as a sacrifice distinct from Calvary and even completing it in some way. Biblical insistence on the once-for-all character of Christ's sacrifice led the Reformers to an almost instinctive denial (or what has been interpreted as denial) of any sacrificial element in the eucharist. (Today the question is being asked whether they were rejecting merely the kind of sacrificial explanations prevalent at the time.)

In England, the Catholic and Reformation influences alternated, but the net effect was to retain a Catholic theory of the eucharist, while explicitly rejecting transubstantiation as describing the method by which the elements of bread and wine are changed into the body and blood.

Reaction of the Council of Trent

The Catholic Church was well aware of the need for reform in many areas, not the least being certain eucharistic practices. But as regards doctrine, the Council of Trent in 1551-52 felt it necessary to restate in detail the Church's teaching on the Mass:

1. After the bread and wine are consecrated, Christ is really, truly and substantially present under the appearances of bread and wine. He is totally present— body, blood, soul and divinity—under each element. Without leaving heaven, he becomes present mysteriously in many places by sacramental presence. This change of the substance of bread and wine into the substance of the body and blood of Christ is most fittingly called transubstantiation by the Church.
2. This sacrament, instituted at the Last Supper, was meant to proclaim his death until the end of the world, to be spiritual food and remedy for sin, to be a pledge of future happiness and glory of heaven, and to be the symbol of unity between Christ and his Church.
3. Because the total Christ is present, the sacred elements are to be adored, and it is proper to have reservation of the blessed sacrament.
4. All are urged to receive communion worthily and frequently. Serious sins must be confessed before reception.
5. The eucharist is also a sacrifice. It is true that Christ offered himself once and for all by his death on the

altar of the cross to God the Father, to accomplish everlasting redemption. But at the Last Supper he left to his Church a visible sacrifice—as the nature of man demands. It is to re-present the bloody sacrifice accomplished once for all on the cross. It is the fulfillment of the prophecy of Malachy 11, 1 and what Paul has in mind in 1 Cor. 10, 21.

6. The Mass is the same sacrifice as Calvary—since both victim and offerer are the same (though Christ now offers through the visible ministry of priests). Only the manner differs: there is no shedding of blood now. This sacrifice of the Church is truly pleasing to God; the benefits of Calvary are received in and through the eucharistic sacrifice, whereby men obtain mercy and grace. But in no way does the eucharistic sacrifice detract from the sacrifice of Calvary.

The sides were now drawn, and bitter controversy caused still further rigidity. For example, Catholic theologians in the century following the Council of Trent spent all kinds of time and devised all sorts of theories of the Mass to prove as vividly as possible just why the Mass *must* be called a sacrifice. Each tried to show how there was some kind of immolation or destruction present, and therefore that each Mass was sacrificial—though indeed always subordinated and relative to the one absolute sacrifice of Calvary. Suarez thought that since Christ by his presence in the host was reduced to the lowly status of food and drink, this was equivalent to death, and could be called sacrifice. Bellarmine pointed to the "destruction" of the eucharistic elements in Communion, another to the twofold words of consecration as a sort of "mystical sword". The more each Mass was viewed as another sacrifice (numerically different, though substantially the same, they insisted), the more each seemed to have an individual worth. Private Masses (with only a server) were not only legitimate but good, and the necessary community worship aspect was not stressed enough.

Furthermore, the theology of transubstantiation became more and more refined, again with various theories attempting to explain the "how" of this mystery, insofar as the human mind can follow it. Study of the exact mode and condition of Christ in his continuing presence in the consecrated host was no doubt a result of the firm belief in his real presence there even after Mass was over. Many today think that Catholics have overemphasized this aspect of a perpetual presence of Christ to be adored, whereas Christ meant the Lord's Supper to be a worshipful event we enter into, food to be received.

Three Centuries of Division

The shameful divisions of Christianity over the past centuries only worsened the initial divisions. Hesitation of Roman Catholics to use the vernacular, to allow more participation by the laity, to develop a good theology of the lay priesthood, to stress the aspect of sacred meal, to stress the role of Scripture and the homily—all these hesitations were at least to some extent due to (unconscious?) fear that any concession would look like a victory for "the enemy".

On the Protestant side, similar exaggerations. Stress on the role of Scripture tended to push aside the Lord's Supper, until in many Churches it was rarely celebrated, perhaps only three or four times a year. Followers of Luther and Calvin forgot that their leaders wanted the Lord's Supper celebrated every Sunday, and wished for all to receive communion. John Wesley, founder of the Methodists in 1740, was a firm believer in the real presence of Christ in the eucharist, and he saw it as a means of grace and spiritual nourishment. He celebrated or received daily whenever possible. Yet modern Methodists have largely forgotten his teaching in regard to the Lord's Supper (only recently beginning to regain an appreciation of the eucharistic liturgy). Anglicans and Lutherans, it is true, have always acknowledged a certain sanctifying power of the sacrament itself. But many Protestants sense a danger of magic in everything sacramental, and some have tended to de-materialize Christianity, doing away with external rites and intermediaries, until sometimes there is no outward worship left. Quakers are a good example of this tendency.

Christ said we must worship "in spirit and in truth". Too many Christians took this to mean worship without formulas, aids and external manifestation. But actually the Hebrew mentality (that of the New Testament) always regarded the spiritual-material combination in man's makeup as necessary, natural and good. What Christ was asking for was a religion which comes from the heart, where the Spirit of God dominates our entire being and all its expression, and opens us to the fullness of truth. In any case, the Protestant trend has been to let the spoken word, whether Scriptures or the pulpit, overshadow the eucharistic table. "Following the service, we will conduct the Lord's Supper. All who can, please stay," used to be a quite frequent announcement.

III. THE SITUATION TODAY:
TRENDS OF EUCHARISTIC THOUGHT

Rather suddenly there is reason for hope. Instead of remaining entrenched in interconfessional polemic, the Christian Churches today are courageously reappraising their doctrines and practices in the light of Scripture and Tradition. There has been great ecumenical progress on the central doctrine of the eucharist. Several things have contributed: (1) a strong liturgical renaissance in many Christian Churches: particularly Lutheran, Anglican, Reformed and Roman Catholic; (2) modern biblical study, which emphasizes the extreme importance of eucharistic worship in the early Church. The ancient Church is seen as a worshipping fellowship and the Lord's Supper is both the means of creating this fellowship and an expression of its present reality. It is the highest actuation of the Church—the Body of Christ; (3) the ecumenical movement accentuates the Lord's Supper in two respects: at every ecumenical gathering, it stands as a witness to the unity which ought to find visible expression, but also as accuser against the schisms still existing. Despite all disagreements (and we must not minimize them), all agree that holy communion is the sacrament of Christian fellowship and unity. Any ecumenical conversations must soon focus on the eucharist.

On the point of the real presence of Christ under the bread and wine, there has been little change from the traditional positions. So far the ecumenical discussions have steered clear of this. But below the surface lie the same tensions and differences.

A second point is equally knotty, namely, the question of ministry. Catholics and Orthodox and Anglicans hold the episcopal ministry and priesthood to be necessary in the Church so that without it, however sincere other Christians are and however similar their services may be, there remains an essential difference. Catholics must even affirm that full sacramental presence of Christ cannot take place except through the ordained priesthood.

We shall also be discussing areas where considerable progress has been made: appreciation of the relation of Word and Sacrament, new emphasis on the Lord's Supper as sacred and family meal, the possibilities and problems of intercommunion, and last but most importantly much progress in the understanding of the Lord's Supper as sacrifice. (This is possible because Roman Catholic theologians have begun to emphasize much more acceptable explanations of the Mass, and because Protestants are beginning to see that the idea of sacrifice belongs more authentically to Christian Tradition than the Reformers were willing to admit.) Under each heading will be some attempt to classify varying doctrines, but detailing the specific belief of every Church separately would be too space-consuming.

Relation of the Word of God to the Sacrament of the Lord's Supper

Protestants have tended to a one-sided stress on the

presence and action of God in the Word; Roman Catholics and Orthodox (and to some extent Anglicans) to a one-sided stress on the presence of Christ and his action in the sacraments—particularly the eucharist. Both views are necessary, and there has been a great deal of reconciliation.

Most basically we can all see that God acts upon the world through his Word—which is creative and powerful. His redemptive Word first came to us encased in human language and in recognizable events (prophetic words, events like the exodus). But most of all the Word became flesh in Jesus Christ. Here the Word of God is both the total person of Christ, and the gospel message he left. Since his death and resurrection, the risen Christ —still the saving Word of God—lives and acts invisibly in the total Church. Here the Word of God takes perceptible form in the Scriptures and preaching of the Church, and visible shape in the sacraments, particularly in the sacrament of the Lord's Supper.

Nearly all Protestants today, then, acknowledge (or are beginning to acknowledge) the central importance of the Lord's Supper; that the integrity of worship demands that we say "scripture, sermon *and sacrament*".

Roman Catholics are now aware that they cannot play down the "liturgy of the Word". The Word of God is all important, and this Word when spoken by the Church is very important. It is one basic way of God's self-communication to us, demanding our response in faith and love. There are other all-important moments when God's self-giving to the believer is actualized (occurs), namely in the sacraments. And the place where the Church is most herself, most Christ living and acting in the world today, is the celebration of the eucharist.

All Christians rejoice at the emphasis the Second Vatican Council has put on Scripture and preaching. The whole first part of the Mass is now called "The Liturgy of the Word", and insists that the faithful must be well instructed so that they can intelligently participate in the Church's worship.

The Lord's Supper as a Sacred Family Meal

From the earliest days of Christianity, the eucharist was clearly regarded as a sacred and family meal, which proclaimed and deepened the union of the whole community in Christ. Roman Catholics have done a lot in their services recently to re-stress this simple meal-structure of the Mass. And they have done even more in their theological literature. Altars again look like tables, and the celebrant does not come to the altar-table until the sacred meal is about to be offered—after the liturgy of the Word. Again, the priest now faces the congregation. All present are urged to participate both in the offering (each putting in his own communion bread at times, members of the group bringing up the bread and wine), in the prayers, and in the actual communion. Communion under both forms of food and drink (as is normal in a meal) has been re-instated for solemn occasions, (many feeling it should always be this way). The new liturgy puts strong emphasis on the family spirit. Many priests feel that it is more important to be part of the visible community worship—especially by concelebration, which is a new feature of the regular liturgy—than by celebration of a so-called "private" Mass.

Similar new emphases are evident in Protestantism. The meal structure was always there, but is now being seen as more important. It should be the normal climax of worship. And family participation is urged.

Most Christians use wheaten bread and grape wine for the Lord's Supper (Roman Catholic, Anglican and Orthodox law insists on these for validity. Wouldn't rice bread do, and some other kind of wine? Does Christ really care about tiny details? Many a Catholic theologian now hesitates to answer—one more example of how old-time legal rigidity is being softened by a re-examination of what Christ did and meant). Some Christian Churches allow either wine or grape juice (*e.g.,* Disciples of Christ); still others insist on grape juice always (Methodists).

Some Have No Lord's Supper

There are some relatively small groups of Christians who do not see the necessity of the Lord's Supper. One is the Quakers (Society of Friends) whose only commitment is to the "Light of Christ" given to the individual soul. They have no outward forms of worship, not even baptism or communion; but they would say: "We believe in the inward experiences these things symbolize". Another well-known group in this category is the Salvation Army (Salvationists). They think the eucharistic practices of Christ and the early Church were carry-overs from Jewish religion, and so not necessary. Will growing understanding about the central place of the Lord's Supper in Christianity bring about changes for these communities? (From now on, we'll be talking only about Christian Churches which admit some form of the Lord's Supper, whatever be the name given to it.)

Is Christ Present in the Bread and Wine of the Lord's Supper?

This is a basic question which always comes up in discussions about the Lord's Supper. The answers vary tremendously: all the way from purely symbolic presence to real, substantial presence of the risen Jesus. Too often the answer is couched in terms that show an attempt to pinpoint one's exact doctrinal position in the face of "erroneous positions", in terms which themselves seem to be misunderstood by others.

Unitarians demand the least here. For them Christ is not divine, and communion is wholly symbolic, a reminder to follow Christ's example. Sometimes the bread and wine are not even given to each, but those present are asked "to partake in spirit", and "eat in remembrance of Christ". Disciples of Christ see the Lord's Supper as sacrament in the sense of a memorial in which Christ is truly present in his saving power but not bodily present in the bread and wine. For Seventh-

Day Adventists the Lord's Supper symbolizes Christ's broken body and spilled blood. Baptists, also, take it in the sense of an external sign, "symbols of the body and blood of Christ partaken of by the members of the Church, in commemoration of the sufferings and death of their Lord".

These Christians hold pretty much the doctrine of Zwingli in Reformation times. So for them there is no real (*i.e.,* bodily) presence of Christ. The words of institution said over the elements bring about no change. The ceremony is more a fraternal religious meal in which one recalls Christ's supreme giving of himself for us. This can serve to stir up faith, and it is through faith that God acts upon us.

A second category of Christian Churches seems to hold a little more—something like the doctrine of John Calvin. Here Christ becomes present in a real way—a real spiritual presence, however. It is as if the spirit and dynamism of the Risen Christ become present to the consecrated elements. No change takes place at the words of consecration, but a real change takes place in the recipient who receives them with a spirit of faith.

Methodists, for example, deny the real substantial presence of the body and blood of Christ, but think of Christ as present "after a heavenly and spiritual manner" which can only be received and eaten by faith. Thus, they come very close to the last classification, and their idea of eucharistic presence of Jesus is mainly subjective, *i.e.,* no presence of Christ independently of the faith of the communicant.

Congregationalists would be pretty much the same. The change from bread and wine to the Lord's body consists "not in a physical change in the material properties of the elements on the altar, but in a moral and spiritual change in the ethical and religious nature of the worshippers assembled before it". With Calvin, they would say that the words of institution do not demand corporeal presence of Jesus. Presbyterians would generally have the same Calvinistic understanding.

Still others are somewhat more realistic-minded. The Evangelical and Reformed Church (now part of the United Church of Christ) tries to combine Calvinist belief that the recipient receives not only bread and wine, but also the spiritual presence of the Lord, with the evangelical (more Lutheran) understanding that one receives the true body and blood of Jesus Christ as nourishment of our new life.

In Canada the newly proposed union of Anglican and United Church of Canada (which will include nearly all non-Catholic Christians) agrees that in the eucharist the faithful receive and partake "spiritually" of the body and blood of Christ.

The third classification includes the Lutherans, Anglicans, Orthodox Christians and Roman Catholics. Whatever be their other differences in eucharistic doctrine, they all affirm the real presence of Christ in or under the form of bread and wine. This means that the risen Jesus is as truly present, body, blood, soul and divinity under the form of bread and wine at the Lord's Supper as he exists in heaven. This is the most "realistic" notion of Christ's presence, and affirms as much as possible. We should note that these Churches see the *total* Christ as present, not just particles of his body and blood. They would affirm that the total person of Christ is present under both bread and wine.

Ecumenically speaking, there seems to be some misunderstanding of this last group among the others—a sort of fear that the realistic beliefs dishonor Christ by making him bodily present, or imply the presence of his crucified and suffering flesh and blood apart from the totality of the risen Christ. It must be said that a good deal of ecumenical dialogue still needs to be done—the kind that has been done beneficially in the area of the sacrificial aspect of the Lord's Supper. (The bogey-man of the Reformation times still hangs heavily over this area.) "Real" presence is ordinarily meant to oppose spiritual presence or symbolic presence. Other times the word "substantial" is used, or even "physical". However, in recent times, some ecumenists want to call any meaningful presence of Christ in the eucharistic service a "real presence". The Faith and Order Conference at Edinburgh in 1937 was trying to formulate a general agreement of Christians regarding the presence of Christ. "We all believe that Christ is truly present in the eucharist, though as to how that presence is manifested and realized we may differ". They obviously did not want to split over the precise nature of the "real presence" or set up any definite interpretation as condition for Church unity.

How Does Christ Become Present, or, What Causes This Presence?

Christians who hold only to symbolic or spiritual presence of Christ see little problem here. It is the faith of the recipient which is all-important. Nothing happens to the elements of bread and wine and Christ is not any more present in the Lord's Supper than in baptism, for example. Nonetheless, the bread and wine are holy symbols to be treated with reverence; any left over after Communion is to be disposed of decently.

Those who believe in real bodily presence are not all agreed on what happens. Lutherans hold that the words of institution bring about no change in the bread and wine; they are not *changed into* the body and blood of Christ. Rather, the total person of the risen Christ becomes present *in,* or *to,* or *under* the forms of bread and wine. How can Christ multiply his physical presence? Well, the risen Jesus in his glorified body somehow partakes of divine qualities of omnipresence; his body is no longer limited by space and time. Many Lutheran theologians used to speak of consubstantiation (presence of substance of bread and wine *together with* the substance of the body of Christ). Luther used this word at times to oppose the Roman Catholic notion of transubstantiation (change of substance of bread and wine into the substance of the body of Christ). But today the tendency is to steer clear of trying to explain this mystery of Christ's real presence in philosophical terms. They would rather assert the fact of this presence (while denying any change in the bread and wine), and leave it at that. "The essential thing in the Lord's Supper is, as Luther held, that just as the eternal Word became incarnate in Christ, so he himself is present in bread and wine to build the Church which is his Body. The real presence of Christ, moreover, is in no way dependent on our faith, but upon the incomprehensible grace by which he wills to give himself to us in the sacrament . . ." (Lutheran position prepared for Lund, 1947).

Again, Lutherans are unwilling to say exactly when Christ becomes so present. Do the words of consecration being about the presence of Christ, or is he present only at the moment of reception? No agreement; but they all agree that Christ is present even apart from the faith of the receiver. And their theology is hazy about how long the presence remains. Probably Christ ceases to be present when the Lord's Supper is over. They do not reserve and adore the consecrated bread that remains. So, in general they hold that Christ is present only when the supper ritual is actually taking place.

Catholics, Orthodox and Anglicans hold the following: that Christ becomes really present at the words of consecration in the Mass. Catholics and Anglicans hold the words of consecration crucial. Orthodox include the invocation of the Holy Spirit (*epiclesis*) as effecting the presence. This happens not because the risen Christ leaves heaven to come down upon the altar, but because the bread and wine are *changed into* the body and blood of Christ. (Here, Anglicans would prefer to be less specific about "change" than about "presence".) Obviously the bread and wine look and act the same as before: the appearances remain; but the inner reality (what makes bread to be bread, etc.) is changed into the reality of Christ. Under *each* form (bread and wine) the total Christ is present—since his glorified body cannot be divided, nor separated from his divine person. And so even if communion is only under one form (bread), the recipient receives the total Christ. Christ is not "attached to" the outward appearances of bread and wine, but is "present to" them. It is a mysterious presence which can only be called sacramental. In spite of his real and substantial presence, one does not touch, chew, or break the body of Jesus. These things are done only to the outward appearances of bread.

A lot of theological writing and even more bitterness has arisen over the notion of transubstantiation—the Roman Catholic attempt to explain how Christ becomes present in the eucharist. Opponents decry the use of rigid philosophical terms (Aristotelian) to explain mysteries. Catholics have long defended the notion of change of substance. Actually it was used as early as 1050, before Aristotle's philosophy was known in the West, and simply meant something like change of "inner reality". The Council of Trent (1551-52) does not seem to demand more when it says that transubstantiation is the most fitting term to describe the change of the substance of bread and wine into the substance of the body and blood of Christ—the change indicated by the words of Christ over the bread and wine: "This is my body . . . this is my blood".

Still, the notion of "substance" inevitably conjures up philosophical problems. Concentration on the precise nature of this mysterious change has served to prolong the divisions of Christians. So the latest Roman Catholic theology of the eucharist spends little or no time on this tangled problem. It holds as strongly as ever to the *fact* of the change, but refuses to get bogged down in formulas that are neither very scriptural nor very contemporary (existential).

How Long Does the Presence of Christ Last in the Bread and Wine?

Most Protestants see little problem here. At the most,

Christ is only present for the duration of the Lord's Supper ceremony. He comes as our spiritual food, so once Communion is over the reason for his presence ceases. These Christians, then, find it difficult to see why Roman Catholics and others keep consecrated hosts upon the altar (in a tabernacle), and adore Christ in this continuing presence. Is this not to take the Lord's Supper out of its original context and make a dynamic thing (the spiritual nourishment of the sacred meal) a mere static presence?

Roman Catholics, Orthodox Christians and many Anglicans firmly maintain the doctrine of the continuing presence of Christ in the host. And how truly believe that this is really Jesus without worshipping and adoring? This belief lies behind Roman Catholic visits to the blessed sacrament, processions with the sacred host, and so on. It starts with the doctrine that once the bread and wine are *changed into* the body and blood of Christ, this presence of Jesus will remain as long as the appearances of these elements remain those of bread and wine. With corruption (through digestion or simply age, etc.) the presence of Christ ceases. Hence the extreme reverence and, indeed, adoration of all consecrated hosts. There is sometimes a regrettable tendency to allow the doctrine of the real presence to obscure the central meaning of the eucharist as primarily sacred and sacrificial meal (so that seeing the host becomes exaggeratedly important, for example). But recent Catholic theology, without in any way denying this continuing presence, has put strong and healthy emphasis on reintegration of all eucharistic devotion around the central core of the Mass.

How Often Should We Celebrate the Lord's Supper?

From opposite extremes two trends of Christian thought are coming to reemphasize the importance of frequent participation in the Lord's Supper. Orthodox, Anglicans, and particularly Roman Catholics have long had frequent and even daily eucharistic celebrations. But only in rather recent times has communion become frequent. Too long the Mass was a mysterious spectacle; that it was a sacred meal of food and drink has (even now) not penetrated very deeply into Catholic consciousness at times. The law of the Church requires it only once a year, but such laxity is considered disgraceful today. Catholics are urged to receive communion at least once a month. Many receive weekly, and some daily. Recent liturgical changes help Roman Catholics to see the Mass more clearly as sacred meal, and point out how their participation is somehow incomplete without reception of communion. Indeed, occasional reception under both forms of bread and wine is now allowed—quite a breakthrough, ecumenically speaking.

From the other extreme, many Protestants had let the Lord's Supper become so occasional a happening that it seemed altogether secondary to the pulpit. The Lord's Supper was celebrated as seldom as once a year in some places. Now there is strong desire (particularly among theologians) to have it much more frequently, even weekly, and to insist that the worship service should culminate in the celebration of the Lord's Supper. Such reemphasis has in fact already taken hold to a significant degree, at least in some Churches.

We now have to speak of two areas that are very important ecumenically. The first is the necessity of ministry for the Lord's Supper—an area that involves clear and serious ecumenical problems. The other is about the sacrificial nature of the Lord's Supper—and here there has been significant progress.

Necessity of Ministry for the Lord's Supper

Protestants in general stress the priesthood of all believers, that through baptism all Christians share in the one priesthood of Christ, and can therefore take full part in Christian worship. However, for good order and because of the social nature of the Church, certain ones are designated (by ordination or appointment), to preside or minister at worship services. He receives no new powers, however. And it is not by reason of anything given to him that Christ becomes present (whether spiritually or really), but simply because Christ wills to become present when the community gathers together under an appointed leader to celebrate the Lord's Supper. A Roman Catholic might like to clarify this position by asking: "Well, would Christ become present if *any* believer said the words of institution? And what if the minister wanted to celebrate all alone, without any community?" The Protestant would find these difficult to answer, partly because the situations are foreign to his practice.

This is much more of a problem for Roman Catholics, Orthodox, and Anglicans. The priesthood of all believers remains important; but this only allows one to participate in the Lord's Supper by offering and receiving once the presence of Christ is a fact. The power to bring about the real change in the bread and wine making it the body and blood of Jesus Christ, belongs only to those who are *ordained* priests in the Church, for ordination brings precisely this power to consecrate. In order to have a truly valid eucharistic service, these Christians firmly believe in the necessity of validly ordained priests. So, as much as they respect the sincerity of other Christians celebrating the Lord's Supper in some other way, they have serious reservations about such communion services, and particularly about the possibility of joining in. Roman Catholics, furthermore, feel that the ordinations of the Anglican Church are invalid by Roman standards, so unfortunately the same problem arises.

Intercommunion

What we have been saying will help explain the different degrees of liberalism or conservatism among the Christian Churches regarding intercommunion: that is, one Church inviting or allowing others to join them in the Lord's Supper, or fully taking part in a common celebration.

The more liberally oriented Churches see little difficulty here. The more intercommunion the better; it will help promote mutual love, understanding and eventual unity. Christ would not want us to deny any sincere Christian. If there is one place we can forget our differences and denominational pride, surely it is at the banquet table of the Lord. Thus, Seventh-Day Adventists, Methodists, United Church of Christ, Presbyterians, and so on, have a relaxed discipline about this.

But there is another way of looking at the whole problem. Here the Lord's Supper is seen primarily as the great culminating sign and seal of Christian unity. It is wrong to pretend and celebrate an intimate fraternal union in Christ that we so flagrantly deny by our manifold differences in doctrine, ministry and church order. Thus, communion should be restricted to those who are already united. Southern Baptists practice rigid, closed communion. Lutherans so far allow intercommunion only among the various Lutheran bodies and not all do even this. (But they see the time as ripe for discussion about some intercommunion with other Christians.) Anglicans, too, tend to be strict, allowing intercommunion, in principle, only to those who believe in the real presence of Christ in communion. Orthodox and Catholics are the strictest of all, till now allowing no intercommunion at all. A recent decision of the Roman Church, however, now encourages occasional communion with the Orthodox Church, since each recognizes the validity of the other's eucharistic service. During the Faith and Order Conference of the World Council of Churches, held at Lund in 1952, an open communion service was held at the Lutheran cathedral. The Orthodox, some Anglicans and a few German and American Lutherans refused to attend, (Catholics would have refused if they had been present.)

Why such rigidity? Well, these Christians feel that it cheapens the Lord's Supper by offering it to the curious, and the superficially friendly. Separation from one another at this sacred time should be a constant thorn which accuses, and which spurs us on to genuine and final reunion. But once this is made clear, many ecumenically minded Anglicans, Lutherans, and even some Roman Catholics see the value of at least occasional intercommunion. "Aware of our basic spiritual unity (despite our division), realizing also the operative power of Christ in the sacrament of union, they could approach the eucharist not as a sign of union in faith and worship, but as an extraordinary supplication for God's intervention in our move toward unity. The whole rite would be a 'qualified intercommunion', a prayer for union, not a proclamation of union."

Is the Lord's Supper a Sacrifice?

Even to mention this question some years ago would have raised a storm of controversy. Our historical sketch pointed out the reasons for this: rigid affirmation of the fact of the Mass as sacrifice (often with exaggerated theological explanations) on the part of Eastern and Roman Churches; just as rigid denial by the opposition of all sacrificial aspect to the Lord's Supper as being totally incompatible with the once-for-all sacrifice of Jesus on Calvary. Even quite recently the *Constitution of the Presbyterian Church in the United States* (1955, p. 77) speaks of the sacrifice of the Mass offered by the Catholic Church as being "most abominably injurious to Christ's one only sacrifice". Yet, these last few years have brought welcome and surprising changes.

On the Catholic side there is a much more healthy, acceptable and biblical approach to the sacrifice of the Mass. It starts with the once-for-allness of Christ's work. Jesus never repeats either his sacrifice or his total offering of himself to the Father. Yet Malachy 11, 1, St. Paul in I Corinthians, and long Christian tradition point to a continuing note of sacrifice in the Church. How reconcile? It must be that somehow the one sacrifice of Christ is made present in the eucharistic liturgy, that the Lord's Supper in a mysterious, sacramental way makes present to us the saving events of Jesus' death and resurrection. One theory holds that this is the precise job of a sacrament—namely, to *cause* what it signifies. And since the eucharist surely signifies the sacrifice of Christ—his broken body and spilled blood—it makes this reality of Calvary somehow present, so that we today can be swept up into it as really as those who first witnessed it in a spirit of faith. Another theory demands even less: that the resurrection is the all-important moment of acceptance of Jesus' sacrificial death by the Father. This moment is eternalized in the glorified existence of our Savior. Thus when he becomes present in the eucharistic service, he becomes present in all the fullness of his accepted sacrifice.

According to these increasingly popular theories, the Mass can add nothing to the work of Jesus on Calvary. If the Mass is called propitiatory by the Council of Trent (*i.e.,* that it makes God look with favor upon us) it is not because of anything we do; it is simply that by this re-actualization of the once-for-all salvific activity of Jesus, into which we willingly enter with the help of God, we become recipients of the saving grace of Christ.

The Eastern Orthodox Church has always insisted that the Mass is a sacrifice. Not a new sacrifice separated from Calvary in content and effect, but a new representation of the once-for-all sacrifice, a new mystical reiteration of it. The belief in heavenly liturgy is strong—that Christ is continually interceding for us in heaven, and showing forth by his glorified wounds his perfect sacrifice. (*See* Hebrews 7, 24-25; 8, 1-5.) In fact, the solemnity and splendor of the Eastern liturgy is to show the Church's visible participation in this heavenly liturgy of the risen Christ.

The Anglican Church today is quite willing to speak of the sacrifice of the eucharist, rejecting all repetition, but affirming the true sacrificial nature of the Lord's Supper. Lutheran theologians are reexamining the position of Luther. Though Luther did not explicitly affirm the Lord's Supper as sacrifice, he did not reject a healthy notion of it. Gustaf Aulén says that in the mind of Luther the living

Lord who is present in the eucharist is none other than the crucified. The finished and eternally valid sacrifice cannot be separated from him. When he comes in holy communion, he actualizes the sacrifice of the New Covenant and makes it effectively present. (*Eucharist and Sacrifice,* p. 203.) Other leading Lutheran theologians state emphatically that the eucharist is the eternal presence in the Church of the sacrifice of Golgotha.

Reformed Church theologian Van de Leeux (Calvinist tradition) agrees: "At the Lord's table the sacrifice of Christ is re-presented and the faithful are called upon to partake of this sacrifice. They cannot receive it and make it their own without giving themselves, without offering up their lives. At the table of the Lord they are not only receivers of the gifts of Christ, but they officiate, they partake, they exercise the priesthood conferred upon them by baptism and confirmation."

We might expect opposition from the less doctrinally orientated Churches. Yet there seems to be a certain measure of agreement—at least among their theologians. One statement submitted by Baptists and other Free Churches in preparation for the Faith and Order Conference in Lund, asserts: "The Lord's Supper is not merely a solemn memorial of Christ's sacrifice of himself, the sacrifice which was once offered on the cross. The Lord's Supper is the dramatic setting forth of this sacrifice, and the means through which we can participate in it and in all its benefits. Because in the sacrament the crucified and risen Savior is himself present to share with us all that is his."

Ecumenical Summaries

When the Faith and Order Conference met at Edinburgh in 1937 the following joint statement of participating Protestants was issued regarding the sacrificial aspect of the Lord's Supper. True, it skims over many difficulties —but at least points to the trend which has grown ever stronger since that time:

"If sacrifice is understood as it was by our Lord and his followers and in the early Church, it includes, not his death only, but the obedience of his earthly ministry, his risen and ascended life, in which he still does his Father's will and ever liveth to make intercession for us. Such a sacrifice can never be repeated, but is proclaimed and set forth in the eucharistic action of the whole Church when we come to God in Christ at the eucharist or Lord's Supper. For us, the secret of joining in that sacrifice is both the worship and the service of God; corporate because we are joined with Christ, and in him to one another (1 Cor. 10, 17); individually because each one of us makes the corporate act of self-oblation his own; and not ceremonially only, but also profoundly ethical, because the keynote of all sacrifice and offering is 'Lo! I come to do thy will, O God'. We believe also that the eucharist is a supreme moment of prayer, because the Lord is the celebrant or minister for us at every celebration, and it is in his prayers for God's gifts and for us all that we join. According to the New Testament accounts of the institution his prayer is itself a giving of thanks; so that the Lord's Supper is both a visible word (*verbum visibile*) of the divine grace, and the supreme thanksgiving (*eucharistia*) of the people of God. . . ."

After years of studying the problem the same Commission of Faith and Order prepared the following clarifications for the meeting at Lund in 1952:

"In his one perfect and sufficient sacrifice of Calvary he (Christ) offered perfect obedience to the Father in atonement for the sin of the whole world. This was the act of expiation made once and for all and is unrepeatable. In his risen and ascended life, he ever makes intercession for us.

"Our response in worship, then, is the praise, prayer, thanksgiving and offering of ourselves in faith and obedience made to the Father in the name of Jesus Christ.

We make the sacrifice of praise and thanksgiving. It is at this point that our greatest difficulties arise as we seek to express just how our worship on earth is related to the eternal intercession of Christ in heaven. We all agree that there is an element of mystery here which can scarce be expressed (Rom. 8, 26).

"Some of us believe that in the Lord's Supper, where they enter into communion with the crucified and risen Lord, they only offer a sacrifice of praise and thanksgiving and obedient service as a response in faith to the benefits the Lord gives us. Others would like to insist, however, that in the holy eucharist the Lord Jesus Christ as God's great High Priest unites the oblation made by his body, the Church, with his own sacrifice, and so takes up her own into the *Sanctus* of the company of heaven. Between these two views are others to which a brief reference may not do full justice . . . "

Catholics and Orthodox have always held that the eucharist is more than just *our* sacrifice of praise and thanks, that it is a mysterious entering into the once-for-all sacrifice of Christ. They would side, then, with the last view in the above quotation. In fact, there has been a surprising amount of support for this viewpoint, particularly in Europe among Lutheran and Reformed theologians (representing between them most of the continental Protestants of Europe) and Anglicans. The following comment of Father Yves Congar is highly interesting. It is from a critique of statements formulated by the Faith and Order Theological Commission at Bossey (Switzerland) in 1963:

"Very positive agreement—as unexpected by Catholics as it was joyfully welcomed—was reached between the Lutherans and Reformed in favor of the sacrificial character of the eucharist. Once the bogey of repetition has been removed, Protestant thought will admit that the eucharist incorporates our sacrifice and is the memorial of

Christ's own unique sacrifice. We have not as yet pursued our dialogue far enough to know just where the parting of the ways occurs—if it does at all. Does Protestant theology about the eucharist as sacrifice mean more than our communion in Christ's sacrifice? And what exactly does Catholic dogma affirm? Certainly it repudiates the notion of the *renewal* of Christ's sacrifice, or a re-commencing. (At least such a notion would have to be very carefully explained.) What exactly does the Mass add to the Cross? It is the celebration *by the Church* under the symbolico-real form of the sacrament of that which Christ has done once for all, and which from that moment has included all that we could do. It is a celebration in which, by the ministry of ordained priests who are indeed ministers of the Body, Christians actualize their union with the death and resurrection of Christ, already pledged by their baptism. Everyone at Bossey had the feeling that on this vitally important issue, a rapprochement should be possible, given prayer and patience.

These ideas on the sacrificial nature of the Lord's Supper may come as a surprise to many, both Catholic and Protestant. This is just one more area where return to Scripture and ecumenical dialogue have put theologians a long distance ahead of the rank and file of churchgoers. Much work remains to be done, but it would be a shame if these large areas of agreement and significant ecumenical advance remained unknown to, and unappreciated by, the average Christian.

Effects of the Lord's Supper

Briefly, all Christians who accept the Lord's Supper would agree that there are two great effects: first, deeper fellowship and union with Jesus Christ; secondly, increased union with the whole Church and fellowship to one another.

First, union with Christ. All would accept the sacraments as outward and visible signs of inward and spiritual grace. For some, it remains a pure sign, to stir up faith and to give assurance of salvation through the sacrifice of Jesus. As we take the bread and wine into our bodies, we indicate our desire to have Christ, whom these signs represent, enter into our hearts. Rather than simply talk about it, we act out our desire to have Christ dwell in our hearts by faith. Others—those who hold to the spiritual presence of Christ—see the Lord's Supper as "containing" the grace that is received through faith (*e.g.,* Lutherans). Still others see it as a "cause" of grace, not only because Christ is as really present here as he was in Palestine, but because sacraments are *acts* of Christ, as surely as when he worked a cure by his touch.

This grace that is given is not some impersonal pouring in of some *thing* each time we receive. It is rather the sustaining and empowering presence of God the Father, Son, and Holy Spirit, given to us through the humanity of Jesus. And it is in a new (or deeper) relation of loving faith that the power of the eucharist emerges into our lives. For God not only communicates himself to us in the life of grace, but produces in us the ability to freely respond to this self-gift of himself. In the Lord's Supper, most of all, we are offered not only closer fellowship with Christ, but an added sharing in his sonship to the Father. We are offered an ever deeper sharing in the very risen life of Jesus.

All who accept the Lord's Supper agree that it has a three-fold dimension of past, present and future: it is vivid memorial of the sacrifice of Jesus Christ; it is somehow a "making present" of this to our lives bringing us the fruits of his once-for-all saving actions (we've seen the various ways in which Christians understand this); and finally, it is a pledge of future glory—when the Christ, who is already united to us in the Supper invisibly, will be with us visibly in all his glory and splendor when we participate fully in the "heavenly banquet", of which the Lord's Supper here is only a foretaste.

Secondly, the Lord's Supper increases our union with

the whole Church and with one another. John Calvin expressed this in the following way:

"The Lord communicates his body to us [in the Lord's Supper] in such a manner that he becomes completely one with us, and we become one with him. Hence, as he has only one body, of which he makes us partakers, it follows, of necessity, that by such participation we also are all made one body; and this union is represented by the bread which is exhibited in the sacrament. For as it is composed of many grains, mixed together in such a manner that one cannot be separated or distinguished from another, in the same manner we ought, likewise, to be connected and united together by such an agreement of minds, as to admit of no dissension or division among us."

Participation in the Lord's Supper surely helps to strengthen and increase the invisible bonds that unite all Christians; and all see it as the symbol of the ultimate complete unity in Jesus Christ that is the aim of the whole ecumenical movement. And sincere communion in their own Churches is certainly a means to the desired unity. As for open communion and intercommunion at this stage, we must remember and try to appreciate the various problems involved.

Interfaith dialogue on the subject of the Lord's Supper should be an exciting, helpful and interesting experience. No categories and classifications can truly capture the living beliefs of Christians, and we apologize for deficiencies which surely exist in this short treatment. It does not serve the true purpose of ecumenism to gloss over the difficult areas of eucharistic dialogue; but we Christians have more in common here than we have often realized.

LIVING ROOM DIALOGUES
Evaluation Sheet

Since this program is a new experiment, those responsible for preparing the material need your help in evaluating it and preparing further materials. *Please* fill out this form (use extra paper if necessary) and mail to: LIVING ROOM DIALOGUES, Room 804, 475 Riverside Drive, New York, N.Y. 10027 or Paulist Press, 304 W. 58th St., New York, N.Y. 10019.

How many were in the group? ———

How many Catholics? ——— Orthodox? ———
   Protestants? ———

How many men? ——— women? ———

What was the average attendance? ———

Did the group continue through the whole series? ——

If not, why?

Which dialogue topics stimulated most discussion among your group?

Which produced the least discussion?

Please list the topics you would like to see covered in the second book for Living Room Dialogues.

Did you follow the suggested format? ———

If not, what changes were helpful? ———

Did you use one leader throughout? ———
   or rotate leadership? ———

What other helps would you like? ———

Did members of the group get new insights? ———

Can you list some of these? ———

Were there positive changes in attitude? ———

What percent of the group reported such changes? ——